AN INTRODUCTION TO SHAKESPEARE'S POEMS

Other books by the author

Disguise and Role-Playing in Ben Jonson's Drama
Discharging the Canon: Cross-cultural Readings in Literature (editor)
Shakespeare: Troilus and Cressida
Saul Bellow
An Introduction to Shakespeare: The Dramatist in his Context

An Introduction to Shakespeare's Poems

Peter Hyland

palgrave
macmillan

First published 2003 by
PALGRAVE MACMILLAN
Houndmills, Basingstoke, Hampshire RG21 6XS and
175 Fifth Avenue, New York, N.Y. 10010
Companies and representatives throughout the world

PALGRAVE MACMILLAN is the global academic imprint of the Palgrave
Macmillan division of St. Martin's Press, LLC and of Palgrave Macmillan Ltd.
Macmillan® is a registered trademark in the United States, United Kingdom
and other countries. Palgrave is a registered trademark in the European
Union and other countries.

ISBN 0–333–72592–1 hardcover
ISBN 0–333–72593–X paperback

This book is printed on paper suitable for recycling and made from fully
managed and sustained forest sources.

A catalogue record for this book is available from the British Library.

Library of Congress Cataloging-in-Publication Data
Hyland, Peter.
     An introduction to Shakespeare's poems / Peter Hyland.
          p.   cm.
     Includes bibliographical references and index.
     ISBN 0–333–72592–1 — ISBN 0–333–72593–X (pbk.)
     1. Shakespeare, William, 1564–1616—Poetic works.   2. Shakespeare,
     William, 1564–1616. Venus and Adonis.   3. Shakespeare, William,
     1564–1616. Rape of Lucrece.   4. Narrative poetry, English—History and
     criticism.   5. Shakespeare, William, 1564–1616. Sonnets.   6. Sonnets,
     English—History and criticism.   7. Adonis (Greek deity) in literature.
     8. Venus (Roman deity) in literature.   9. Lucretia—In literature.
     I. Title.

     PR2984 .H95 2002
     822.3'4—dc21

                                                            2002075255

10   9   8   7   6   5   4   3   2   1
12 11 10 09 08 07 06 05 04 03

Printed in China

Contents

     Sonnet 1: A Reading   151
     Breeding Immortality   154
     Gender-Bending   159
     Is Love Love?   162

  9 **Reading Shakespeare's *Sonnets*: 2**   **168**
     The 'Black' Mistress   168
     'Will' and the Poet   175
     Time's Tyranny and the Poet's Pen   181
     Conclusions   185
     Coda: 'A Lover's Complaint'   187

 10 **Various Poems**   **194**

     Conclusion   **214**

     Notes   216

     Suggested Reading   224

     Index   228

Acknowledgements

For uniformity of reference, all quotations from Shakespeare's works are from Stephen Greenblatt, Walter Cohen, Jean E. Howard and Katharine Eisaman Maus (eds), *The Norton Shakespeare* (New York and London: W. W. Norton, 1997). The Norton edition is based on the Oxford Shakespeare, edited by Stanley Wells and Gary Taylor, so the reader seeking specific references should find no difficulty.

Part of Chapter 5 appeared in a different form in *The Upstart Crow*, 18 (1998).

Introduction

William Shakespeare is generally known as the most significant poet to have written in English, though most people think of his poetry mainly from his plays. As these plays are written predominantly in verse, it might at first sight seem unnecessary to make a distinction between 'the poetry' and 'the poetry of the plays'. We can choose bits of poems and bits of plays and show that they seem really to be the same sort of thing. Take, for example, these two passages:

> Shall I compare thee to a summer's day?
> Thou art more lovely and more temperate.
> Rough winds do shake the darling buds of May,
> And summer's lease hath all too short a date.

These are the opening lines of Sonnet 18, probably the most familiar of the sonnets. In them one person praises another through hyperbolic comparison with an aspect of nature; with no other evidence to go on we might suppose the speaker to be a man addressing the woman he loves. Anyone with the slightest knowledge of English prosody will recognize that the lines are iambic pentameter, and that the first and third lines rhyme, as do the second and fourth. Compare this passage with the following:

> Things base and vile, holding no quantity,
> Love can transpose to form and dignity,
> Love looks not with the eyes, but with the mind,
> And therefore is winged Cupid painted blind.

These are lines from the opening scene of *A Midsummer Night's Dream*. In a sense, the speaker is commenting on the kind of attitude reflected in the first passage: love does not see what is there, but through fancy can transform the worthless into the beautiful, making it possible for a lover to speak of an ordinary person as lovelier than a summer's day. These lines too are written in iambic pentameter, this time in rhyming couplets. We recognize both of them as poetry,

1

and, without the larger context of the texts from which they are extracted, we can say that they appear to be preoccupied with similar concerns.

The inclination to treat Shakespeare's plays as 'poetry', as if plays were the same sort of thing as poems, is encouraged by the fact that even though many stage and (increasingly) film performances of the plays are available, for most of us our first experience of them comes from printed texts. Consequently we perceive the printed play and the printed poem as if they were materially equivalent when indeed they are not, for in Shakespeare's time they filled quite different cultural needs. The result, though, is that Shakespeare the poet is defined for us by his plays, while most of us are unacquainted with his poems. With the exception of a few sonnets, they are amongst the least known of his works, aligned with plays like *Love's Labour's Lost* and *Titus Andronicus*, which were until recently on the unfamiliar margins of Shakespeare's canon. The reworking of these lesser-known plays into films has shown that texts produced for one verbal–visual medium can be reproduced more or less successfully in another, in ways that open them up to new readings. The non-dramatic poems on the other hand, even though some of them have been dramatized, are denied such broader publicity. This, I think, is justification for a book that confines itself to these poems.

There is, however, a larger justification for a book about this poetry, and it relates to the cultural value that has accrued around the idea of Shakespeare. Few would disagree that for most of us the reading and writing of poetry are at best marginalized activities, and yet the idea of the poet Shakespeare permeates our culture to such a degree that even those who do not know much about him are nevertheless at the end of a tradition that has stressed his transcendent genius' and the 'universality' of his writings. We might know some of the phrases that reinforce this characteriza-tion. 'He was not of an age, but for all time,' according to his contemporary Ben Jonson; later in the seventeenth century John Milton saw him as 'Fancy's child', who 'warbled his native wood-notes wild'. Shakespeare's eighteenth-century editor Samuel Johnson wrote of him:

When Learning's Triumph o'er her barb'rous Foes
First rear'd the Stage, immortal SHAKESPEAR rose;
Each Change of many-colour'd Life he drew,
Exhausted Worlds, and then imagin'd new.

For the nineteenth-century poet and critic Matthew Arnold, Shake-speare towered omniscient above ordinary human beings, 'Out-topping knowledge'. The result of this history is that Shakespeare stands at the centre of Western (or even 'world') culture as its greatest poet. We need to be aware, however, that in spite of the idealizing language of these descriptions, there is no *absolute* truth to them. We can see this if we relocate Shakespeare in his own context.

To restate my earlier point: the Shakespearean poetry that is most familiar to modern readers was not originally written as 'poetry'. It was the script for a medium of entertainment and communication in which it was only one (though no doubt the most important) of a number of elements of performance such as acting, music, costume, dance and clowning. As organized language, that is, its function was to be dramatic rather than poetic, and to be dramatic in a way that would appeal to a large audience that embraced most social levels. This is not to say that the plays were *not* poetry, but that Shake-speare understood them as something different from his non-dramatic poetry. Of this he produced only a small amount, over an unknown number of years, probably starting around 1592. It was primarily directed toward powerful elite court circles, and consists of two long narrative poems, *Venus and Adonis* and *The Rape of Lucrece*; 154 sonnets, published as a sequence in 1609; and a handful of minor poems.

In this book, I want to focus on these non-dramatic poems, setting them in their original context, a dynamic and often dangerous milieu where poetry performed important social and cultural work. Shakespeare is often represented as a defender of the narrow conservative interests of an elite establishment, but that is too simple a characterization. He was a child of his time, which was vastly dif-ferent from our own, though similar in more ways than we might like to think. In spite of the fact that England had a female monarch when Shakespeare wrote most of his poetry, the state was a patri-archy, and his writings reflect the tensions generated by this anomaly. He also lived at a time when English adventurers were moving out into newly discovered lands, and when the meaning of 'English-ness' as something distinct and definable was still being determined; like other English men and women he had to find ways of coming to terms with the fantastic implications of these discoveries, and per-haps he did not always do this in ways that satisfy our modern liberal or radical sensibilities. And to say that he upheld the values of aristocracy may be simply to acknowledge that he recognized the precariousness of his position amongst the harsh political realities within which he existed.

The image of Shakespeare as 'conservative' has, in my opinion, too often distorted readings of his works. He has been understood as a writer who could not have imagined a society that did not have the class divisions that were fundamental to the one in which he lived. Shakespeare, of course, was on the inferior side of the class barrier, and if the orthodox, anti-populist perspective that some critics have found in the plays is really there, how much more true must that be of the poems. The plays, after all, were written for an audience that included very many common people, but the poems were written primarily for an elite readership. These are issues that I will consider in Chapter 1, but I will offer here the suggestion that Shakespeare's lower-class background, insofar as it must have limited his access to elite circles, must also have generated in him some scepticism about them. The rigidity of the class system, especially the resistance of aristocratic circles to penetration by their inferiors, was a source of frustration and resentment for clever young men from the lower classes and the provinces. The myth of the talented young man from these margins of society coming to the big city in search of a fortune and achieving so much success that he can buy a Tudor mansion and socialize with aristocrats and even with royalty has ceased to be a myth in the modern age. Actors, popular singers and football players (not all of them talented) do it all the time. Shakespeare, of course, appears to fit into the myth: a glover's son from a small provincial town who left his wife and children behind to make it big in London, became very rich from his writing, and was a favourite of Queen Elizabeth herself. The myth did not work quite so well for Shakespeare as it does for his modern counter-part, however. Although he became rich from his work in a popular cultural medium, penetrating the tight world of the Elizabethan establishment was not quite so easy.

Consider the character of Feste in *Twelfth Night*. Within the world of the play he is a professional entertainer, and even though he is its superior intelligence he is also its fool. He is Olivia's jester, but he moves freely between the play's two aristocratic households, offering his wit in exchange for money, and working very hard at it. As an entertainer of the powerful he is used and tolerated, even valued, but at the end of the play he is left alone on the stage, essentially an outsider, singing a song that insistently dissipates illusion. We might see this as a kind of allegory for Shakespeare's own position. There is no doubt that as an entertainer he was very successful with the rich and powerful as well as with the popular audience. But he must have been aware, like Feste, that there was a line that he would never be able to cross. This was, after all, a society so obsessed with social distinctions that the government enacted sumptuary laws, dictating the quality of clothing that could be worn by each social rank in an attempt to render these distinctions visible. Shakespeare, like Feste, would always be a servant: 'And we'll strive to please you every day.'

To some degree the theatre dissolved social distinctions, or at least gave the appearance of doing so, since it embraced the whole spectrum of society in its audience. When Shakespeare wrote his narrative poems and sonnets, he was writing for a much more exclusive body of readers. The primary consumers of poetry were 'the great and the good' who inhabited court circles, and their tastes dictated literary fashion. *Venus and Adonis* and *The Rape of Lucrece* were both dedicated to the Earl of Southampton. Sonnet sequences were in vogue for a decade or more after the publication in 1591 of Sir Philip Sidney's *Astrophil and Stella*. Of course, aristocratic fashions were emulated, especially in London, by the growing numbers of wealthy merchants and professionals, but the market for volumes of poetry was necessarily small, if for no other reason than that they were expensive, and the successful poet had little choice but to direct his work toward those who influenced artistic fashion.

Without doubt, Shakespeare was ambitious; that is why he left Stratford-upon-Avon for the broader opportunities that London offered. We cannot know what the balance in him between artistic and social ambition might have been, but it would be a naive romantic illusion if we were to think of him as driven solely by his need to create. He must have seen that his only instrument of power in this metropolitan society was his pen, the channel of his literary and theatrical genius. He was adept at giving his audience what it wanted (or at making his audience want what he gave it). We can imagine that he must have spent a lot of time thinking about how to turn aesthetic power into social power. And he must have seen how difficult such a transformation was going to be. In the end he made a lot of money, but as early as 1597 he bought New Place, a large house in Stratford, presumably knowing already that it was there and not in London that he would spend his retirement as a local worthy.

As one might expect from all of this, I think that Shakespeare's poetry reflects a set of attitudes too complex, even contradictory, to be described simply as 'conservative'. I think that underlying all of his major non-dramatic poems is a fierce scepticism about aristocratic power and values. Both his narrative poems are about the destructive nature of desire, and both are about what happens when a socially powerful individual attempts to impose his or her will on an inferior. His sonnets present an apparently more personal and private, and finally more disillusioned, account of hierarchical relationships and willful appetite. Quite radically, he takes poetic genres and attitudes that were currently fashionable, and he redirects them into channels that can surely be seen as potentially subversive.

In what follows I will consider from this broad perspective all of Shakespeare's non-dramatic poetry: his two long narrative poems, *Venus and Adonis* and *The Rape of Lucrece*; his *Sonnets*; and the few other poems usually considered to be his, as well as some that have recently (though not unanimously) been attributed to him. Where it is helpful to do so I will also consider how the style and content of his plays relate to this non-dramatic verse, especially when they seem thematically and chronologically relevant to his poems. To do this I will set his poems within the context of his life and times, examining (among other things) the place of poetry within the culture of Elizabethan England, and the importance of the patronage system and the rivalry and competition that it fostered amongst those writers who struggled to make a living for themselves in a marketplace that was sometimes rewarding, often hostile, and never easy.

1
Shakespeare Becomes a Poet

How did William Shakespeare begin the career that made him one of Elizabethan and Jacobean London's theatrical and literary successes? We know that in February of 1585 he was still living in Stratford-upon-Avon, the town of his birth. He was not quite 21 years old (born, perhaps, on 23 April 1564, baptized, certainly, on 26 April), the father of new-born twins Hamnet and Judith, who were christened on 2 February of that year, as well as of Susannah who had been born two years earlier. William's father was John Shakespeare, a glover and leather-dresser, who had been prosperous and had held various prominent political offices in the town, but who got into debt around 1576, after which he appears to have been unable to pull his life together again. William's mother, Mary Arden, came from a wealthy Catholic family; the Ardens were landowners who were members of the minor gentry. William had married Anne Hathaway in November 1582. Anne was seven or eight years older than William and was pregnant at the time of their marriage. We know that in 1592 Shakespeare was living in London, for the first reference to him as a writer, in a pamphlet by Robert Greene, appeared in that year. It is clear from Greene's remarks that Shakespeare had been working in the theatre for some years, though we cannot tell from them how long. Also in 1592 Shakespeare began writing *Venus and Adonis*, the first of his two narrative poems. We know nothing of substance about his life between 1585 and 1592.

These seven years have been designated the 'lost years', and there has been much speculation about them. Shakespeare almost certainly attended the King's New School in Stratford; although there is no documentary evidence to confirm it, the range of knowledge and cultural reference in the plays is what we might expect of a bright grammar-school educated man who had learned how to learn. At this grammar school he would have received an excellent education, including a training in rhetoric, logic and history; in Latin literature as well as contemporary European humanist writing; and even in Greek. Although his family had Catholic connections, he would have had an orthodox Protestant religious education which equipped him with a comprehensive knowledge of the Bible, the Prayer Book, and the *Homilies*. Such an education obviously provided a sound grounding for an ambitious man who wanted to be a writer. We know nothing about Shakespeare's domestic life, nor do we know how, or even if, he earned a living during these years. We do not know why he decided to leave Stratford for London, although it is easy to conjecture that a talented young man, burdened with a family and caught in what must have seemed to him a wearying provincial life, would find it difficult to resist the temptations of the increasingly magnetic metropolis. We do not know when he went to London, although it was probably during the last three of four years of the 1580s, for by 1592 he was apparently already a playwright with a measure of success and so must have been there for some years.[1]

I will not have much to say here about the speculation that has gone on concerning the lost years; for this the interested reader can seek out the intriguing work of E.A.J. Honigmann. I will, however, try to imagine what might have been the attitudes and expectations of a bright young man from a small provincial town as he confronted the complexities of the capital, where he hoped to carve out a living and a name for himself. Obviously, he was ambitious in ways that could not be fulfilled in Stratford or the area around it: his education might have equipped him to be a schoolteacher, or given him the skills to find clerical or other secretarial work in some local 'great house', but the opportunities for either of these things were severely limited and could not have been very appealing to someone with the aspirations that Shakespeare clearly had. Like many intelligent, educated and energetic young men from the provinces (women, I need not point out, were far too restricted in the freedoms allowed to them to have been able to enter a literary profession), he must have seen London as the only possible market for his abilities. This meant, however, that he entered the city, dynamic centre of a burgeoning culture, as a figure unequivocally from the margins.

It is not very likely that Shakespeare simply packed his bags and went off to join the London theatre without having made some prior connection to it. London acting companies sometimes toured the provinces, and a number of them visited Stratford during Shakespeare's youthful years. Amongst these was the company known as the Earl of Leicester's Men, led by James Burbage. James Burbage is a very important figure in the development of the early

English theatre because he built the first significant public playhouse in London. He was also the father of Richard Burbage, leading actor in the Lord Chamberlain's Men (later the King's Men), the company for which Shakespeare wrote most of his plays. These links suggest one obvious possibility, that Leicester's Men provided Shakespeare with an entry into his career, probably as an actor, though this is no more than speculation. What is more important is that Shakespeare's chosen profession intensified his marginal status. Although in the late 1580s the theatres were immensely popular, the men who worked in them had not really shaken off the stigma associated with acting, which from the early Tudor period had identified travelling players as outlaws. The mobility of players in a strictly stratified society made them suspect, and this suspicion was aggravated by the fact that when the playhouses were built (the first was opened in 1576), they were located in entertainment quarters where brothels and taverns already existed – essentially outlaw areas. The players' profession made them, paradoxically, popular and disreputable at the same time. The paradox was resolved in part through a form of patronage. In 1572, a law was enacted declaring that companies of players without a patron were rogues and vagabonds; companies found protection in the house of a powerful aristocrat (such as the Earl of Leicester) where they were allowed to wear his livery and call themselves his servants. This freed then from outlaw status, but confirmed their low place on the social scale. This was as true for those who wrote for the popular theatre as for those who acted in it.

London was the seat of the royal court, which was not only the centre of government and therefore of power, but also, for those who were interested in such things, of culture and fashion. It was the attractive focus for many men like Shakespeare, who were ambitious, educated and mainly from those strata of society immediately beneath the gentry; to enter into the ranks of the elite by attaining the title of 'gentlemen' was the aspiration of many of these outsiders. The elite of Elizabethan England was actually a very small segment of society, consisting of the nobility and the gentry. 'Nobility' embraced the lay peers, whose rank was hereditary, and beneath them the knights, whose titles were given for reasons of military, political or personal service. The gentry was made up of esquires and gentleman who had extensive land and wealth and were entitled to a coat of arms. The lower orders had, at their upper level, yeomen (landowners who, though wealthy, farmed their own land), and burgesses (wealthy townsmen who held civic positions and were usually members of the rising classes of merchants and tradesmen). Below these were husbandmen, who were tenants rather than owners of the land they worked, and below the husbandmen were crafts-men, day-labourers and farm-workers. They were at the bottom of recognized society, but beneath them was a vast underclass of vaga-bonds and masterless men. The exact proportion of English society made up by the nobility and gentry is not known, but it is estimated to have been no more than 2 per cent.[2] It was, however, a very powerful and very privileged group, and it is hardly surprising that there was such intense desire amongst men like Shakespeare to pene-trate it (Shakespeare's family applied for a coat of arms in 1596, and presumably this was a reflection of his own aspiration). There was, certainly, a degree of mobility around the line that divided gentry from commoners, but that mobility was resented and resisted by those who held the power.

The pathway to admission into the gentry led through the court. The court was itself a place of paradox, simultaneously brilliantly bright, with the queen at its luminous centre; and dark and shadowed with the plots and machinations, anxieties and disap-pointments of those jostling for favour. Advancement, though, was virtually impossible except by way of the court and its complex web of patronage relationships, so ambitious men were obliged to attempt to breach its borders. Many found themselves left outside, and became embittered by their belief that their superior talents were not recognized. The 'malcontent', a character driven by a sense of injured merit and usually willing to sell himself as a spy, intriguer or murderer, became a staple of Elizabethan and Jacobean plays. He was not, however, simply a conventional dramatic character; he was a representation of a real social issue. There are malcontents in many of Shakespeare's plays, and while it is possible that he was simply dramatizing a social type that he was familiar with, it is more prob-able that his malcontents reflect in some way his own social experi-ence. Think, for example, of the bastard Edmund in *King Lear*. He is the play's chief villain, and his unrelenting attack on established values is deeply disturbing. At the same time, a degree of sympathy is surely generated with him because of the injustice that lies behind his resentment over the favours bestowed on his legitimate brother:

> Wherefore should I
> Stand in the plague of custom and permit
> The curiosity of nations to deprive me

For that I am some twelve or fourteen moonshines
Lag of a brother? Why 'bastard'? Wherefore 'base',
When my dimensions are as well compact
My mind as generous, and my shape as true
As honest madam's issue?

(1.2.2–9)

In articulating his frustration with the social exclusiveness that refuses to recognize his abilities, Edmund could well be speaking for all those who are marginalized by an inequitable social structure, and this is a kind of frustration that Shakespeare himself must have known, at least at the outset of his career.

Shakespeare eventually became a successful playwright and a very prosperous man, but most of his material rewards came from his investments (he owned a share of the acting company for which he worked, the Lord Chamberlain's Men, renamed as the King's Men when James I acceded to the throne, as well as in the Globe Theatre) and from other lines of business, not from his writing. It is interesting that although he lived and worked in London for more than 20 years, he bought expensive properties in Stratford-upon-Avon so that he could retire comfortably there – the metropolitan attractions that had brought him to London as a young man were apparently not sufficient to keep him there as an old one. Almost all Shakespeare's plays are set in courts and concerned with the activities of representatives of the nobility, of kings and princesses, dukes and knights, characters who are often glamorized and whose position might appear to be endorsed by the dramatist. But it is the nature of the medium to embrace a range of voices and therefore to set out competing ideological positions, and it is surely reasonable to infer that the realities of London life, when seen from the margins of the city and the court, rather quickly generated a degree of scepticism in the idealistic young writer, and that the inequities and arrogance of hierarchy exposed by Edmund (and many other characters who inhabit the margins of the societies of Shakespeare's plays, from Shylock through Thersites to Caliban) were of at least as much concern to him as its majesty. Such characters present a critical or dissenting view of legitimacy or orthodoxy, and while their voices are sometimes, though not always, silenced by the end of the play, the questions they raise remain with the audience.

I am stressing Shakespeare's social marginality along with his ambition because it is easy to see how the collision of these could lead to scepticism and disenchantment, and because much Shakespeare criticism has downplayed these aspects of his work. Most constructions of the kind of mind Shakespeare must have had have been built from his plays, and there is a long (though not uncontested) critical history that represents Shakespeare as an apologist for aristocratic values who worked in an essentially conservative medium. One major manifestation of this history is best represented by the work of E.M.W. Tillyard, who in 1943 published what in its time became a very influential book, *The Elizabethan World Picture*. Noting that Elizabethan writing reflects a deep concern with order, Tillyard fabricated an Elizabethan 'collective mind' that was incapable of dissent, so fearful was it of any threat of disorder.[3] Tillyard had his critics, of course, most notably A.P. Rossiter, and over the past three decades his arguments have been resurrected in order to be discounted by new critical theories, but they have sometimes been replaced by arguments that continue to make dissent an impossibility for Elizabethans, replacing psychological inhibitions with political ones. For example, the Marxist critic Terry Eagleton begins his study of Shakespeare with this statement: 'Even those who know very little about Shakespeare might be vaguely aware that his plays value social order and stability'.[4] Well yes, they do, but not at all costs. The new historicist critic Leonard Tennenhouse claims that Shakespeare's theatre was allowed to exist only as long as it served court ideology, and argues that Shakespeare could not have imagined any political reality different from that in which he lived; he could not have conceived of 'one where the community of blood was not separated by an immutable principle from the people, or even one in which the power relations of the two social bodies were inverted'.[5] Such a position imposes severe limits on Shakespeare's imagination, however, and has been countered by, among others, Annabel Patterson, who finds its totalitarian assumptions 'condescending to Shakespeare' who, she thinks, is 'unlikely to have unquestioningly adopted an anti-popular myth as his own'.[6]

It is probably sufficiently evident that my sympathies lie with Patterson's position here, and I do not think that the complex pressures apparent in Shakespeare's writing, both dramatic and non-dramatic, can be explained by a conservative historicist model. This is important, because the plays were written for a broad, mixed audience of which the upper classes formed a comparatively small segment. It is true that at certain levels the plays embody the conservative ideology proposed by critics like Tennenhouse, and this is also true of the non-dramatic poems, which were written primarily for a more select readership. Shakespeare's choice of materials and the success of these poems indicate how well in touch he was with the values of this elite readership. I want to argue, nevertheless, that his sceptical stance is apparent in these writings too, though it might be more guardedly expressed. No writer who depends on the good opinion of his readers wants to alienate them. The market of book-buyers in Tudor England was necessarily small. Most writers who had no other source of income (that is, 'professionals') were obliged to sell their talents to wealthy patrons, which meant that writing became an arena in which writers fought for attention and favour. Since this put them in the position of writing into the culture of the rich and powerful it might appear that such a situation must indeed lead to work that was at best strictly controlled and at worst obsequiously supportive of these established interests. Shakespeare was fascinated by the lives and values of the powerful, but his own position on the margins could hardly have allowed him to embrace them uncritically. The poet I am presenting here is one whose struggle is to balance the need to please his readers (who did not necessarily share a uniform perspective) with the competing need to interrogate established values, and who found covert and ironic methods of doing this.

It is often assumed that Shakespeare's genius was so conspicuous that his passage into the London literary world of the late 1580s was an easy one, particularly as, when he turned to writing narrative poetry, he apparently had no difficulty finding a prominent patron in the Earl of Southampton. I can see no reason, however, why Shakespeare's struggle to establish himself in his career should have been any easier than any other writer's. To penetrate the limits of the court was not easy for men who came from outside its culture; as Colin Burrow describes it:

> The closed circle of the court, which by the end of Elizabeth's reign was open only to a tiny group of noblemen, was the gravitational center of Tudor literature, and like all gravitational centers it was so powerful that few could survive for long at its heart – but writing grew from its excluded margins.[7]

These men on the margins, as I have noted, were forced to find ways to distinguish themselves, and it was not a comfortable process. I think that it is of more than passing interest that the first reference

to Shakespeare's presence in London, Robert Greene's sneering
attack on him as a parvenu and perhaps a plagiarist in the theatrical
profession, should have appeared in the year in which Shakespeare
temporarily diverted his literary energies from plays to poems:

> there is an upstart crow, beautified with our feathers, that with his *Tiger's
> heart wrapt in a player's hide*, supposes he is as well able to bombast out
> a blank verse as the best of you; and being an absolute *Johannes Factotum*,
> is in his own conceit the only Shake-scene in a country.[8]

Greene's words have been exhaustively analysed, and they probably tell us more about Greene than about his victim. Nevertheless,
it is worth considering what effect they might have had on the novice
playwright, presumably still unsure about the wisdom of trying to
make a living with his pen in a city where a university-educated
man like Greene, a versatile and not inconsiderable writer of plays,
poems, pamphlets and prose romances, could come to the embittered end that is shadowed in his deathbed book. If the world of
professional writing had so little to offer Greene, what could it offer
Shakespeare?

Documentation of Shakespeare's theatrical career prior to Greene's
reference to him remains a blank, but it is reasonable to assume that
he had by that time written the three parts of *Henry VI* (Greene's jibe
about the tiger's heart alludes to *3 Henry VI*), and perhaps *Richard III*,
The Comedy of Errors, *The Two Gentlemen of Verona*, and *Titus Andronicus*.
His plays had clearly brought him some celebrity, or there would
have been no reason for Greene's resentment. However, as I have
noted, the profession of playwright was not then a lucrative one,
and it was subject to occasional disruption, for the city of London
authorities closed down the playhouses whenever there was a severe
outbreak of the bubonic plague, and sometimes also when there was
fear of public disorder. On 23 June 1592, the playhouses were closed,
partly because of the plague, but also because of rioting by groups of
apprentices. On 28 January 1593, a restraint was imposed upon
public gatherings in general, and it was not until early in 1594 that
the playhouses were finally able to reopen. The uncertainty of his
profession must have distressed Shakespeare, for he could not have
known how long this disruption would be, and no matter what
success he was beginning to experience, he could hardly have had
enough money to sit around waiting for it to end. The writing for
publication of non-dramatic poetry was not in itself a way of making

much money, since the market for volumes of verse was necessarily small. The penurious writer had to find a patron, as Shakespeare did in the Earl of Southampton, to whom he dedicated *Venus and Adonis* (1593) and *The Rape of Lucrece* (1594). Despite the many romantic theories that have been built around this connection we do not know how Shakespeare came into contact with Southampton, nor do we know how intimate their relationship was. What we do know is that as soon as it became possible for Shakespeare to get back to the playhouse he did so, and he seems to have shown little further interest in writing for the more prestigious market represented by his patron.

This, on the face of it, is odd, because numerous editions of both poems were printed in Shakespeare's lifetime, which attests to their great popularity. While no kind of professional writing was respect-able, there was a difference, measured in social legitimacy, between writing for the tiny sophisticated (or would-be sophisticated) minority who bought volumes of poetry, and writing for the rowdy masses who frequented the public playhouses. In his lengthy career, Shakespeare's contemporary Ben Jonson often complained about having to write for what he called 'the loathed stage'; he got away from it whenever he could find a patron, though he was often forced back into it by financial need. Jonson tried to elevate his plays into poems by giving their printing and publication the same detailed attention that he gave his poems and by blurring the distinction between the two by calling them 'Works'. Even so, as he told William Drummond, 'Of all his plays he never gained two hundred pounds'.[9] It is clear that Shakespeare was no less ambitious than Jonson, and in 1592 he had not yet had the chance to discover in himself the business acumen that would eventually allow him to make much more money out of the theatre than writing for it could have done. Why, then, did he not pursue, as Jonson would certainly have done, the possibilities he had opened up for himself with the contact he had made with Southampton and the popular success of the two narrative poems? Why did he return to the undeniably risky business of writing plays?

First, it is necessary to be clear that despite the widespread assumption that Elizabethans placed 'poems' above 'plays', the matter is not in fact a simple one. Much has been made of Shakespeare's claim in his dedication to *Venus and Adonis* that it is the first heir of his invention, and to the fact that he apparently carefully supervised the printing of both narrative poems but showed no interest whatever in the publication of his plays. Dennis Kay presents the general view about this:

> We have to remember the low status accorded to play texts in this period, and recognize that Shakespeare, as a man of his time, saw scripts as inescapably transient and collaborative efforts; they were to be distinguished from a work of art, an altogether loftier enterprise and something grounded upon the idea, the 'foreconceit,' the *concetto*, the 'invention' of the poet.[10]

It seems to me that this statement conflates two different things. We cannot take Shakespeare's lack of involvement in the publication of his scripts as an indication that he did not think of them as 'works of art'. His relationship to his play-texts was limited by the realities of his profession. Once a play was written it was sold to an acting company and remained their property for so long as they wanted to stage it. It was usually released for publication only when it no longer had the power to bring an audience into the theatre or in circumstances when the acting company was in dire need, or when a pirated version had been printed. In any case this usually happened some years after the play's composition. The dramatist no longer had a financial stake in its publication, and was probably sufficiently distanced from it to have no aesthetic stake in it either. Not until Ben Jonson conceived the idea of recuperating his plays by reconstructing them as literary texts for his 1616 Folio did any dramatist find a way to reassert control over his work. Since Shakespeare died in that year he could hardly profit from the example, but there is no reason to believe that he would not have been delighted by the publication by Heminges and Condell of his own First Folio, whether or not their primary motives were commercial.

Indeed, the hierarchical superiority of poems to plays that is implied by Jonson's struggle to give his plays the dignity of poems is not as clear a matter as it appears. While it is certainly true that Jonson was far more aware of aesthetic issues than were most of his contemporaries, it is often difficult to separate his artistic theories from his social hunger. The main reason that he loathed writing for the stage was that it forced him to cater to the tastes of what he called the 'vulgar' or the 'world', the broad public audience that frequented the playhouses. His printed works reached a different, smaller and more affluent market of readers (he called them 'understanders'), a social and intellectual elite that he desperately wanted to join. But many of these wealthier understanders also attended playhouses and probably would not have drawn the distinction between poems and plays as clearly as Jonson did, though they might have been flattered by Jonson's characterization of them. While I have no doubt that Jonson believed in his literary theories, I think also that they fitted with his social ambition. Shakespeare would have been as aware of these distinctions as Jonson was, but that does not necessarily mean that he was as sensitive about them.

For most of Shakespeare's contemporaries the term 'poetry' meant roughly what the term 'literature' means today. A decade before Shakespeare made his brief shift to non-dramatic poetry Sir Philip Sidney had struggled in his *Apology for Poetry* with the problem of raising the reputation of poetry, by which he clearly meant something broader than the term now implies. Indeed, he laboured to distinguish poetry from history and philosophy, which do not depend on fancy or imagination, but when he surveyed literary genres as reflected in the then-contemporary English canon he included plays. He said that Elizabethan plays were 'not without cause' condemned, but this was not because he did not regard plays as literature, but because these particular plays did not observe generic conventions; he made an exception of *Gorboduc*, however, which 'obtain[s] the very end of poesy'.[11] Plays, that is, could be as aesthetically valuable as poems. The difference lay not so much in the object as in the audience. In spite of his effort to make the *writing of* poetry more respectable, Sidney himself did not differ from other aristocratic poets in his attitude toward its *publication*. In court circles more writing circulated in manuscripts than as printed books; some courtiers themselves wrote poetry that was intended for small cliques of their friends, and for them the idea of the widespread publication of their work would have been offensive. Indeed, such manuscript circulation kept elite culture exclusive, one of the means whereby aristocratic power was preserved. None of Sidney's writings was published during his lifetime, but during the 1590s, partly in response to the publication of pirated copies of his works and partly as a means of reviving Sidney's image, his family began to release authorized editions of his works, and the prestige attached to the Sidney name began to remove something of the stigma attached to 'professional' writing.

Shakespeare perhaps began to write his sonnets at about the same time that he wrote *Venus and Adonis*, and the first seventeen, the so-called 'marriage group', concern issues that have a link with that narrative poem. The circulation of Sidney's *Astrophel and Stella*, and its subsequent publication in 1591, had triggered a fashion for sonnet sequences. Shakespeare probably composed most of his sonnets between 1593 and 1603, although some may have been written as early as the late 1580s; on the known evidence more accurate dating is hardly possible. Some were circulating in manuscript by 1598, as we know from a reference by Francis Meres. Meres was a literary enthusiast whose *Palladis Tamia: Wit's Treasury* was registered in that year; it was essentially a compilation of classical and modern literary extracts that he thought were of rhetorical interest. Amongst them he included a brief account of the current state of English letters, where he refers to Shakespeare's 'sugared Sonnets among his private friends'.[12] We do not know which sonnets, however, nor do we know which friends were reading them. In 1599 William Jaggard published a slim miscellany of twenty poems as '*The Passionate Pilgrim* by W. Shakespeare'. Five of these poems are certainly by Shakespeare; two appear in the *Sonnets*, with slight modifications, as 138 and 144, and three were lifted from *Love's Labour's Lost*. The remainder probably are not Shakespeare's (some certainly are not); Jaggard presumably hoped to sell them on the strength of Shakespeare's name, and had some success since he issued a second printing in the same year.

The full text of the 154 sonnets was first published by a stationer called Thomas Thorpe in 1609. There has been much scholarly disagreement about whether or not the edition was authorized by Shakespeare, but it probably was. It is difficult to explain, though, why Shakespeare chose to publish his sequence so long after the fashion for sonnets had worn itself out. In 1609 the theatres were once again closed because of a severe outbreak of the plague, and it is tempting to suggest that he needed an alternative source of income, as had been the case with his two narrative poems. However, by 1609 he was much more secure in the theatre, as sharer in the Globe and as a member of the acting company that had become the King's Servants; furthermore, he had substantial income from businesses in Stratford. Perhaps it was simply a matter of pride in his work, but whatever the reason, the *Sonnets* appear not to have been well received, for no other edition was issued during Shakespeare's lifetime.

These are Shakespeare's major non-dramatic poems. Apart from them, a few other, minor poems were ascribed to him during his lifetime. Along with the *Sonnets* Thorpe published a narrative poem entitled *A Lover's Complaint*, claiming that it too was the work of Shakespeare. Until recently a majority of critics questioned the authenticity of this poem, but modern scholarship, especially that concerned with the analysis of diction, has found much in the poem to confirm it as Shakespeare's. In 1601 the puzzling allegorical poem 'The Phoenix and the Turtle' was included in a volume entitled *Love's Martyr*. This was a collection of allegorical poems on the subject of the myth of the phoenix and its self-renewal; apart from the long title-poem, by Robert Chester, the volume included poems by John Marston, George Chapman and Ben Jonson.

In Elizabethan England, publishing was a disorganized and often unscrupulous business. Sometimes poems were published anonymously. Sometimes poems were pirated. Sometimes the poems of one writer were published as the work of another more successful one in order to increase the likelihood of good sales. It is consequently impossible to say that the poems described above were all that Shakespeare wrote, and recently there have been claims on behalf of other poems not previously attributed to him. We can, however, be certain of little beyond the fact of the major burst of non-dramatic writing that can be located between about 1592 and 1594, and it seems that his interest in writing non-dramatic poems diminished once the theatres reopened; perhaps his excursion into writing for a patron had not provided him with an attractive living. In 1594, he became a member of the Lord Chamberlain's Men (subsequently renamed King's Men) and as far as we can know, he redirected all his energies to writing for his acting company until his retirement to Stratford in 1612, from which he emerged to collaborate on the writing of plays only a couple of times before his death on 23 April 1616.

2

Shakespeare and the Literary Marketplace

We can try to imagine Shakespeare's position in that dreadful June of 1592 when he was deprived of the source of his livelihood. How else could he make a living with his pen? Apart from the theatre, which was one of the most lucrative outlets for writers, there were other more or less disreputable forms of writing from which a little money could be made. Various kinds of poetry were fashionable. There was also a vogue of prose romances that developed in court circles and spread beyond them. Prose romances have a place in the early development of the English novel, though they were distinguished by self-consciously elegant style and an interest in abstract debate rather than by developed plot and characters. At a less literary level there was pamphleteering, a forerunner of journalism. Pamphlets were short tracts, usually on controversial political or religious matters, or relating sensational stories about the criminal underworld. Many writers, as Robert Greene did, tried their hand at more than one of these. But if we think of a profession as a calling, a more or less honorable means of earning a living, then writing as a profession barely existed at all. In some ways the last years of the reign of Elizabeth can be understood as a time when a few writers began the lengthy struggle to establish their work as a respectable activity; these were all, in effect, upstart crows, from Spenser through to Jonson. Some of them never even thought of themselves primarily as writers; writing was a means to an end, an enterprise that they hoped would get them into service in the court through the patronage system. Almost all writers depended in some way upon patronage. Aristocratic households were still large, and maintained the medieval practice of counting amongst their servants artists and entertainers such as writers, actors, musicians, or dancing teachers. The relationship between benefactor and artist was of profound cultural importance because it indicated the social and political power of the patron. In return for some degree (usually not large) of financial or material support (such as board and lodging) writers provided their patrons with poems or dedicated writings to them. The obvious demand for flattery limited what we might think of as the writer's 'artistic freedom', but it did provide him with an income. So in 1592 Shakespeare, with his main source of income cut off, found his patron.

It is absolutely essential to keep in mind that, however great an artist he might have been, Shakespeare's first motivation was to make a living, and he sold what he produced in a particular marketplace. The commercial implications of the idea of a literary marketplace might seem to be in opposition to the whole idea of what today we think of as poetry, but a marketplace is simply a space in which commodities are provided for consumption by others, and all writers write for consumers of their work who will give them payment in some form. The theatre itself is a marketplace in this sense. When Shakespeare was writing, the book trade was still in the very early stages of its development. The first printing press in England had been established by William Caxton in 1477, hardly more than a century before Shakespeare began his literary career. Even in London the writer's market was limited. Books were very expensive and the percentage of the population that was literate was still small, though increasing. The demand for printed books was likewise small, and while there was an enthusiastic readership willing to pay for the kinds of poetry that were in fashion, a poet who depended for his living on people buying his books could hardly expect to flourish.

We have to think of the market for writers in a broader sense. The circulation of texts was a very complex business, and the object sold was not necessarily a printed text or book, nor was the payment for it necessarily money. Shakespeare's plays were sold in manuscript form to his acting company, and were then transmuted into performances for auditor-spectators; they did eventually reach print, but they no longer belonged to their author. His two narrative poems must have been offered to Southampton in manuscript form, and for that dedication he presumably received a monetary reward, but payment could well have been, as it was for many 'professional' writers, some other form of support or preferment. His two poems were also printed to be sold to a popular but affluent readership that would have been much impressed by the fact that they had attracted such distinguished patronage; Southampton's name would certainly have increased their value in the commercial market.

Which did Shakespeare value more, the endorsement of his poems by Southampton, or their acceptance by the wider readership?

The answer to this question might seem obvious, but the fact is that there were strong connections between the concerns of English literary culture and the concerns of the powerful elites. The middle-class audience, determined to be 'upwardly mobile', was fascinated by the interests of its 'betters', and so the poet's dedication of work to a fashionable aristocrat acted as a kind of advertisement for the poem. Furthermore, most professional writers were themselves anxious to be upwardly mobile, so the attention given to a manuscript by an influential patron was potentially worth much more than the money brought in by the sale of a printed book. The dream of upward movement, sadly, was only too frequently no more than a dream; nevertheless, it is true that the success of most professional writers of Elizabethan literature depended to some degree on how they reflected the interests of the upper classes.

In actually trying to sell his work the writer must have felt the greatest frustration. He was usually at the mercy of the stationers who controlled the publishing business. There was no system of royalties, and so he depended on the bargain he could strike with the publisher; a volume of poetry might bring its author as little as two pounds. The writer was always in the weaker position. There is only a little exaggeration in the statement by Phoebe Sheavyn that 'the average stationer drove hard bargains, preferred inferior work, snubbed and insulted the writer, and when possible, stole his manuscripts from him'.[1] It is possible that Shakespeare returned to writing for the stage as soon as he could because it took him out of the grasp of these men; this might also be the reason why he delayed so long the publication of his sonnets. We do not know much about his dealings with publishers, but like most writers of poetry he probably saw the value of printed volumes of his work mainly in the boost they gave to his reputation. Even this idea is problematic, however, for in the early 1590s there was still a stigma attached to the idea of poetry as a profession and to the act of publication. This was connected to the fact that many noblemen were themselves producers of poetry.

During the latter part of the reign of Elizabeth the writing of poetry had become fashionable in the court, and a significant number of nobles prided themselves upon their talent and literary sophistication. They wished only to impress their peers, however, and their poems were circulated in manuscript amongst their aristocratic and powerful friends. They would have considered as contemptible the idea of exposing their writings to the masses through print. These poets were 'amateurs' in the original sense of the word, which did not have the derogatory implications of superficiality or ineptitude that it sometimes has today. They wrote their poetry for a very privileged 'market' of consumers who were admirers, not buyers. So at its highest social levels the literary marketplace hardly looked like a marketplace at all, since texts were circulated with the specific intention of keeping them away from a large readership. Literary documents were produced for and passed around inside elite groups within the court and within aristocratic families and circles (sometimes called 'coteries'), and such manuscript circulation was emulated by groups in other powerful environments such as the Inns of Court, the universities, and wealthier middle-class households. Harold Love calls such circulation 'a mode of social bonding', and says the 'choice of scribal publication in preference to print might well be dictated by a sense of identification with a particular community and a desire to nourish its corporate ideology'.[2] Particularly in elite groups the circulation of literary texts became a means both of transmission and of control of the ideas, beliefs and attitudes, the aesthetic and ideological positions that defined the specialness of the group. For the aristocratic writer literary manuscripts became a means of negotiation or endorsement of status within the community of power; that is, they earned not money, but cultural capital.

This does not mean that the writing of aristocratic poets never got into print. As I have noted, London's rising wealthy class of merchants and others with access to a good education had a deep curiosity about aristocratic fashions and tastes, and also had the means to emulate them. It often happened that manuscripts found their way out of the privileged cliques for which they were produced and into the hands of these new classes, and inevitably into unauthorized print. An instructive illustration of this is the fate of the work of Sir Philip Sidney. The most celebrated of Elizabethan aristocratic writers, Sidney was a member of one of the most powerful and respected noble families in England, and was often characterized by his contemporaries as the ideal Renaissance man. He was deeply involved in public and military affairs, and his recklessness and outspokenness at one point made him so offensive to the queen that between 1580 and 1583 he retired from the court, living principally at Wilton House, the home of his sister Mary, Countess of Pembroke. During that period he produced a body of writing that was to become extraordinarily influential, including the sonnet sequence *Astrophil and Stella*, which inspired the fashion for sonnet sequences of the 1590s; the *Arcadia*, a prose romance with verse interludes; and *An Apology for Poetry* (also known as *The Defense of Poesy*), the first serious attempt in English to justify the kind of imaginative writing that we would now include under the larger heading of 'literature'. He wrote them to be circulated within his coterie of courtly friends, perhaps for no loftier motive than the hope that through them he might catch the attention of the queen and regain her favour. As I mentioned earlier, he certainly had no intention of releasing them into print; but although none was published before his death in 1586, by the early 1590s all had been printed. Indeed, the prestige attached to his name was so great that the publication of his works helped to remove the stigma attached to publication in general.

Aristocratic attitudes to writers who, like Shakespeare, were not born into privileged circles were obviously ambivalent. In court circles poetry was a highly regarded commodity, circulated within a small community; it reflected the desires and beliefs of the court, and its value was not perceived as material. But the noble consumer's desire for novelty, for new and exciting poetry, was often mixed with a degree of distaste for those who produced it if they came from outside the 'community of blood'. The professional poet was working with very potent and volatile materials, the significance of which was intimately connected to the ideology of the elites within the court and to the way in which they perceived themselves and wished to be perceived. He could, therefore, be dangerous. As we have seen, Shakespeare's way into the system was through the Earl of Southampton, but we do not know what, if anything, he gained from this relationship. However, he clearly had no misgivings about publishing the poems he dedicated to his patron, no doubt feeling himself unable to afford any well-bred disdain for the tastes or the money of the common reader.

PATRONAGE

Before I consider Shakespeare's connection with Southampton I must say more about patronage, for the significance of its effects on writing in the Elizabethan period can hardly be overestimated. 'Patronage' refers to a culture in which a monarch, statesman, nobleman (or woman: literary and artistic patronage was one area of activity in which aristocratic women were influential), or other wealthy, powerful individual gives rewards to favourites or clients, usually in return for some kind of support or service. In Renaissance England the political and social organization was given coherence by a pervasive system of patronage. It was a structure through which power could be disseminated and controlled; the prizes of patronage were rich and varied and connected to all important institutions. They included 'cash, titles and honors, lands, leases, grants, licences, monopolies, pensions, educational and ecclesiastical positions, parliamentary seats, and places in the employ of the nobility, government officials, and the monarch'.[3] In return for these gifts the patron expected loyal service from the recipient. At a simple level patronage can be understood as a means whereby those in power sustained their power by buying allegiance.

In most periods there has to be some form of support for artists to allow them to make a living, and in the Renaissance artistic patronage was inextricably connected to political patronage (though this connection is almost always a component of patronage at some level). As we have already seen, for writers in Shakespeare's time there was no great commercial demand for what they sold, but the reign of Elizabeth I, and to a lesser degree that of her successor James I, saw the greatest flourishing of patronage to writers and other artists in English history. We cannot understand the significance of this, however, if we try to separate artistic patronage from other kinds. The court was the central marketplace for patronage and a magnet for the ambitious of all ranks. Michael Brennan writes, 'The attendance of a large number of wealthy and influential patrons at court, including aristocrats, leading churchmen, military commanders and distinguished members of the professions, ensured that it became the goal of a host of lesser mortals who hoped to engage their interest and favour'.[4] Amongst these lesser mortals there were always writers.

Given the subservient and inhibited position of the writer in such a relationship, the obvious question to suggest itself here concerns what today we like to think of as 'artistic freedom of expression': what freedom can an artist have if he is competing against others for the favour of the powerful? Undeniably, the system imposed constraints, though I might note in passing that in modern societies support for artists often comes in the form of grants from foundations and government agencies, and often these grants are limited by specific guidelines about the moral or political content of artifacts. This, of course, means that contemporary artists too might be dependent on what is essentially a form of political patronage. The fact is that some Elizabethan writers who did not wish to flatter or to toe the orthodox line found ironic or oblique ways of writing. It was certainly not uncommon for a controversial or uncooperative writer to be dropped by a patron.

What kind of support could Elizabethan writers expect? For the most part it was monetary, and could range from a small sum for a specific dedication, to a modest pension for a writer who had drawn the right kind of attention to himself: Edmund Spenser received 50 pounds a year after the publication of *The Faerie Queene*. Support might also be food and lodging (Ben Jonson is known to have lived in a number of wealthy households) or other kinds of protection and encouragement. At best it might furnish the writer with a professional position suitable for his skills, such as tutor, secretary or chaplain. A rare, perhaps uniquely-fortunate example of a writer who received patronage throughout his life was Samuel Daniel. Appointed servant to the ambassador to France, he was also employed as an agent in France for Sir Francis Walsingham. On his return to England he was appointed tutor to William Herbert, son of Mary Sidney, and later to Lady Anne Clifford, daughter of the Earl of Cumberland. He was also given support by the Earls of Essex and Southampton. All this support gave him the leisure to produce a large, varied, and in its time influential body of writing.

Why should a system based on a patron–client relationship that fostered obligation and dependency have flourished under Elizabeth? A part of the answer is that although the Tudor monarchy supplanted medieval feudalism, it was still essentially a hierarchical system. Most of the families that constituted the Tudor aristocracy had themselves been ennobled by the Tudors, and the patronage system was a means of binding them to the monarch by ties of obligation. They, in their turn, handed out gifts and favours to their supporters. Patronage in one form or another thus permeated the entire society in something like a trickle-down effect. The source of everything was the sovereign, whose gifts by and large went directly to the aristocratic members of the court: they within their own households passed on this largesse. Outside the court, the system was replicated in wealthy circles, and city officials, churchmen, lawyers, merchants and members of companies all dispensed patronage in emulation of their superiors.

Patronage, then, was essential as a means of tying together the social and political structure, but it had another important function. For those who had power, patronage became a matter of prestige, a means of reflecting their power. The simple ability to dispense favours was the most conspicuous aspect of this, but another effective use of patronage was to create images of substance and splendour by linking it to art. Gordon Kipling has shown that Henry VII, Elizabeth's grandfather and the founder of the Tudor line, was the first English monarch to offer 'widespread and systematic patronage to artists and men of letters'. In instituting his own court he tried to emulate the splendour of continental courts, and his household included 'librarians, portrait painters, tapestry weavers, poets, players, glaziers, and the devisers of masques and revels'.[5] This was not simply a matter of show, however; Henry was well aware of the importance of literary sophistication in the education of those who would be successful governors. His son, the future Henry VIII, was tutored by the poet and dramatist John Skelton.

Elizabeth inherited this shrewd awareness of the necessity of scholarship and education. She read widely and was herself a writer and linguist of some ability, and her attitudes and interests influenced the things that were valued in her court. She was also aware of the mythic potential of a carefully-manipulated public image, and much of the artistic energy of her court was directed towards her transformation into Gloriana, the Virgin Queen, embodiment of English magnificence, symbol of national unity, pride and power. This image was presented and elaborated in pageants, plays and entertainments, in paintings and in poems. For the writer who wanted to be a beneficiary of court patronage, some commitment to its values was necessary, and some degree of compromise was impossible to avoid. At the same time, without patronage there could not have been the great explosion of literature that characterized the Elizabethan age.

Within Elizabeth's court a number of powerful figures had control over patronage, most notably two members of the Cecil family, William, Lord Burghley, and Robert, Earl of Salisbury, but their interests were almost exclusively political. There were other patrons who were genuinely knowledgeable and interested in poetry, but even those whose concern might be thought of as aesthetic also had pragmatic concerns that were essentially ideological. During his short life Sir Philip Sidney was an active promoter of the idea that England needed a literature in its native language, and his sister Mary carried his message on long after his death. Sidney's uncle, the

Earl of Leicester, cultivated literary men, though he was especially interested in using literature to further the Protestant cause. Another of the queen's favourites, Robert Devereux, Earl of Essex, gave sincere encouragement to writers, but this was inextricable from his concern to further his own ambitions, which were supported by his close associate the Earl of Southampton, Shakespeare's patron.

While it is clear that the motives of patrons were never simple, the positive effects of patronage in generating an English literature are undeniable. One of the most generous households in its treatment of writers was that of the Herbert family, the Earls of Pembroke, for whom almost 250 authors are known to have written dedications or literary tributes.[6] In 1623 the posthumous First Folio of Shakespeare's plays was dedicated to William, third Earl of Pembroke, and his brother Philip. The mother of William and Philip was Sir Philip Sidney's sister Mary, Countess of Pembroke. Mary Sidney had a keen interest in the promotion of literature, which in the first place revealed itself in her efforts to perpetuate the name and reputation of her dead brother. But she was herself a talented writer at a time when writing by women was not encouraged, and since patronage at least allowed women to make some contribution to the developing literature, she also directed her creative energies into helping to sustain the writing of others.

The Pembrokes came as close to a generous ideal as the patronage system allowed, but we cannot assume that in all cases the patron really valued what the writer had to offer. Equally, we cannot assume that ambitious young men trying to break their way into court circles always cared more about the quality of what they wrote than about their own self-advancement; as the historian Lawrence Stone has pointed out, literary patronage offered 'the necessary leverage to thrust them into comfortable jobs in the Church, the universities, and royal administration'.[7] This is not as materialistic as it might appear. Many courtiers wrote poetry, but only as one of many things that occupied their time. The idea that anyone would see writing as a full-time vocation was still novel. Writing was a means to other ends, not an end in itself. This is not to deny, of course, that there were writers for whom poetry was a deeply serious and engaging matter. The idea that the poet is the conduit of truth is an ancient one, and was revived with the rediscovery of classical thought that came with the Renaissance. Sidney pointed out that the ancient Romans called a poet *vates*, 'which is as much as a diviner, fore-seer, or prophet' (*Apology*, p. 219). Authors like Ben Jonson had a lofty view of the calling of the poet; Jonson was not afraid to tell King James I himself that 'Poets are of rarer birth than Kings'. For such a writer, the pursuit of patronage was as constantly frustrating as it was necessary.

The reality of patronage was that the client needed the patron more than the patron needed the client, and as far as writing was concerned there were always more poets than there were individuals anxious to support them. The degree of self-interest that existed on both sides of most patron–client relationships meant that the successful writer was the one most willing or able to provide whatever pleased the patron. As a result, there was fierce competition. This had the positive effect of forcing writers to greater effort, and is one of the reasons why there remains such a large body of powerful literature from the period. As Gary Taylor has recently argued, 'Diversifying competition intensely and directly among a group of talented contemporaries provides the best possible breeding ground for works that will be able, in turn, to survive competition with centuries of yet unborn rivals'.[8] This competition also had the negative effect of favouring those writers who were the most willing to flatter, or to offer their services to the pragmatic rather than artistic end of polemical justification of religious or political causes.

Perhaps the worst effect of the system was that for most serious writers it could generate only disillusionment and bitterness. While appearing to hold out glittering prizes it usually led to disappointment. Its gifts were unpredictable, insecure and limited, and the poet who expected too much from the system might be destroyed by it. A case in point is Edmund Spenser. Born in 1552 the son of a London cloth-worker, Spenser attended Pembroke Hall, Cambridge, where he was befriended by Gabriel Harvey. Harvey introduced him to Sidney, who was deeply impressed by his writing. Taken into Sidney's coterie, which included the aristocratic poets Fulke Greville and Sir Edward Dyer, Spenser reached the fringes of the court. In 1580 he received, probably through patronage, an appointment in Ireland as private secretary to Lord Grey, but although he worked hard to make the situation comfortable, and amassed a great deal of property, this was always to him a kind of cultural exile, and he desperately wanted to return to London and court life.

Spenser produced poetry that amazed his own time, and he thought it should be rewarded with more than simple attention. *The Faerie Queene*, monumental even in its uncompleted state, represents the most astonishing literary bid for royal patronage of the period. It did not lead to the advancement he hoped for, however, providing nothing much beyond his meagre pension. In 1591 (only a year before Shakespeare was to turn to writing the kind of poetry that needed a patron) Spenser published 'Mother Hubberd's Tale', with its bitter account of the realities of existence for those who need to seek preferment at court:

> Full little knowest thou that hast not tride,
> What hell it is, in suing long to bide:
> To loose good dayes, that might be better spent;
> To wast long nights in pensive discontent;
> To speed today, to be put back tomorrow;
> To feed on hope, to pine with feare and sorrow;
> To have thy Princes grace, yet want her Peeres;
> To have thy asking, yet waite manie yeeres;
> To fret thy soule with crosses and with cares;
> To eate thy heart through comfortlesse dispaires;
> To fawne, to crowche, to waite, to ride, to ronne,
> To spend, to give, to want, to be undonne.
> Unhappie wight, borne to desastrous end,
> That doth his life in so long tendance spend.
>
>   (895–908)[9]

Unsuccessful in all efforts to draw official approval upon himself, he was forced back to England by the Irish uprising of 1598 and died penniless in the following year.

This was the reality of patronage for many, perhaps most, writers. How deeply did it affect Shakespeare? As a member of an acting company he was already inside the structure of patronage, since the companies were employed in noble households. It is possible that in his early years in London he worked with the Earl of Leicester's Men or Lord Strange's Men. Although this employment obliged the companies to entertain the important guests of their noble patrons, its most beneficial effect was to protect them against legal persecution, since without it actors were defined by the law as vagabonds. The dependency of the acting companies on this kind of patronage was legal rather than financial, however, because most of their income came from the public playhouses. They had therefore a degree of freedom that was not available to writers who had to seek more direct patronage. When the plague caused the closing of the playhouses and Shakespeare found himself adrift, it is not surprising that he approached the Earl of Southampton, who had already proved himself generous to writers.

SHAKESPEARE AND SOUTHAMPTON

Henry Wriothesley succeeded to his title as the third Earl of Southampton in 1581, when he was eight years old. In 1593, the year that Shakespeare published *Venus and Adonis*, he was 19; Shakespeare was 28. It is reasonable to suppose that Shakespeare came into contact with Southampton through the patronage connections he made in the acting companies, but there is no evidence to confirm this. In 1592, when the playhouses were closed, Shakespeare must have been somewhat oppressed by the need to seek an income elsewhere. Southampton was a brilliant young man who encouraged a number of writers and scholars; he is known to have given support to Barnabe Barnes, Gervase Markham, Samuel Daniel and Thomas Nashe, and without doubt there were others. It is possible that some of Shakespeare's sonnets were already circulating in manuscript, and his plays were gaining him a reputation, as we know from Greene's attack on him.

When he offered *Venus and Adonis* to Southampton, would Shakespeare have had good reason to suppose that the young Earl would be flattered by his gift? The tone of the dedication that prefaces the poem is what one might expect from a reasonably self-confident writer approaching a patron whom he does not know but from whom he might expect a sympathetic judgement:

> Right Honourable, I know not how I shall offend in dedicating my unpolished lines to your lordship, nor how the world will censure me for choosing so strong a prop to support so weak a burden. Only, if your honour seem but pleased, I account my self highly praised, and vow to take advantage of all idle hours till I have honoured you with some graver labour. But if the first heir of my invention prove deformed, I shall be sorry it had so noble a godfather, and never after ear so barren a land, for fear it yield me still so bad a harvest. I leave it to your honourable survey, and your Honour to your heart's content, which I wish may always answer your own wish, and the world's hopeful expectation.

YOUR HONOUR'S IN ALL DUTY,

WILLIAM SHAKESPEARE

The attitude is properly modest, and we do not have to believe that Shakespeare really considered his lines to be 'unpolished'. He sets up a distinction between 'the world', common opinion, that will censure him for offering such a poor gift to a patron, and Southampton himself, whose more discriminating taste might perceive something of value in the poem. If Southampton likes the poem Shakespeare will write him another, better one – 'some graver labour' – if not, he will stop writing poetry. The witty way in which he puts his fate into Southampton's hands indicates that he does not expect his gift to be rejected.

This is not to say that Shakespeare feels no discomfort in this dedication. He is very clear about the hierarchical structure of power that orders the relationship between patron and client; in different ways it reflects the relationship between reader and writer or between audience and playwright. In the final line of the Prologue to *Henry V Shakespeare*, speaking through the Chorus, asks the audience 'Gently to hear, kindly to judge, our play', and this is not merely a rhetorical gesture, for the audience does have the authority to make the play fail. The vulnerability of the writer–client is intensified by the extreme social superiority of the reader–patron, and the dedication firmly acknowledges that all power is in the hands of the poem's 'noble godfather'. Embedded in the dedication, then, is a reflection of the poet's understanding of the precise location of the poem in a network of cultural forces. The poet is confident of the value of his work, in spite of his ironic self-disparagement, but at the same time he is aware that he needs the patron's approval for a number of reasons. Primary amongst these is the material support that Southampton might give; beyond this, however, is the need to appeal to the wider audience demanded by print publication, and the approval of a fashionable figure like Southampton would certainly have helped to make the poem fashionable. It did, indeed, go through nine editions during the writer's lifetime, and the fact that very few copies survive is an indication of its popularity.

Even though he was only 19 in 1593, Southampton, was already a generous benefactor to writers and scholars, and it is not extraordinary that Shakespeare should have dedicated his poem to a man from whom he might have expected financial support. The dedication itself has come under intense scholarly scrutiny in attempts to establish what it might or might not imply about Shakespeare's relationship with Southampton. Some scholars have found in its tone a sense of relaxed ease that suggests to them that Shakespeare was already relatively intimate with Southampton when he published the poem, an interpretation which fuels the argument that Southampton is the youth addressed in the *Sonnets*. This belief raises the difficult question of how the dramatist, a young man from a small provincial town who was still only beginning to establish a reputation as a writer for the playhouses, could have achieved such intimacy with so powerful a figure. In my own view, the dedication provides no evidence to support this interpretation. It rather shows that Shakespeare was well aware of the kind of thing that should be said to gain the favour of a potential patron.

Shakespeare's second narrative poem, *The Rape of Lucrece*, was dedicated to the Earl of Southampton in the following year:

> The love I dedicate to your lordship is without end, whereof this pamphlet without beginning is but a superfluous moiety. The warrant I have of your honourable disposition, not the worth of my untutored lines, makes it assured of acceptance. What I have done is yours; what I have to do is yours, being part in all I have, devoted yours. Were my worth greater my duty would show greater, meantime, as it is, it is bound to your lordship, to whom I wish long life still lengthened with all happiness.
>
> YOUR LORDSHIP'S IN ALL DUTY,
>
> WILLIAM SHAKESPEARE

There are scholars who have detected in this dedication a more familiar tone than in the earlier one, and have conjectured from it an increasingly intimate relationship between Shakespeare and his young patron. However, even if the tone is more familiar (and I do not think it is clear that it is), it might mean no more than that Shakespeare felt more confident about dedicating this second poem to a man who had already accepted his first. I think we need to understand that dedications were in themselves a kind of genre, with conventions of their own. Like the dedication to *Venus and Adonis*, this one places the power of judgment in the hands of the aristocrat: it is the nobility of Southampton, the poet claims, rather than the quality of the 'untutored lines', that will ensure the poem's acceptance by the patron. Again, this was not truly Shakespeare's estimation of the worth of his work. A dedication acted as a kind of advertisement for the text it prefaced; it was written not just for the dedicatee, but also with an eye on the larger market of potential buyers. It was obviously in the interest of the poet to give an impression of familiarity, whatever the true state of the case might have been.

There is not really much more that can be said about Shakespeare's relationship with his patron, though a whole history has been constructed by speculative scholars and critics who have mined biographical material from the *Sonnets* because they have assumed that Southampton is the young man of the *Sonnets*. There is no documentary evidence of any reward that Shakespeare received for his work, and certainly no record of any close and long-standing association. There is a story, apparently originating with the dramatist Sir William Davenant, that Southampton gave Shakespeare 1000 pounds. Davenant is not a reliable witness (he also claimed to be Shakespeare's illegitimate son), and if we set that sum beside the 50 pounds pension given to Spenser, it seems highly improbable. Because of the rigid hierarchic divisions in Elizabethan society it is unlikely, though not impossible, that Shakespeare was welcomed into Southampton's circle. If the connection lasted for any number of years (as must have been the case if Southampton really was the youth of the *Sonnets*, but there is no other evidence of it) it would have been a risky one, for in 1598 Southampton married Elizabeth Vernon, cousin of the Earl of Essex, thus incurring the wrath of Queen Elizabeth. Three years later he was implicated in Essex's doomed rebellion against the queen, and was sentenced to death. This was commuted to life imprisonment, and he was released when James I came to the throne in 1603. Thereafter he spent most of his energies in support of colonial adventures.

SHAKESPEARE ON COURT POETRY AND PATRONAGE

Because Shakespeare's *Sonnets* have been so frequently used as evidence of an intimate relationship between Shakespeare and Southampton (which I think is no more than a romantic myth), a common assumption has been that Shakespeare found a patron easily. I find this hard to credit, however. By 1592, he was developing a reputation as a playwright (though the absence of any reference to him prior to Greene's makes it reasonable to assume that it was not yet great). Even if a few of his sonnets were in circulation, as far as is known he had no reputation at all as a poet. There is no reason to believe that Southampton was the only patron that Shakespeare approached. Nor is there any evidence that the poet did not suffer the frustration and humiliation described by Spenser as the common experience of poets, the suing and waiting, the fawning and running. Spenser's experience came in spite of his having far more powerful connections than Shakespeare could have had. If Shakespeare did suffer any of these discouraging experiences, it would not be surprising if he got out of the patronage trap as quickly as he could.

Unlike Jonson, Shakespeare left no explicit statements about his attitude to the various aspects of his profession, but there are poet-figures in a number of his plays. We might reasonably ask what can be derived from his treatment of them, but this leads us into problematic territory, since any statement in a play must be identified primarily with the character who utters it rather than with the dramatist who wrote it. What we find, however, is what Ekbert Faas has characterized as a 'consistently negative portrayal of poets in his work'.[10] Now of course, our judgement of any such portrayal will depend on the context in which it is presented. Nevertheless, this insistent hostility has been apparent to others: Katherine Duncan-Jones, in her recent edition of the *Sonnets*, asks, 'How do we reconcile Shakespeare's consistently scornful allusions to sonnets and sonneteering in his plays with the fact of his having composed one of the longest sonnet sequences of the period?'[11] There is, of course, more than one possible answer to this question, but one thing that should be noted is that Faas simplifies through generalization, for while it is true that Shakespeare's portrayal of poets is (fairly) consistently negative, they are treated in different ways, and the greatest mockery is directed at fashionable, courtly poets.

With the possible exception of *The Two Gentlemen of Verona* Shakespeare's poets appear in plays written after his own experience as a poet. His best-known statement about poets and poetry is the speech by Duke Theseus in the last act of *A Midsummer Night's Dream*, and the hostility is surely there. Having listened to the strange story told by the young lovers, Theseus weighs it with 'cool reason', and dismisses it, on the grounds that love generates the same delusions, the same 'shaping fantasies', as madness. He then goes on, perhaps rather arbitrarily, to lump the poet in with the lunatic and the lover, condemning him for indulging in the same excesses. Theseus tells us:

> The poet's eye, in a fine frenzy rolling,
> Doth glance from heaven to earth, from earth to heaven,
> And as imagination bodies forth
> The forms of things unknown, the poet's pen
> Turns them to shapes, and gives to airy nothing
> A local habitation and a name.
> Such tricks hath strong imagination
> That if it would but apprehend some joy;
> It comprehends some bringer of that joy;

Or in the night, imagining some fear,
How easy is a bush supposed a bear!

(5.1.12–22)

We might respond that Theseus is here confusing two different
operations of the imagination, confounding illusion with delusion,
since the poet actively uses his imagination to give shape to airy
nothing, while the lunatic and the lover are passive victims of theirs.
Furthermore, as audience, we have seen the things that he is denying
in the name of his conception of 'reality'. Theseus has often been
taken as the authoritative voice in *A Midsummer Night's Dream*, but
the context of this speech seems to prevent us from uncritically
accepting his view of things, and we might (using our own 'cool
reason') conclude that Shakespeare expects us to reject this dismissal
of the poet as a manifestation of aristocratic arrogance.

I think that this is indeed the response that Shakespeare expects of
us, if for no other reason than that Theseus's words would condemn
A Midsummer Night's Dream itself. Nevertheless, if we place his comments in the context of Shakespeare's treatment of poet-characters
in other plays, the distance of the dramatist's position from the
Thesean attitude is not quite so evident as we might wish to suppose. Any praise of poetry is usually undercut through being located
in an ironic context, and poets themselves are always mocked, sometimes harshly. For example, in *The Two Gentlemen of Verona* poetry is
described as 'heaven-bred', its magical powers originating in the
figure of Orpheus, 'Whose golden touch could soften steel and
stones, / Make tigers tame, and huge leviathans / Forsake unsounded
deeps to dance on sands' (3.2.78–80). This, however, is an attempt to
persuade the fool Thurio to write a sonnet with the hope of winning
Sylvia, bringing 'heaven-bred' poesy sharply down to earth. As
a type of the gentleman-amateur (albeit a sham one) Thurio stands
as a sort of mock version of the courtly poet who by Shakespeare's
time had made Petrarchan love poetry fashionable to the point
where it had effectively been emptied of meaning.

The poetic myth known as Petrarchism developed from the writing of the Italian scholar and poet Francesco Petrarca (1304–1374),
known in England as Petrarch. Petrarch self-consciously constructed
an image of himself as a person in exile in a transient world.
Although he spent his early years in the Papal court at Avignon and
developed a wide circle of acquaintances amongst the powerful
figures of his own day, eventually accepting the laurel crown that

established him as the Italian national poet, he liked to represent himself as a marginalized figure, a wanderer. At the centre of his writing is the metaphor of the journey; he often imagines himself as a storm-tossed ship. His sonnets were included in his *Canzoniere*, a collection of 366 poems in a number of lyric forms. Fundamental to this collection is the poet's love for the woman Laura, whom he claims to have met in church on Good Friday 1327. His idealization of this woman, expressed in conceits that became conventional in the description of feminine beauty and virtue, and his presentation of the desire and hopelessness prompted in him by her refusal of him, with its language of paradox and oxymoron, of freezing fire and burning ice, can be understood as a way of speaking about any ideal, alluring because it can be imagined, but painful because it is unreachable. Although there was an historical Laura, Petrarch's 'Laura' can best be understood as a pretext rather than as a person. Thus, he is able to use her to write about human love, but the religious associations of his first meeting with her also allow him to write about her as the embodiment of a spiritual ideal. The fact that she remains unattainable by him allows him to examine his own experience of alienation.

These ideas were imported into England in the early part of the sixteenth century, and were received with such enthusiasm that they shortly became clichés. At the centre of Petrarchism is the relationship between the male speaker of the poems and the beautiful woman he loves. Her beauty is a Platonic reflection of her virtue, and it is this for which he loves her, but this same virtue causes her to reject the speaker's pleas: if she were to give in to him she would be discarding what makes her desirable. The speaker is thus trapped inside a paradox, forced to love what he cannot have, and this is why so much Petrarchan imagery presents paradoxes of the interdependence of pain and pleasure. Because communication between the two is always frustrated and the woman remains at a distance, she is perceived by the speaker as an object. He therefore describes her physical beauty rather mechanically in terms of emblematic perfection: her eyes like the sun, her hair like gold, her skin like snow or lilies. On the other hand, he is acutely self-aware, minutely examining his own responses to what he perceives as the cold cruelty of this ideal figure. This set of conventions was easily integrated into the literary culture of 'courtly love', which had been established in England in the Middle Ages and still had a powerful attraction for the Elizabethan court. The courtly lover expressed his esteem for the lady in terms of a feudal model of selfless loyalty, serving her as a knight served his lord. Thus, although the lover was always a warrior, and the language of love often couched in terms of a military campaign, love was expressed as a refining experience, repressing the more brutal aspects of 'chivalric' action.

It should be apparent that this system is open to self-indulgent abuse, and by the mid-1590s it was somewhat tarnished. In *As You Like It* the young gentleman Orlando is also entrapped by Petrarchism in an artificial view of love. He hangs poems on trees to express his love for Rosalind, and is only freed to win her after she has shown him how far divorced from reality his literary understanding of love is: 'Men have died from time to time, and worms have eaten them, but not for love'(4.1.91–92). This play appears to suggest, perhaps more gently, that poetry can be dangerous if it prevents us from seeing what is really there. Of course, we have to remember that the plays themselves are poetry, and presumably Shakespeare is not mounting a serious attack on the source of his own livelihood. Perhaps his laughter is really directed against the aristocratic concept of the amateur poet rather than against poetry itself.

Shakespeare's most extensive treatment of this kind of poet comes in *Love's Labour's Lost*, in which four young aristocrats try to use poetry as a means of wooing four young women. Their endeavour ends in failure, and they are mocked by the women whom they seek to impress. The main reason for this is the extreme affectation of their language, in which display has taken the place of substance. Biron, the lover whose scepticism puts him closest to 'reality', is eventually led to renounce the linguistic ornamentation that the young men have believed to be the essence of poetry:

> O, never will I trust to speeches penned,
> Nor to the motion of a schoolboy's tongue,
> Nor never come in visor to my friend,
> Nor woo in rhyme, like a blind harper's song.
> Taffeta phrases, silken terms precise,
> Three-piled hyperboles, spruce affectation,
> Figures pedantical – these summer flies
> Have blown me full of maggot ostentation.
> I do forswear them, and I here protest,
> By this white glove – how white the hand, God knows –
> Henceforth my wooing mind shall be expressed
> In russet yeas, and honest kersey noes

And to begin, wench, so God help me, law!
My love to thee is sound, sans crack or flaw.

                                                      (5.2.402–15)

There are many ironies here. Although these lines are part of
a slightly longer speech, they constitute a sonnet: Biron expresses
his renunciation of literary artifice in one of the most elaborately
artificial of verse forms. There are other blatant rhetorical devices –
the self-conscious patterning of the first four lines, the linguistic
affectation, the Petrarchan cliché of the white hand. Biron claims to
recognize them as a disease, yet he is unable to cure himself of them.
At best, we can take from the treatment of the four young aristocrats
the idea that an interest in poetry is a sign of an immature and
incomplete approach to life.

In the same play, however, there are 'poets' whose treatment
cannot be quite so easily interpreted. Nathaniel and Holofernes
present a play for their noble superiors which in its ineptitude rivals
Peter Quince's most lamentable comedy. The aristocrats, like those
in *A Midsummer Night's Dream*, provide a mocking and disruptive
commentary, but the purpose of the scene seems less to mock the
two 'dramatists' than to expose the callow attitudes of their supposedly well-bred audience, and when Holofernes chides them with
'This is not generous, not gentle, not humble' (5.2.617) we are
inclined to agree with him. *Love's Labour's Lost* can be seen not so
much as presenting a negative portrayal of poets as mocking poetic
amateurism and revealing the humiliations of those at the receiving
end of the patronage system. It foreshadows the frustrations of
Quince and Bottom and their friends as they try to reflect refined
values back to their aristocratic audience.

There are two other plays in which poets make a significant
appearance, *Julius Caesar* and *Timon of Athens*. In *Julius Caesar*
Shakespeare gives us two poets. In the first case the poet Cinna,
a supporter of Julius Caesar, is mistaken by the Roman mob for the
conspirator Cinna. The mob threatens to tear him to pieces; when he
tries to defend himself by insisting on his identity as Cinna the poet,
they instead decide to 'Tear him for his bad verses' (3.3.29). It might
be that Shakespeare merely wished to show the undiscriminating
ugliness of mob violence here, but the tone of the scene, dark as it is,
is nevertheless comic: Cinna falls victim to an extreme act of literary
criticism. Two scenes later a different poet, labeled 'cynic' by Cassius,
approaches Brutus and Cassius, who have just reconciled after

a bitter quarrel. His marginal position seems to make him a 'professional', even a Jonsonian poet, and he has come as healer, offering
the wisdom of his years, to beg them to 'Love and be friends'
(4.2.183). The response of the two generals is to dismiss him with
mockery and contempt. Shakespeare gives these two poets together
hardly more than a dozen lines, and we might want to ask why he
bothered to include them at all. In the case of the cynic-poet, Brutus
and Cassius have already made up their quarrel, so his presence
appears particularly redundant. Perhaps this is Shakespeare's point,
however. The question asked by Brutus, 'What should the wars do
with these jigging fools?' (4.2.189), indicates the political ineffectuality
of poets, and in this play they are scorned at both ends of the social
hierarchy, by the plebeian mob and by the aristocratic conspirators.

The one play that unquestionably presents a 'professional' poet is
Timon of Athens. Here, the Poet seeks patronage from Timon for his
living, selling his dedications as the Jeweller and the Merchant sell
their wares, while acknowledging the duplicity that betrays his art:
'When we for recompense have praised the vile, / It stains the glory
in that happy verse / Which aptly sings the good' (1.1.15–17). On the
one hand, he presents himself as a satirist, a single honest voice pre-
dicting that Timon will fall and be abandoned by his suitors; on the
other, he is revealed by Apemantus and finally dismissed by Timon
as a mere flatterer, an alchemist whose art is directed only at the
making of gold and therefore no different from the 'infinite flatteries
that follow youth and opulency' (5.1.33–34) that he purports to
reveal. While Timon's rage is partially explained by a misanthropy
that finally collapses into madness, the Poet's honesty is certainly
compromised by his involvement in the general materialism.

If, however, we set this Poet and the second Poet in *Julius Caesar*
(it is perhaps significant that neither is given an identity beyond his
professional one) alongside the various aristocratic poets of the earlier
plays, we might see that while it is true, as Faas and Duncan-Jones
argue, that the treatment of all poets is negative or scornful, there is
an important difference here. Most of the poets who are mocked are
courtly amateurs who play at being poets. These two Poets have
a different relationship to their work; one hesitates to call it 'serious',
given the way in which they are treated, but underlying it is a sense
of frustration at the position of the professional poet within the
class-dominated social system that made it difficult for him to be
heard, and impossible for him to earn a living and retain integrity at
the same time. The plays' mockery, that is, is directed at the whole

situation in which poetry is dominated by the self-absorbed amateurism of the courtly poet; the obverse of this is the contempt in
which the professional poet is held by those from whom he needs to
seek patronage – a contempt that appears justified in that the
dependent writer is forced into 'infinite flatteries' if he is to avoid
starvation. Perhaps Shakespeare's brief experience in the toils of the
patronage system was, in spite of the success of the poems he produced, sufficient to repel him from continuing in it once he could
escape it. The comparative freedom of the public stage also allowed
for a comparative honesty of self-expression.

Such a reading allows us once again to question the view, far
too frequently expressed, that Shakespeare is an apologist for aristocratic values. On the contrary, most of his plays offer us a position,
like that of Holofernes, that resists elitist narrowness and contempt.
It might, like Thersites, counter contempt with contempt, but it must
be understood for what it is. In this light we can see that it is entirely
appropriate that both Shakespeare's narrative poems expose the
destructiveness of aristocratic arrogance and irresponsible self-love.
His views on poetry, it appears, cannot be divorced from a sceptical
ideological position, a position, we can hardly doubt, that was
painfully earned.

3
The Art of Poetry

What I have so far had to say about Elizabethan poetry has emphasized its material value, its value as cultural or political currency.
This is not to say that poetry was not 'art' or not recognized as such,
for indeed there was a conscious effort in the latter half of the sixteenth century to establish and justify an 'art of English poetry'.
Tudor poetry, indeed, had its foundations in educational tradition,
for it was one of the products of the philosophical movement that is
now known as humanism. Humanist studies had their roots in the
Middle Ages, in a programme of education based on the *trivium*
(grammar, logic, rhetoric) and *quadrivium* (geometry, arithmetic,
astronomy, music) that had essentially formed the education system
in ancient Rome. This system, with its heavy emphasis on the proper
use of language, was the foundation of the Renaissance 'rebirth' of
interest in the Latin and Greek classics and the moral and intellectual ideas to be found in them. A major initiator of this interest was
Petrarch, who sought to unearth and disseminate Greek and Latin
texts, and to implant their ideals through his own Latin writings and
his imitations of classical literature. Throughout the fourteenth and
fifteenth centuries the humanist endeavour continued to rediscover
classical texts and, increasingly, to propagate their ideas. The
humanist project effectively reached England at the end of the
fifteenth century through the teachings of Desiderius Erasmus and
Sir Thomas More.

If I may describe simply a complex set of ideas, the humanist
study of secular classics led to an empirical and sceptical understanding of the value of human experience, and especially of the
relationship between the individual and God. This promotion of
individual intellectual freedom inevitably brought humanistic inquiry
close to the ferment of challenges to authority, especially the authority of Church dogma, that led to the Reformation. The humanists'
emphasis on human dignity did not mean that humanist teaching
was incompatible with religious belief, and indeed scholars like
Erasmus attempted to identify correspondences between classical

42

and Christian thought. It did, however, mean that apprehension of the ideal or transcendental was sought in sources other than those established by mediaeval Church authority. One of the results of this was the growth, especially amongst courtly humanists, of what we might think of as a cult of beauty, in which the spiritual was closely tied to the aesthetic. Poetry became one of the means of expressing this apprehension of beauty.

The Italian humanists, in particular Marsilio Ficino (1433–1499), sought an alternative to the rationalistic philosophy of Aristotle that had formed a dominant strain in mediaeval thought. This they found in the idealistic writings of Plato and his later follower and interpreter Plotinus. Ficino, who undertook the translation of all of Plato's works into Latin, drew from them a body of thought which, in his important work the *Theologica Platonica*, he combined with Christian theology into a version of Neoplatonism. Fundamental to Ficino's Neoplatonism is Plato's insistence on the immortality of the human soul, which is located at the centre of creation, between the abstract world of Ideas and the physical world of things. In Plato's terms, it is the world of Ideas that is 'real' because it is eternal, unchanging, and therefore perfect; the world we know through our senses is merely a copy of the Ideal. The human soul, which comes from the Ideal world but is enclosed by the body in the physical world, seeks to return to its source, an end to be achieved through contemplation.

Although they cannot really be separated I am concerned here with the aesthetic rather than the theological implications of Platonism because of the Neoplatonic concern with the love of Beauty, which took on profound significance for Renaissance courtiers and poets. In the *Symposium* Plato taught that the two worlds are connected by erotic love. Love of the beauty of another leads us in a progression from a general love of physical beauty to a love of moral beauty, thence to a love of intellectual beauty, and finally to the love of Beauty. From this progression Ficino developed the concept of Platonic love, in which the love between God and the individual soul is replicated in the individual's spiritual love of another person. This doctrine of Platonic love made it possible for writers and artists to explore sexual love in terms of spiritual relationships. It was a doctrine that imposed near-impossible demands on a poet-lover, of course, promoting continence through its insistence on translating erotic desire into spiritual love, and so it also allowed the writer to explore the conflicting, even paradoxical, relationships between body and soul, between human and spiritual need. In this it had clear affinities with what we might call the myth of poetic and spiritual desire that grew from the writings of the earlier humanist Petrarch.

In spite of the philosophical seriousness of humanist thought, the project of establishing an English literature cannot be separated from political imperatives related to nationalistic and aristocratic desire. It must by now be clear that the cultural status of poetry was complex and ambiguous, and I will say something more about how it developed. When around 1580 Sidney began to write his *Apology for Poetry*, it was possible for him to ask 'why England (the mother of excellent minds) should be grown so hard a step-mother to poets', and to lament that poetry 'should only find in our time a hard welcome in England' (*Apology*, p. 257). What he meant by 'a hard welcome' was not just general indifference, but an increasing moral hostility, a pressure of censure from positions that combined the Puritan condemnation of poetry as a source of corruption with the Neoplatonic dismissal (using Plato's *Republic* as authority) of artists as liars who promote the illusory over the real. In his essay Sidney countered these attacks and championed poetry over the more pragmatic modes of discourse represented by philosophy and history. I am not here concerned with how Sidney defended and sought to promote poetry, however, but rather with why he felt it necessary to do so.

Although Sidney follows the neo-Aristotelian developments of such continental theorists as Julius Scaliger, the impulse underlying the *Apology* is in fact nationalistic. His essay presents itself as a general statement about the value of poetry, but what he is really concerned to do is to foster *English* poetry: this explains the insistence of his statement that it is England who is the hard stepmother, England who offers a hard welcome to poets. When he looked at the corpus (we can hardly call it a 'canon') of English poetry as it then existed he did not, in fact, see very much. In his essay he praises Chaucer (for *Troilus and Criseyde*, but making no mention of *The Canterbury Tales*) in whose writing he nevertheless finds faults which he thinks only to be expected in work so antique. Nearer to his own time, all he can find to praise is the work of the Earl of Surrey, first published in 1557, and *The Mirror for Magistrates* (1559). He dismisses all plays except *Gorboduc* (1561), and even that he finds defective in its defiance of the unities of place and time. Of contemporary writing the only work he commends is Spenser's *The Shepheardes Calendar* (1579).

Sidney's account of the 'great tradition' of English poetry as he perceived it in 1580 raises certain questions. The most conspicuous one concerns the yawning 150-year gap between Chaucer, who died in 1400, and the Earl of Surrey. Was there really no poetry during that period? Well, obviously there was, but presumably Sidney did not recognize it as such, or if he did he did not value it. To understand this we need to consider changes that had taken place in the English language and in attitudes to it since Chaucer's time; these were part of a much larger structure of changes between medieval England and the early modern period. Chaucer wrote in Middle English in the latter part of the medieval period, the stretch of a little more than four centuries that followed the Norman conquest of England in 1066. During that period, culture in the native English language survived largely as an oral practice, although the written remains of it from before the second half of the fourteenth century, which appear to be largely of popular origin, suggest that it was characterized by vitality if not variety. Court culture was associated mainly with the Norman French of the ruling classes, while Latin persisted as the language of the learned. The evolution of the vernacular language, enriched by borrowings from French and Latin, was inevitable, however, and Chaucer was not the only writer of his time to recognize its literary potential. Since all writing of the period existed only in manuscript form, much must have been lost, but works by the anonymous author of *Sir Gawain and the Green Knight* remain, as does *The Vision of Piers Plowman* by William Langland, and the works of Chaucer's friend John Gower. From the early part of the fifteenth century we can add to these the work of numerous imitators of Chaucer, including John Lydgate, and Sir Thomas Malory's versions of Arthurian romances.

Sidney must have been aware of more than *Troilus and Criseyde*; Chaucer's *Canterbury Tales*, Malory's Arthurian stories and Gower's *Confessio Amantis* were amongst the first works printed in English by Caxton, and achieved fairly wide circulation. From them, however, he could find only one work to praise, presumably because he did not find anything else to be of literary interest. Part of the reason for this is that various changes had taken place in the pronunciation of English after Chaucer's time. The most notable of these was what is known as the Great Vowel Shift; all Middle English long vowels had undergone significant modification, so that for Sidney and his contemporaries, who were not aware of the changes, it had become impossible to know how Middle English poetry was to be read.[1]

It consequently appeared to them rough, graceless and vulgar. Something of the frustration that this caused is reflected in the poems of the early sixteenth-century poet John Skelton, a writer ignored by Sidney. Skelton saw that while there were problems with the English vernacular as a vehicle for poetry, it nevertheless had the potential for great vitality, as his own poetry demonstrated. In *Philip Sparrow* (1505) he wrote:

> Our natural tongue is rude
> And hard to be enneude
> With polished terms lusty;
> Our language is so rusty,
> So cankered, and so full
> Of frowards, and so dull,
> That if I would apply
> To write ornately,
> I wot not where to find
> Terms to serve my mind.

(774–83)[2]

In *The Arte of English Poesie* (1589), the most notable critical work subsequent to Sidney's, George Puttenham wrote that Skelton was 'a rude and railing rhymer & all his doings ridiculous, he used both short distances and short measures pleasing only the popular ear: in our courtly maker we banish them utterly'.[3]

What is significant here is Puttenham's opposition of the courtly to the popular and his clear promotion of the courtly. Like Sidney in the *Apology* he was articulating the interests of a particular group, the aristocratic sophisticates who wanted England to have a literature that could rival those in other European languages, especially Italian and French. This entailed, first of all, dispelling anxieties about the adequacy of the English language as a vehicle for poetry. Sidney insisted that 'for the uttering sweetly, and properly the conceits of the mind, which is the end of speech, that hath [English] equally with any other tongue in the world' (*Apology*, p. 268). Following Sidney, Puttenham wrote of the English tongue that 'at this day it will be found our nation is in nothing inferior to the French or Italian for copie of language, subtlety of device, good method and proportion in any form of poem, but that they may compare with the most, and perchance pass a great many of them' (*Arte*, p. 59). The English poetry that Sidney and Puttenham and others like them desired was consciously conceived of in ideological terms, as a poetry that could creditably represent England as a nation, which to them primarily meant aristocratic England. There is a degree of unconscious irony, however, in the fact that their tastes suggested that the English aristocracy had more in common with the aristocracy of European nations than with the English masses. Puttenham praised Sir Thomas Wyatt and the Earl of Surrey for their adaptation of Italian forms into English: 'they greatly polished our rude and homely manner of vulgar Poesy, from that it had been before, and for that cause may justly be said the first reformers of our English metre and style' (*Arte*, p. 60).

This desire for a distinguished literature was deeply rooted in national political history. The endeavours of Henry VIII to extricate himself from his marriage to Catherine of Aragon had initiated momentous changes in England's sense of her identity. During the Middle Ages England, like all European nations, had been subject to the Roman Catholic church, and therefore a small part of a great transnational political and religious body. The separation of England from the Roman church was marked in 1533 by the Act of Supremacy. As part of his project to reinforce Tudor power Henry VIII declared himself 'Protector and only Supreme Head of the Church and Clergy of England'. In so doing he denied papal sovereignty and curtailed the power of Catholicism, not only initiating the Protestant Reformation in England, but fostering the growing sense of a distinct national identity. During his daughter Elizabeth's reign the powerful Puritan faction at court, led by Sidney's uncle the Earl of Leicester, began to develop a vision of a destiny for Tudor England as the leader of a league of Protestant states that would counter Roman power. Part of their intensely patriotic project was the creation of a body of English writing that would have the dignity of literary excellence but that would also reflect the moral, religious and national aspirations of England as they saw it. Sidney himself became the central figure in a group of courtiers, thinkers and poets who imagined an English literature that would express these larger ideological needs.

There is a peculiar paradox in the fact that this drive to create a recognizably English culture should have derived much of its energy from continental models. The influence of one book in particular, Baldassare Castiglione's *Il Cortegiano*, (published 1528, translated into English by Sir Thomas Hoby as *The Courtier*, 1561), can hardly be overestimated. Castiglione's book taught the arts of the courtier – arts of ambiguity and deception, as well as of play and self-display, and these had clear affinities with the arts of poetry. In his account of the rhetorical figure *allegoria*, George Puttenham reveals very clearly the intimate connection of the courtier's and the poet's art; of the courtier, he says:

> that he could dissemble his conceits as well as his countenances, so as he never speak as he thinks, or think as he speaks, and that in any matter of importance his words and his meaning very seldom meet: for so as I remember it was concluded by us setting forth the figure *Allegoria*, which therefore not impertinently we call the Courtier or figure of fair semblant, or is it not perchance more requisite our courtly Poet do dissemble not only his countenances and conceits, but also all his ordinary actions of behaviour, or the most part of them, whereby the better to win his purposes and good advantages.
>
> (*Arte*, pp. 229–300)

This appears to be a rather sinister view of courtly and poetic activities, but it is connected to the notion of *sprezzatura*, also introduced by *The Courtier*, which taught that the most difficult feats should appear to be achieved without effort. This fostering of courtly gracefulness was, further, an aspect of the idealistic Neoplatonic conception of love and beauty that Castiglione advanced.[4]

All of these aspects of Castiglione's doctrine went well within the particular context of the court of Elizabeth I. Amongst the many myths constructed to strengthen the queen's hold on power was the cult of Gloriana the Virgin Queen. Elizabeth as the Virgin Queen had multiple identities: she was Diana or Cynthia, goddess of chastity and constancy; she was Venus-as-Virgo, embodiment of love and beauty. She was, in a sense, the Neoplatonic ideal, and as such was a figure to be served by her courtiers, who played an elaborate game of courtship. One way in which some of them served her was by writing poetry that elaborated her myth. The whole Petrarchan system underlying the sonnet sequences that flourished during the last two decades of her reign, the serious game of service dedicated to an unattainable ideal woman, was peculiarly well designed for this court. The darker realities of the courtier's life were translated into an erotic literary game in which the idealizations of Petrarchism found competition from the rather more licentious example of Ovid. There was, of course, a variety of poetic fashions, but Petrarch provided the impetus for sonnet sequences and Ovid for erotic narrative poems. It was not only courtly poets who were obliged to play the game; so were those on the margins, the would-be courtiers like Spenser whose *Faerie Queene* represents poetic courtship on the largest scale. Shakespeare tried his hand at both Petrarchan and Ovidian poems.

This weighty influence of courtly interests obviously had a profound effect on the development of poetry both as an art and as a profession. Poetic art reflected the preoccupations of courtier-poets that I have outlined above. The poetic profession, in the short run at least, was largely moulded by these same tastes, since what got published reflected the interest of a broader public in what they understood of courtly fashion. In an appendix to her book on the Elizabethan literary profession Phoebe Sheavyn provides an analysis of the social status of 200 poets who wrote at some time between 1525 and 1625 (it is by no means a complete record, but it is reasonably representative).[5] Of these 200 poets, 38 were courtiers, 20 were country gentlemen (that is, men with independent means and private estates), and 37 were members of the elite institutions of church and university. 33 were members of other occupations, ranging from physician to waterman. 49 were what Sheavyn defines as 'courtly satellites', by which she means anyone who served the court in such functions as secretary, tutor, chaplain, agent, musician, and so on, that is, writers who depended on patronage or who used their writing as a lever for a more substantial position. Only 18 out of the 200 (Shakespeare among them) are identified primarily as writers.

The most problematic category is that of the courtly satellites, and here it is necessary to question some of Sheavyn's allocations. She includes in this group such writers as Spenser and Jonson; she places Spenser there because he earned almost nothing as a writer, and Jonson, apparently, because he served the court in a number of capacities, even though he was often able to live on his earnings. However, it is better to try to see writers like these two as they saw themselves. Whatever other activities they might have been forced into, neither Spenser nor Jonson saw writing as a diversion or as primarily a means of winning patronage. It is true that both men hoped that their works would bring them such advancement, but both also believed in writing as a higher calling, a serious life-long activity that should be recognized as such. This consciousness of writing as a vocation was something new, and it is an essential component in the development of writing as a profession.

Even when we make adjustments to Sheavyn's categories, what is notable about them is the imbalance in numbers between amateur and professional writers. At least half the writers can be identified as members of the nobility and the gentry, men of independent means. Another quarter of them were men who were seeking entry into the elite through patronage. Fewer than one-tenth of the total (and not much more even if we add in writers like Spenser and Jonson) were professional writers, and most of these were playwrights. Of course, as time passed the balance shifted somewhat, but the conclusion to be drawn is clear: courtly tastes dominated the field of poetry, since those who were seeking advancement were obliged to write for the court culture. Only the marginal group, playwrights and pamphleteers, were writing for less exalted tastes. The implications of this for the subsequent development of poetry are vast; for example, Antony Easthope has shown that something as apparently natural to English poetry as iambic pentameter was promoted during this period with the purpose of emulating classical models, and of excluding older, 'popular' metres (like those used by Skelton); in other words, iambic pentameter became the fundamental line of English poetry for ideological reasons.[6] The excellence of 'poetry', that is, was intimately related to, and indeed depended on, social difference.

None of this diminishes the significance of this literature as 'art'. Just the opposite, in fact, for the desire for a courtly literature led to a conscious and rigorous examination of sources and materials and of ways of writing. Almost three decades before Sidney wrote the *Apology* Thomas Wilson, himself a Protestant politician, had written *The Arte of Rhetorique* (1553), the first of many books that offered models for the thoughtful writer to emulate. One of the doctrines of the humanist movement was that writers should imitate the language and style of Greek and Latin authors, for classical texts were judged to embody also the highest moral ideals. The study of rhetoric, as we have seen, had been fundamental to English education even in the Middle Ages when it was one of the three areas of learning that made up the *trivium*, taught in monastic schools. The study of rhetoric in the West began with the Greek Sophists in the fifth century BC, and although this study was followed and modified by Isocrates and Plato, it was Aristotle who developed it into a method of systematic analysis. For the Renaissance humanists, however, the Roman writers Cicero and Quintilian provided the most significant models as they offered a system for the art of writing as well as the art of speaking that could both generate and evaluate texts. Cicero in particular took on heroic stature, because in combining the roles of orator and politician he embodied his teachings in his life. For Cicero, excellent speaking could not be separated from excellent thinking; mastering the arts of rhetoric meant becoming a man of virtue. As Ben Jonson put it in the epistle prefacing his play *Volpone*, 'if men will impartially, and not asquint, look toward the offices and function of a poet, they will easily conclude to themselves the impossibility of any man's being the good poet, without first being a good man'.[7]

In taking such a systematic approach to understanding the capabilities of language, rhetoric was a very complex field. It involved the classification of language, and the analysis of models by division into parts. It taught, through the imitation of these models, the skills (essentially formulae) necessary for the effective organization of an argument. It taught the range and function of tropes and figures of speech that could be used to make such argumentation pleasant. For ultimately, the end of rhetoric is to persuade; as Cicero wrote: 'The supreme orator is the one whose speech instructs, delights, and moves the minds of his audience'.[8] This is very close to the injunction in Horace's *Ars Poetica*, repeated so frequently in the Renaissance that it became a commonplace, that the aim of poetry is to teach and delight. As Puttenham puts it, 'the Poet is of all other the most ancient Orator, as he that by good and pleasant persuasions first reduced the wild and beastly people into public societies and civility of life, insinuating unto them, under fictions with sweet and coloured speeches, many wholesome lessons and doctrines' (*Arte*, p. 196).

Puttenham here is making very large claims for poetic rhetoric. His view of the poet as the creator of civilization is replicated in the courtly acceptance of rhetoric as a source of refinement. However, his use of the word 'insinuating' suggests a certain unease about what he is saying. 'Sweet and coloured speeches' may well offer wholesome lessons, but there is a fundamental contradiction obscured by humanist rhetorical theory: that there is in fact no necessary connection between linguistic effectiveness and moral truth. If the stated purpose of the poet's rhetoric is to lead its readers to something the writer is presenting as 'truth', then its implied purpose is to take control of the readers, to exert power over them. 'Delighting' is therefore a form of domination, and can as easily be used to *mis*lead the reader (in the *Apology* Sidney shows some discomfort in his attempts to dismiss the Neoplatonic arguments about the potential negative persuasiveness of poetry). In Sonnet 82 Shakespeare's speaker compares his own praise of his young subject to the 'dedicated words' of other writers:

> when they have devised,
> What strained touches rhetoric can lend,
> Thou, truly fair, wert truly sympathized
> In true plain words, by thy true-telling friend.

His opposition of rhetoric to truth here is made clear by his repetitions of the latter term, and while he is not necessarily saying that rhetoric is always opposed to truth he is certainly showing his awareness of its dangers.

An understanding of the dangers of rhetoric as a vehicle for duplicity can lead to a serious questioning of the relationship of words to meaning. At the end of *Troilus and Cressida*, Troilus receives a letter from Cressida which he dismisses as 'Words, words, mere words, no matter from the heart' (5.4.110). What is the connection between words and matter? For some writers rhetoric became increasingly a question of ornamentation. We have already seen how Shakespeare dealt with this issue in *Love's Labour's Lost*. He was responding in part to the elaborately affected style that became fashionable after the publication by John Lyly of two books, *Euphues, or the Anatomy of Wit* (1578) and *Euphues and his England* (1580). As a literary style, 'euphuism' is characterized by its obtrusive use of rhetorical figures, and while it certainly played a part in the development of English prose style, its more immediate effect was to open up poetry to the potential for empty self-display.

From all of this it will be apparent that the driving forces that led to the generation of Elizabethan poetry were various and often conflicted. There is an intimate connection between the growth of early modern English literature and the consciousness of a need for a national identity, but the concept of that identity, at least as it is reflected in the literature that remains, was largely in the hands of those in power. Elizabethan poetry consequently embodied primarily the ideals of the court, which was itself a place of fictions and myths designed in part to mediate the fact of Elizabeth herself, a woman at the head of a patriarchy. Underlying the poetry are patterns of courtship which are controlled by elaborate sets of rules; thus are systems of rhetoric and systems of manners interconnected into an 'art of poetry'.

I have stressed the influence of court and other elite interests on the development of English poetry as it was at the moment when Shakespeare turned from his plays to writing non-dramatic poetry. This is not intended to suggest that there was no popular poetry (in the sense of a poetry not designed to appeal primarily to upper class circles) because obviously there was a great deal of it. The songs in many of Shakespeare's plays are a reflection of a vast body of popular material and indicate Shakespeare's own delight in it. It is particularly interesting that *Love's Labour's Lost*, which is largely about courtly poetry and culture, should end with a song ('When daisies pied') that is unashamedly about lower-class life. Another kind of popular poetry was the broadside ballad, so-called because it was printed on one side of a folio sheet; this was a cheap form of publication, and the ballads themselves usually presented a kind of sensational material related to jest books and rogue pamphlets, which were also forms of popular literature.

In fact, this 'popular' literature was popular in the broadest sense, since the upper classes also enjoyed it, just as they enjoyed popular theatre. But we need to note a distinction (one that can less easily be made today) between the popular and the fashionable. As we can see from the work of Puttenham and others like him, a conscious effort was being made to develop a literature that could be clearly distinguished from the vulgar or the 'rude and homely'. There were powerful ideological forces behind this enterprise, and it was inevitable that the 'high' culture envisaged by these men would triumph, given that courtly poetry or poetry that emulated its values was more likely than popular poetry to find its way into print and therefore to establish itself as the standard. Consequently, as we have seen, the incentive for ambitious writers like Shakespeare to underwrite these fashions was great.

Where does this leave Shakespeare? Clearly, as a man who needed to make money out of his writing he had to find a way into the patronage system, and this meant that he had to write the kind of poetry that would appeal to a noble patron, something he was apparently able to do with ease. This does not by any means require that he fully endorsed the values of those for whom he wrote. As we have seen, the courtly world that was the primary consumer of this poetry did not often offer much in the way of comfort for the professional poets who came from outside it, and Shakespeare must have viewed it with some scepticism or even, if we can recognize anything of his own experience in the complaint of the Poet in *Timon of Athens* about praising the vile for recompense, with resentment. In that case, we might expect to find evidence of Shakespeare's conflicted responses in his poetry.

The only power Shakespeare could wield over his fashionable readers lay in his pen, and he used it in subtly critical ways. The two poems that he dedicated to Southampton fulfil very well the requirements of the Ovidian erotic narrative and as such were designed to appeal to sophisticated tastes. In both of them, however, Shakespeare examines how power works within a hierarchy of relationships, and reveals the ways in which the powerful attempt to exert control over the bodies and lives of others. In neither can he be said to be sympathetic towards the arrogance of power. In the *Sonnets* he uses the idealized codes that were the conventions of Petrarchan poetry while at the same time mounting a violent attack on them and effectively undermining them. In these non-dramatic poems, that is, Shakespeare, counters the social power of those for whom he wrote with his own aesthetic power. In a different time and place these poems might have been understood as being profoundly subversive.

4

Shakespeare and Ovidian Poetry

THE EPYLLION

If we set aside the small body of verse that Shakespeare produced in lyric and elegiac forms, his main contributions to non-dramatic poetry are to two poetic sub-genres that were fashionable in the early 1590s and that are at almost opposite extremes of the poetic spectrum (though both allowed for a display of literary virtuosity): the sonnet sequence, and the extended narrative poem. The sonnet-form is effectively fixed by its fourteen lines and set rhyme-schemes, and therefore demands great rigour in control and concentration. The extended narrative poem, as it developed in Shakespeare's time, might seem to have encouraged the opposite of concentration. It had no prescribed verse- or stanza-form, no real limit to its length, and it therefore allowed the writer considerable freedom not only for amplification, ornamentation and digression, but also for the inclusion of generic elements of other forms. It does not even have a handy designation, although the term 'epyllion', meaning 'minor epic' is sometimes applied to it. Even this term is a little misleading, however, because the sources and models for most of these narrative poems are not the Homeric or Virgilian epics, but the erotic writings of Ovid.

Such narrative poems were in fashion in Elizabethan and early Jacobean England for about three decades, though their vogue, like that of the sonnet sequence, was at its most intense during the 1590s. It began with the publication in 1589 of Thomas Lodge's *Scilla's Metamorphosis*. Lodge, like Robert Greene, was a member of a group of young men, known as the 'University Wits', who in the 1580s sought to turn their university education into a means of earning a living through their writing. These were men of the middle classes who made connections that put them on the fringes of court life, but who as writers needed to reach a more general audience.

Lodge himself was the son of a Lord Mayor of London, educated at Trinity College, Oxford and at Lincoln's Inn, but disinherited by his father because of his writing. To make his living he turned his hand to most available forms, and was moderately successful as a writer of plays and pamphlets, as well as poetry, though in frustration he eventually gave up writing to become a physician. In *Scilla's Metamorphosis*, making use of the contemporary enthusiasm for Ovid, he took Ovid's brief account (in *Metamorphoses* XIII) of this story of erotic desire and transformation, and expanded it to 786 lines, producing a poem that pretended, in proper Horatian fashion, to mix profit with pleasure. The title page says that the poem is 'very fit for young courtiers to peruse, and coy dames to remember', presumably offering titillation to the young men and a lesson for the young ladies. The poem in fact seems more concerned to offer pleasure than profit, however, and is directed firmly at courtly taste.

The most significant example of the genre (almost certainly written prior to *Venus and Adonis*, though the date of its composition is unknown) is Christopher Marlowe's *Hero and Leander*. Marlowe's interest in Ovid was evident in the 1580s, when he began his translation of the *Amores*, a collection of short erotic elegies not published until after his death; it was considered so provocative that in 1599 it was banned and burned on the order of the Bishop of London. *Hero and Leander* was entered in the Stationers' Register (a catalogue of the titles of all books intended for publication) on 28 September 1593, and although it too remained unpublished until after Marlowe's death there is some evidence that it was circulating in manuscript form before then. Shakespeare, at any rate, was familiar with it, as is reflected in both *Venus and Adonis* and *The Rape of Lucrece*. Marlowe's poem more than rivals both of them in sophistication and energy.

The tragic story of Leander's love of the beautiful Hero that caused him to swim by night across the Hellespont to her tower, until he was drowned in a storm, can be found in Ovid's *Heroides*; however, Marlowe based his version on a Greek poem by the fifth-century Alexandrian poet Musaeus who, like Ovid, told the story as tragedy. Marlowe's poem does something different, because he ends his story before Leander's tragic death. Many readers have assumed that the poem is unfinished, and the Elizabethan dramatist and translator George Chapman wrote a completion of it for its publication in 1598. However, I believe that it was not Marlowe's intention to write more, for by concluding the story where he did, he contrived to make it into something much more complex. By turns harsh and sympathetic, the poem develops an ironic treatment of the two young lovers, finding in their naive vulnerability both comedy and pathos, and setting them in a larger mythic world of destructively contradictory passions; as his narrator says, 'Love is not full of pity (as men say), / But deaf and cruel where he means to prey' (287–8).[1] Marlowe narrative voice is one of the sources of the poem's complexity: sometimes mocking the poem's characters, sometimes mocking the reader, it leads and misleads. The poem is deeply transgressive; Marlowe seems to have intended to make it as outrageous as possible, stimulating both heterosexual and homosexual erotic interest. Above all, it is a vehicle for an astonishing demonstration of rhetorical skill.

I have given this extended description of *Hero and Leander* because I think it presented a mark against which Shakespeare had to measure himself. Shakespeare makes clear his familiarity with Marlowe's poem on a number of occasions, but particularly in the opening lines of *Venus and Adonis*, where his reference to 'Rose-cheeked Adonis' (3) surely alludes directly to an account in the earlier poem of an annual festival kept 'For his sake whom their goddess held so dear, /Rose-cheeked Adonis' (*Hero and Leander* 92–3). Why did Shakespeare do this? Dennis Kay suggests that 'he is operating within the decorums of 1590s writing in signalling debts, modifying contexts, indicating twists and turns of genre'.[2] It seems to me more likely, however, that Shakespeare deliberately invited comparison with Marlowe's poem as a challenge, not as a debt, responding to the undeniable element of self-display in it. He was, after all, moving into a literary area that was unfamiliar to him. He had to appeal to those readers whom Marlowe had already charmed, and we must remember that in 1592 Marlowe's reputation as a playwright, and certainly as a poet, was better established than Shakespeare's. To outdo Marlowe at his own Ovidian game would have been a notable feat.

Like the sonnet sequence, the Ovidian narrative poem was a genre that saw its high point in the late Elizabethan period, even though it extended into the reign of James I. Shakespeare's two poems, *Venus and Adonis* (1593) and *The Rape of Lucrece* (1594), contributed to its establishment; the following are notable examples, though few of them are read today:

1594   Thomas Heywood, *Oenone and Paris*
1595   George Chapman, *Ovid's Banquet of Sense*
        Michael Drayton, *Endymion and Phoebe: Idea's Latmus*
        Thomas Edwards, *Cephalus and Procris*

1598   John Marston, *Metamorphosis of Pygmalion's Image*
1600   John Weever, *Faunus and Meliflora*
1602   Francis Beaumont, *Salmacis and Hermaphroditus*

The form continued to attract writers for another two decades, and Shakespeare's poems were reissued many times, but the innovative energy that drove it was burnt out by 1603.

Some of the reasons for the burst of creative energy that shaped the genre have been touched on in the preceding chapter. With the exception of Lodge, the writers listed above were young men from the provinces who had come to London to make their fortune. Most were from comparatively substantial families and had the benefit of a university education. They made social connections at university that allowed them to attach themselves to the literary cliques that operated on the margins of court society, and they became the producers of literature for their fashionable friends, but it was literature that also discovered a wider audience. They found themselves involved in the ongoing struggle, mentioned earlier in relation to Sir Philip Sidney, to establish the credibility of imaginative literature against the attacks of Puritan moralists. Most of them, as did Lodge, paid lip service to the Horatian injunction that poetry should mix profit with pleasure; but they knew that the rigorous persuasive power of rhetoric was not necessarily hostile to sensuous language, especially when attached to an ostensibly moral tale. This is one of the reasons why Ovid provided such an attractive model to them.

SHAKESPEARE AND OVID

Ovid provided a particularly attractive model for Shakespeare, as even his contemporaries noted. Frances Meres in his *Palladis Tamia* had this to say about Shakespeare: 'As the soul of *Euphorbus* was thought to live in *Pythagoras*: so the sweet witty soul of Ovid lives in mellifluous & honey-tongued *Shakespeare*, witness his *Venus and Adonis*, his *Lucrece*, his sugared *Sonnets*'.[3] Whether this was Meres' own perception, or whether he was simply voicing a commonplace view, his connection of Shakespeare to Ovid contained a deep truth. In his poems Ovid provided a wide range of compelling narratives and, more important, a sustained model of dazzling rhetorical mastery. His writing reverberates throughout Shakespeare's works, both plays and poems.

Some measure of the importance of Ovid to Shakespeare can be seen in the fact that the first words the reader sees on opening Shakespeare's first published work are not Shakespeare's but Ovid's: he chose as the epigraph to *Venus and Adonis* lines taken from the *Amores*: '*Vilia Miretur vulgus; mihi flavus Apollo / Pocula Castalia plena ministret aqua*' ('Let the rabble wonder at what is cheap; may golden Apollo serve me bowls filled with Castilian water'). In this act of deference Shakespeare appears to be associating himself with Ovid's high conception of poetry as divine inspiration (Apollo was the Roman god of poetry, the Castilian spring was sacred to the Muses). In *Love's Labour's Lost* Shakespeare has the comic pedant Holofernes characterize Ovid by 'the elegancy, facility, and golden cadence of poesy' (4.2.114–15), and it is hardly possible to doubt that Shakespeare himself saw these qualities in the Latin poet. He used the *Metamorphoses* as the source for *Venus and Adonis* and the *Fasti* as the main source of *The Rape of Lucrece*. The stories themselves, dealing as they do with the hazards of desire, must have made Ovid attractive to him; however, what was of even greater interest was what Meres described, perhaps ineptly, as Ovid's 'sweet witty soul', the enchanting power of his language.

Many classical poets influenced early modern English writing, but none exerted such intense yet troubled influence as Ovid. His life itself could be understood as a kind of metaphor for the status of poetry at the time. Publius Ovidius Naso, born 43 BC, was a part of the great literary flowering of Rome under the Emperor Augustus that produced, along with many minor writers, the epic poet Virgil, the historian Livy, and the rational and satirical poet Horace. This was a time of order and restraint, and Ovid's urbane writing, including the *Amores*, the *Fasti* and the *Metamorphoses*, gave him both social and literary success. In 8 AD, however, Augustus became enraged with Ovid, banished him from Rome, and banned all his works from public libraries. The pretext for this was the poet's *Ars Amatoria*, which taught men how to seduce women and, rather worse, encouraged female licentiousness. The poem had been written some years earlier, however, and there appear to have been more immediate political reasons for the exile, mysteriously related to the adultery of the Emperor's granddaughter Julia, who was banished in the same year. Whatever the reason, Ovid remained in exile, writing poems reflecting his desire to return home, until his death around 17 AD.

Ovid's unfortunate career can be seen to exemplify the danger of transgression inherent in all poetry, since the pleasure that poetry produces is often in conflict with the needs of authority. Ben Jonson, in his play *Poetaster* (1601), actually used the story of Ovid's banishment to examine the social and moral functions of different kinds of poetry, especially as they relate to the interests of the state. In Jonson's play Ovid is attractive because of his subversive energies, but he is set up as counter to the loftier, more reasonable poets Virgil and Horace. The play accepts Ovid's banishment as being necessary because he has given himself up to an empty and socially destructive ideal in embracing the sensual rather than the moral. However, in presenting Ovid as libertine, Jonson really offers only one side of the Latin poet as the Elizabethans saw him, for the early modern English attitude to Ovid was deeply divided. To some, he was a teacher of great wisdom and learning, a presenter of universal truth in the guise of mythological stories. To others he was a dissolute and dangerous misleader of youth, a sensualist who seduced by combining the erotic pleasures of the body with the rhetorical pleasures of the text. The problem of redeeming this latter Ovid was not new in the Renaissance; disquiet about the erotic facets of his poetry had been widespread, though not universal, during the Middle Ages. Medieval commentators solved the problem by making Ovid's work conform to Christian moral ideas, partly by presenting him as an ironist, and especially by reading his works as allegorical, so that even the *Ars Amatoria* could be construed as a work that 'detests lechery and lecherous love, and describes how we may love virtuously'.[4] In this way Ovid was made sufficiently respectable that many of his works could be used as textbooks for teaching rhetoric as well as source-books for mythological materials.

Ovid's works became a staple part of the Tudor grammar school curriculum, where they were used to teach the elements of writing. The education that gave Shakespeare what Jonson characterized as his 'little Latin' would have included, at the very least, reading and memorization of much of the *Metamorphoses* and extracts from the *Fasti* and the *Heroides*.[5] Although Shakespeare used an English translation of the *Metamorphoses* for *Venus and Adonis*, he appears also to have consulted the Latin text, and for *The Rape of Lucrece* he must have gone directly to the Latin text of *Fasti*, since no translation of this was published until some years after his death. By the time Shakespeare wrote these two poems, however, Ovid was not confined to the schools, for his popularity had vastly increased as a result of translations of his works.

The first to be translated was the *Metamorphoses*, a series of 15 books of mythological narratives taken by Ovid from various sources, but unified by a general concern with shape-changing and other kinds of transformation. Given their prevalence in the schools, the *Metamorphoses* must have been widely familiar in literate circles, but they became fashionable after the publication in 1565 of Arthur Golding's verse translation of the first four books, which was followed in 1567 by his translation of all 15 books. Golding's translation became so popular that it went into nine editions before 1612, and was often used by Elizabethan poets as a source for their narratives. Golding himself was a serious-minded Puritan whose other translations included writings by the extreme Protestant John Calvin, and he was probably in tune with the medieval habit of reading Ovid as allegory. Indeed, he was apparently uneasy about the discordant aspects of Ovid, which he attempted to harmonize in a letter dedicating the first edition of his translation to the Earl of Leicester. He describes the *Metamorphoses* as: 'purporting outwardly most pleasant tales and delectable histories, and fraughted inwardly with most pithy instructions and wholesome examples, and containing both ways most exquisite cunning and deep knowledge'.[6] Here Golding is recasting the Horatian dictum, as familiar to his readers as by now it is to mine, that poetry should mix profit with pleasure, to make palatable the wholesome instruction by presenting it in a seductive wrapping. It is difficult to resist the feeling, however, that the Elizabethan readers of Ovidian poetry were rather more engaged by the seductive pleasures of the texts than by any moral lesson they might hold. This is almost certainly what initiated Marlowe's interest in translating the *Amores*. The ecclesiastical disapproval that led to the suppression of this translation was essentially a re-enactment of the banishment of Ovid, and an indication of how difficult it still was to rescue him from the unsavoury aspects of his reputation. However, sophisticated poets wrote for a sophisticated audience and, whatever official disapproval there might have been, Elizabethan readers craved Ovidian stories.

What did sophisticated Elizabethan poets and readers find in Ovid that was so irresistible? Fundamental to all of his poetry, not just the *Metamorphoses*, is the idea of transformation. There is the literal transformation of men or women into trees or animals, as Adonis is changed into an anemone at the end of *Venus and Adonis*, and at the simplest level many readers must have been affected by this appeal to wonder. Ovid's tales offer much more than this, however, because what interested him (and what clearly interested Elizabethan writers) was psychological transformation. This is clearly true for Shakespeare: the transformation of Adonis is the indirect result of far more complex and intriguing changes in Venus. She is transformed by sexual desire from goddess of love into a lustful predator who also becomes the comic victim of her own obsession. The implications of this process are both sinister and absurd, and Shakespeare is passionately interested in this conflicted state. Tarquin in *The Rape of Lucrece* exhibits a similar conflicted psychological state, except that in his case Shakespeare is concerned entirely with the sinister or disturbing aspects of the transformations wrought by desire.

It is perhaps not surprising that Ovid's poetry, concerned as it is with what we might think of as a theatrical conception of identity in which the self is not fixed, but fluid and shifting, should have been so significant at a time when theatre was being established in London as a generator of cultural meanings. Much has been written recently about 'self-fashioning' in early modern England; as the influential critic Stephen Greenblatt has it: 'in the sixteenth century there appears to be an increased self-consciousness about the fashioning of human identity as a manipulable, artful process'.[7] The literature of the time, and not only dramatic writing, was fascinated by the possibilities that are opened up when we see the self as a role (perhaps the most spectacular example is John Donne's *Songs and Sonnets*), and Ovid's narratives of metamorphosis offered perfect material on which to build explorations of the performance of identity.

As much as this, however, it was Ovid's 'sweet witty soul', the elegance and flexibility of his verse forms, the copious and playful use of rhetorical devices, the easy scepticism of his attitude, that drew Elizabethan poets to him. What his example offered to them was wide scope for self-display. We have already seen how the study of rhetoric, an important component of the humanist education project, became a fundamental part of poetic theory. The extensive nature of the pseudo-Ovidian epyllion gave writers the opportunity to show their command of a broad range of rhetorical devices. In Marlowe's *Hero and Leander*, Leander attempts to seduce Hero in a lengthy speech that is, in fact, a bravura display of rhetorical skill. When he has finished Hero says to him: 'Who taught thee rhetoric to deceive a maid? /Aye me, such words as these should

I abhor, / And yet I like them for the orator' (338–40). Hero is well aware that rhetoric is as deceptive as it is delightful, but she chooses to ignore the deception, so her lines here present Leander's speeches as a kind of microcosm of the poem. Behind the 'orator' Leander stands the poet Marlowe, and in allowing Hero to praise Leander's skill Marlowe actually draws attention to his own. Thus Leander's rhetorical seduction of Hero represents the poem's seduction of the reader.

At the same time, the lines also indicate the dangers of rhetoric, in that what is delightful has the power to deceive precisely because it *is* delightful. The presence of persuasive rhetoric, that is, returns us to the troubling question of the relationships between language and truth, and language and power. Leander's speech has a practical purpose: to take control of Hero's body. By analogy, Marlowe's poem wants to assert control over its readers, to misdirect their understanding of its intentions. Like Marlowe, Shakespeare was attracted by the seductive possibilities of rhetorical abundance and ambiguity; he was also seriously preoccupied with the damage that the treacherous duplicity of language can cause. Tarquin, in *The Rape of Lucrece*, wishes, like Leander, to take control of a woman's body, but before he can approach Lucrece he must first seduce himself, transform himself through rhetoric: 'Such hazard now must doting Tarquin make, / Pawning his honour to obtain his lust, / That for himself himself he must forsake' (155–7). In alienating himself from himself Tarquin debases language and motive: desire here is lust, seduction is rape.

Ovid's exile from Rome came about because his erotic writing set him against the chilly authoritarianism of powerful interests. Elizabethan England did not lack its own authoritarian elements, and it was not difficult for writers to fall foul of them. Perhaps there was a political component to the interest that Ovid held for these poets, in that his non-conformity reflected a yearning for independence in a society where independence was a commodity in limited supply. Whatever the reasons, the poets brought the erotic Ovid out of exile and transformed him. They took his stories and expanded them, changing them to suit their own needs and those of their readers. They shared his delight in language, and saw how his rhetorical playfulness might be adapted to the needs of a developing English literature. Taken together, Shakespeare's two Ovidian poems show what a broad range of possibilities were opened up by the Latin poet.

THE TEXTS

Venus and Adonis and *The Rape of Lucrece* were written between 1592 and 1594. As I have noted, it is generally supposed that Shakespeare turned to poetry because of the closure of the playhouses in July 1592 as a result of an outbreak of the plague. Shakespeare could not have known how long the epidemic would last, and this explains his vow in the dedication of *Venus and Adonis* 'to take advantage of all idle hours'. It is possible that from the outset he conceived of the two poems as a pair, a comic and a tragic examination of the destructive potential of erotic desire that provided a powerful critique of fashionable Petrarchism, for in the same dedication he promises to honour Southampton with 'some graver labour'. Presumably he expected that both poems would appeal to the same audience. If so he was, apparently, mistaken, for around 1598 the writer Gabriel Harvey noted in a copy of an edition of Chaucer: 'The younger sort takes much delight in Shakespeare's *Venus and Adonis*: but his Lucrece, & his tragedy of Hamlet, Prince of Denmark, have it in them, to please the wiser sort'.[8] I might add that if Harvey was correct, the younger sort must have been more numerous that the wiser sort; if we are to judge from the number of editions each poem went into before 1640, it would appear that *Venus and Adonis* was much the more popular.

Venus and Adonis was registered at Stationers' Hall on 18 April 1593. The first extant quarto edition (and the first work by Shakespeare to appear in print) was printed by Richard Field, a contemporary of Shakespeare's from Stratford who had a shop in the Blackfriars district, and sold by John Harrison at his bookstall in St Paul's Churchyard, where on 12 June 1593 an elderly gentleman named Richard Stonley bought a copy for sixpence, the first known purchase of a publication by Shakespeare.[9] The volume was well printed, probably from the poet's manuscript. Only one copy of this first printing survives. After two editions Field relinquished his rights to the poem to Harrison, and the poem went into at least 16 editions before 1640. There are very few surviving copies of any of the editions, which is usually taken as a sign that a publication was very popular. *The Rape of Lucrece*, Shakespeare's 'graver labour', was entered in the Stationers' Register on 9 May 1594. This also was printed by Field and sold by Harrison and, like *Venus and Adonis*, contains very few errors. On the title page the poem is called *Lucrece*, but the head title and running titles call it *The Rape of Lucrece*. Though not as popular as *Venus and Adonis*, *The Rape of Lucrece* nevertheless went through six editions in Shakespeare's lifetime. There are 11 surviving copies, two of which contain slight differences; since proofreading was done during the printing process, it is probable that these are uncorrected versions.

THE DEDICATIONS

I have discussed Shakespeare's relationship with Southampton, and I do not wish to revisit the question here beyond noting that Shakespeare would have been well aware of the kind of thing that should be said to gain the favour of a potential patron. It could not have been too difficult for a clever young man, reasonably well-versed in the classics (at least two of his earliest plays, *The Comedy of Errors* and *Titus Andronicus*, were based on classical sources), who had already begun to explore the possibilities, comic and tragic, of erotic confusion, to produce the kind of poem that had become the rage of sophisticated circles. In dedicating *Venus and Adonis* to Southampton, Shakespeare made exactly the right move: the suggestion that the young Earl was the ideal reader of the poem would have been a wonderful advertisement to recommend the work (and its successor) to a wider public that liked to think of itself as fashionable and cultivated. Who made up this 'wider public'? Literary innovation, we know, became literary fashion when it aroused the interest of courtiers and law students at the inns of court, and was then eagerly taken up by ambitious members of the middle class. It appears from the complaints of contemporary moralizers about the danger to women of reading poems like *Venus and Adonis* that women in fact were a substantial part of the readership. Thus the erotic nature of epyllia might reflect the desire of women to see beyond the limits of action imposed upon them by Elizabethan society as much as it reflects the 'daring' or prurient tastes of male courtiers and students.

One other question arising from this dedication concerns what Shakespeare might have meant when he called *Venus and Adonis* 'the first heir of my invention'. Taken literally, the phrase suggests that the poem was his earliest work, but this seems unlikely because of the poem's assurance, although it is possible that he began it early in his career and revised it extensively when he prepared it for publication. The phrase is open to a different interpretation, however, for Shakespeare's words might well reflect something we have already seen, that as published texts, poems had a higher value than plays in elite Elizabethan society. The text of *Venus and Adonis* that the poet dedicated to Southampton was carefully printed, probably under his own supervision, and indicates his sense of its cultural importance. In contrast, as we have seen, there is no evidence that he had any involvement in the publication of any of his plays, and consequently we do not know how highly he valued them. It is possible that, like most of his contemporaries, he thought of plays (especially those written for the public playhouses) as ephemeral, and never tried to give them the more permanent life of print. Those plays that were published during his lifetime were often carelessly printed, and we cannot say how closely or distantly they matched his manuscripts. In calling *Venus and Adonis* the first heir of his invention Shakespeare may have been erasing all the plays he had already written in order to intensify the sense of the poem's significance. This does not mean that he really regarded it more highly than his plays, but he was clearly aware of the demands of his intended readership.

5

Venus and Adonis

Venus and Adonis, Shakespeare's retelling of the well-known myth of the doomed desire of the goddess of love for a young mortal, is an exuberant erotic narrative and a playful display of linguistic virtuosity in which Shakespeare contrives to tell a tragic story with a vitality of manner that often propels his material towards the comic. Like much Elizabethan poetry it is a product of the Renaissance fascination with classical myths, a concern that to a modern reader might seem to be distant and obscure. However, in early modern Europe, classical thought was widely held to contain the sources of intellectual and aesthetic truth, while the myths themselves could be reinterpreted for contemporary needs. The story of *Venus and Adonis* thus provided Shakespeare with a situation of intense dramatic conflict that he was able to exploit to illuminate questions that were germane to the real, everyday experience of his readers, and that retain equal, though perhaps different, interest for modern readers. *Venus and Adonis* concerns human relationships at their most elemental and frustrating level. It raises questions about the meaning of desire, about the relationship between self and other, about the troubled connections between comedy and tragedy, and about the connections between beauty, love and death. Underlying all of these concerns is the question of the relationship between language and power. As we can infer from the demeanor of Shakespeare's approach to Southampton in the dedication ('if your honour seem but pleased, I account myself highly praised'), the poet recognized that the only means he had of influencing powerful interests was the manipulative power of his own rhetoric, and one of the concerns of *Venus and Adonis* is not simply to display the attractions of rhetoric, but also to examine its dangers and limitations.

Venus and Adonis is a poem of 1194 lines, consisting of 199 six-line stanzas of iambic pentameter rhymed *ababcc*, a stanza-form known technically as a sixain. This might seem to be a fairly simple form, but it held a particular cultural significance at that time, for the six-line stanza had something of a vogue in the Elizabethan court, having been used by a number of aristocratic poets, including Sir Philip Sidney, Sir Walter Ralegh and Sir Edward Dyer. Edmund Spenser, who inhabited the fringe of the courtly group that included Sidney and Dyer, used it for the opening and closing eclogues of *The Shepheardes Calendar*, doubtless hoping to impart some aristocratic cachet to his poem. Lodge employed it for *Scilla's Metamorphosis*, probably for the same reason. Shakespeare could, presumably, have followed Marlowe's lead in *Hero and Leander* and used rhyming couplets; his choice of the sixain form suggests that he too was well in tune with aristocratic tastes. The stanza has further significance in that it mimics the last six lines of the English form of the sonnet that Shakespeare took for his own sonnet sequence, and I think he almost certainly intended his readers to have in mind the gender politics underlying the Petrarchan preoccupations of the conventional sonnet sequence, which concern the attempts of a male 'protagonist' to win the affection of an adamantly resistant woman. Shakespeare's poem inverts this situation by making the aggressor female and making the source of her frustration male.

I am going to ask an essentially unanswerable question here: why didn't Shakespeare write one more stanza, which would have given the poem 1200 lines and 200 stanzas? That, surely, would have offered to our desire for formal satisfaction a more pleasing sense of completeness. The answer that I would propose is that in some ways the poem is *about* frustration, and not only the frustrated desire of the goddess; frustration is a part of both its content and its manner. It has frequently been noted that *Venus and Adonis* lacks closure, or that its tragic ending fails to satisfy the expectations raised by its comic method. As Catherine Belsey puts it, the poem 'prompts in the reader a desire for action it fails to gratify. Meanwhile, the critical tradition in its turn, tantalized by the poem's lack of closure, has sought to make something happen, at least at the thematic level'.[1] The poem's refusal to satisfy Venus's erotic desire is thus parallelled by a refusal to satisfy the reader's desire for closure. It is, of course, possible that Shakespeare had no conscious awareness of with holding that two-hundredth stanza, but I think it is more satisfying to interpret its absence as a subtle part of Shakespeare's frustration of the reader. I will return to this matter.

Shakespeare took the main outline of his story of *Venus and Adonis* from Ovid's *Metamorphoses* Book X (519–59 and 708–39). It is clear that he consulted Golding's translation, because there are verbal echoes in his poem, but the story was widely known and frequently retold; Spenser, for example, used it extensively in Book III of *The Faerie Queene*. Ovid's version is brief and rudimentary in comparison to Shakespeare's, and offers little in the way of development of either of the characters. It tells how Venus, accidentally wounded by one of her son Cupid's arrows, falls obsessively in love with the young mortal Adonis. As he grows to manhood and becomes interested in hunting she begins to fear for his safety, and warns him of the dangers of wild animals, especially lions and boars. Adonis disregards her advice, however, and one day he hunts down a boar, which mortally wounds him in the groin. The grieving Venus causes drops of Adonis's blood to be transformed into an anemone, a flower notable for its fragility. From two other narratives that he found in the *Metamorphoses* Shakespeare took elements that offered him hints for his development of the characters. The story of Narcissus and Echo in Book III (340–500) concerns a beautiful youth who strongly resists the advances of a young woman, falling victim instead to the enchantment of his own reflection. Since he cannot have what he wants, he wastes away and dies, and like Adonis he is transformed into a flower. Finally, the story of Salmacis and Hermaphroditus in Book IV (287–390) presents in Salmacis a woman who, lusting after a beautiful youth, pursues him aggressively and physically.

Shakespeare combined and modified this Ovidian material to a number of ends. His most apparent changes relate to the figure of Adonis. Far from having reached manhood, Shakespeare's Adonis is barely adolescent, and he resists all Venus's attempts to win his love. Shakespeare incorporated into Adonis elements of the character of Narcissus, making his rejection of Venus at least in part an effect of his self-absorption. From the story of Salmacis he took the idea of aggressive female sexuality and made it fundamental to his characterization of Venus; he may also have taken hints for Venus from the character of Echo, whom Ovid describes as a compulsive chatterer. Shakespeare's Venus appears in the guise of a mature woman lusting after an Adonis who appears as a petulant child. Her forceful physical sexuality is supported by a predatory verbal assertiveness and a virtuoso use of seductive rhetoric, in a reversal of gender roles as Elizabethan readers of Petrarchan poetry conventionally understood them. In addition to the two central characters, Shakespeare provides a narrative voice that incorporates the urbane knowingness of the Ovidian narrator, but through his manipulation of it he achieves very complex effects.

This narrative voice introduces the poem: as the sun rises, he tells us, the goddess Venus, 'sick-thoughted' (5), approaches the youthful 'Rose-cheeked Adonis' (3) who is setting out for the hunt, with the intention of seducing him. She begins by praising him as a paragon of beauty, 'the fields' chief flower' (8), and invites him to join her in the 'thousand honey secrets' (16) of love-play, but her impatience to have her way drives her to pull him from his horse and the two lie on the ground, though Adonis, 'red for shame, but frosty in desire' (36), resists her advances. She counters this resistance by forcing her kisses upon him, her own passion becoming increasingly ravenous, but seeing him unmoved she begins a rhetorical attack (95–174). She first boasts of her erotic capture of Mars, and then goes on to praise her own beauty as 'having no defects' (138); she cannot understand how he can reject such a gift, and asks if he is like Narcissus, locked up in love of himself. If so, she says, he should learn his natural obligation, which is to pass on his beauty through procreation: 'Thou wast begot; to get it is thy duty' (168). Titan, the sun-god himself, envies Adonis, but the youth is unmoved, responding simply, 'Fie, no more of love! / The sun doth burn my face; I must remove' (185–6). Venus resumes her campaign (187–216), offering to protect him from the sun, and when he continues to be unyielding she chides him for his inhuman lack of feeling: 'Fie, lifeless picture, cold and senseless stone' (211). Once again she tries a physical approach, locking him in her arms, and when he struggles she makes her most powerful erotic offer (29–40). Still he resists, pulling away from her and making for his horse.

Before Adonis can mount his steed, a 'breeding jennet, lusty, young and proud' (260) bursts on to the scene, and in a lengthy set-piece (257–324) the narrator describes a response to the urges of nature rather different from that of Adonis. The two horses run off into the woods, and Adonis is left angrily cursing his 'boist'rous and unruly beast' (326), but Venus takes the opportunity to point a lesson: 'Thy palfrey, as he should, / Welcomes the warm approach of sweet desire' (385–6). Adonis remains adamant, though in the longest speech he has yet made (409–26) he finally offers some explanation for his resistance to love: 'I have heard it is a life in death' (413). Venus by now is beginning to fear failure, and she makes one more rhetorical attack, presenting Adonis as a banquet for all the senses (427–50). However, she can read his hostile response in his face, and she falls to the ground in an apparent faint. Adonis is tricked into attempting to revive her with a kiss, which brings the goddess to an immediate recovery and an account of the healing power of his kisses (493–522). Adonis is now somewhat contrite, and although he still resists Venus he tells her to attribute this resistance to his 'unripe years' (524). He offers her a goodnight kiss, but she responds with a 'glutton-like' enthusiasm (538–76).

Having achieved so much Venus agrees to let Adonis go, asking if they can meet on the morrow. However, when he tells her of his intention to hunt the boar she is fearful and falls to the ground, pulling him with her, and 'He on her belly falls, she on her back' (594). They are now in the position she has sought all along, but 'He will not manage her, although he mount her' (598). When he tries once more to escape, Venus embarks on another of the poem's set pieces (613–768). In an attempt to dissuade him from the hunt she first constructs a horrifying image of the boar as a figure of death: 'His snout digs sepulchres where'er he goes' (622). If Adonis must hunt, she says, let him hunt the 'timorous, flying hare' (674), and she gives a powerful account of that creature's terror (673–708). This serves only to irritate Adonis further: his friends await him, it is now dark, and he might fall. Venus seizes upon this to urge him once again to think about what the world will lose if he dies in 'fruitless chastity' (751). Adonis responds to this with the closest thing to a real argument that he has yet made (769–810). He makes a distinction between the real love that was born in heaven and the 'sweating lust' that has usurped love's name on earth (794), and while he does not say so explicitly, he implies that Venus is associated with lust. After this he finally makes his escape, leaving Venus to spend the night grieving her frustration in a 'heavy anthem' (839) at which the landscape itself seems to echo her grief.

The next day begins on a note of hope as the lark sings and the sun washes the world in gold (853–64). Venus can find no sign of Adonis, but when she hears the sound of a hunt, she races through the wood until she comes upon the boar, its 'frothy mouth, bepainted all with red, / Like milk and blood being mingled both together' (901–2). Running on, she encounters Adonis's hounds, and fearing the worst she berates death, the 'Grim-grinning ghost, earth's worm' (933). She now gives full vent to her grief (955–72), until she hears the sound of a huntsman in the distance and, telling herself that Adonis is not dead, 'she unweaves the web that she has wrought' (991) and apologises to death. Running towards the sound, she finds the gored body of Adonis, the 'foul boar's conquest' (1030). At first unable to comprehend what she sees, she attempts to find meaning for it in a lament over the body (1069–1120). She reconstructs Adonis as a youth loved by all creatures except the boar, which she now sees as her rival in a fearful kind of love: 'If he did see his face, why then, I know / He thought to kiss him, and hath killed him so' (1109–10). She then utters a prophecy that from this time on love will always lead to sorrow and jealousy and will be the cause of wars and discord (1133–64). At this the body of Adonis disappears, and a purple and white flower grows from his blood, which Venus plucks and carries off to her home on the island of Paphos, 'where the queen / Means to immure herself, and not be seen' (1194).

SOME READERS

The history of the poem's reception is a history of competing and contradictory readings. Is it tragic or comic, or should we call it tragi-comedy? Is it about love or lust? Should we see Venus as divine or human, predatory or nurturing, a lover or a mother? Is Adonis a representation of moral idealism or a self-absorbed and petulant child? What vision of nature is embodied in the boar? What authority is given to the narrative voice? Is the eroticism excessive? Can we make its frank sensuality render a serious account of human relationships? These questions and many more have been posed. There are no conclusive answers to most of them. Shakespeare might have intended a specific reading of the poem, but that intention is not available to us, and his contemporary readers could well have read his poem in a manner different from his intention. We, as postmodern readers, can look back over the poem's history and benefit from earlier readings; they will enrich our response, but will not take us closer to any 'truth'.

For some of the poem's readers, its erotic elements have actually appeared pornographic. As I have noted, the number of editions of *Venus and Adonis* issued during Shakespeare's lifetime testifies to its popularity, and no doubt many of its early readers would have been as uncritical as Frances Meres was in 1598. There seems to be a note of disapproval in Gabriel Harvey's comment in the same year, quoted above, about the delight taken in *Venus and Adonis* by the 'younger sort'. The jealous Harebrain in Thomas Middleton's 1608 play *A Mad World, My Masters* confiscates the poem from his wife because he fears the aphrodisiac effect it might have on her: 'I have convey'd away all her wanton pamphlets, as *Hero and Leander, Venus and Adonis*; oh, two luscious mary-bone pies for a young married wife!'(1.2.47–50).[2] To Harebrain, though presumably not to Middleton, the poem is pornographic. Three years later John Davies of Hereford tried to find a balance of the two aspects of the poem: 'Fine wit is shown therein; but finer 'twere / If not attired in such bawdy gear'.[3] One cannot help feeling that he deplored the bawdry more than he valued the wit.

Increasingly during the seventeenth century the poem was read and either enjoyed or condemned for its lascivious content. Perhaps it was disquiet about this latter aspect that led to an apparent decline in interest during the eighteenth century, when the poem was excluded from most editions of Shakespeare's works. In the five volumes of the *Critical Heritage* series dedicated to Shakespeare's reputation in that century the editor includes only ten references to *Venus and Adonis*. The last of these is to the great editor Edmond Malone, who in 1780 wrote of the poem, 'This first essay of Shakespeare's Muse does not appear to me so entirely void of poetical merit as it has been represented'.[4] He was looking back over a period when the tradition of the poem's wantonness had obliterated any sense of its poetic value. Some thirty-seven years later the poet Coleridge found much to praise in both the matter and the manner of *Venus and Adonis*. He thought that Shakespeare's essentially dramatic instincts allowed him to remain detached from his work, so that the reader never feels any sympathy with 'the animal impulse' represented in it: 'though the very subject cannot but detract from the pleasure of a delicate mind, yet never was poem less dangerous on a moral account'.[5]

We do not have to agree with Coleridge about the poet's detachment in order to disagree with the attacks on the poem's sensuality, and certainly today few people are likely to feel themselves corrupted by it. Even in the twentieth century, however, critics have often generated moralizing readings that seek unity for the poem through mythic, allegorical or symbolic readings in which *Venus and Adonis* embody opposed forces that illustrate some large idea that they believe Shakespeare wanted to explicate. Such moralizing readings of the poem tend to ignore its intricacy and its potential for a multiplicity of meanings. Lu Emily Pearson, for example, claimed that 'Venus is shown as the destructive agent of sensual love; Adonis is reason in love. The one sullies whatever it touches; the other honors and makes it beautiful. The one is false and evil; the other is all truth, all good'.[6] Many of the readings that see the poem in terms of such binary oppositions find in it some form of Neo-platonism, with Adonis representing 'Beauty or true Love refusing to be won by Venus-Lust to propagation'.[7] In a variation of this Norman Rabkin finds his opposition between 'earthbound Venus whose love never reaches beyond apotheosized animality' and 'self-denying Adonis whose definition of love leads him in search of a purity attainable only in death'.[8] All of these readings are based upon something that can be found in the poem, but they distort it by simplification: Venus is a complex collection of desires and faults, but she is not 'evil'; Adonis is not in search of purity, he is in search of a boar.

These readings reflect a continuing discomfort with the poem's sensuality, and an anxiety to show that Shakespeare had it under control within the confines of moral allegory. We might sympathize with Kenneth Muir in his dismissal of what he calls 'Neoplatonic nonsense', but it is not enough simply to reverse the polarity, as he does, and present Adonis as a prig whose self-centred behaviour causes us to pity the naturally passionate Venus.[9] Eugene Cantalupe goes further in liberating the poem from rigid construction by arguing that it should be seen as a work of comic irony, burlesquing conventional Neoplatonic versions of the story.[10] Moralizing readings have rarely been able to come to terms with the poem's comic tone, but as Rufus Putney noted, if we assume 'that *Venus and Adonis* was meant to be amusing, all that before seemed ridiculous and inept is transmuted into mirth'.[11] Putney did push his own argument a little far, but he also helped release the poem from some of its more earnest interpreters.

Putney's work opens up the question of the relationship between the poem's content and its tone. Is it a tragedy or a comedy? Since it presents the death of Adonis, and ends with Venus mourning her loss, we would have to say that in form or structure it is a tragedy. But its playfulness undercuts the darker elements, and we might feel somewhat uncomfortable with the boundaries that the word 'tragedy' suggests. There seems to be a disjunction between form and mood. Muir, weighing problems of definition in an essay appro-priately entitled '*Venus and Adonis*: Comedy or Tragedy?', found that 'We are driven to conclude that the poem cannot easily be categor-ized'.[12] The word 'driven' suggests Muir's unease with his conclu-sion, however, and other critics have worried about the poem's categorical elusiveness. For John Buxton, the question comes down to a matter of decorum, as the poem is insufficiently elevated for its serious mythic material: 'For the story [Shakespeare] has to tell he makes his characters too human, and too dramatic: he thinks of Venus only as more powerful than Adonis, when he should describe her as more divine; they are not enough idealized; and they talk too much'.[13] This prescriptive kind of criticism, in which Shakespeare is chastised for not writing the poem that the critic thinks he should have written, is not very helpful, since it deflects attention from what the poet might actually have been doing. Shakespeare knew *Hero and Leander*, and he could easily have emulated Marlowe by terminating his story before the catastrophe, in which case he could have left Venus comically frustrated without risking the harsher shading that this darker matter brings to his poem. But he did not. He was aiming, with this fine incongruity between content and method, for complex and even contradictory effects.

Much fruitful work has recently been produced on the poem's concerns with the dangers and excesses of rhetoric, beginning with Richard Lanham's important study of the relations between motive and language.[14] Heather Dubrow has shown that *Venus and Adonis*, like most of Shakespeare's non-dramatic poetry, is 'deeply involved with the uses and abuses of power and of language;' while A.D. Cousins, rather unusually, defines the rhetorical implications of the almost-silent Adonis as a 'rhetoric of chastity'.[15] The important point to be noted is that the poem's rhetoric is not simply a matter of Shakespeare's being carried away by his own poetic powers, as some earlier critics thought, but is fundamental to his concept of his characters and of how language works in relationships and communities. As Anthony Mortimer puts it, '*Venus and Adonis* exist in and not behind their rhetoric'.[16]

To return briefly to the history of allegorical and symbolic readings of *Venus and Adonis*: one of the attractions of them was that they allowed the imposition of a neat pattern, a sense of completed form, on a frustrating, unruly narrative. As I noted earlier, some recent readers like Catherine Belsey have concentrated on its resistance to such desire for closure. Richard Halpern, who sees the poem as being directed to a predominantly female readership, says 'Just as Adonis' beauty arouses Venus but refuses to satisfy her, so Shakespeare's poem aims to arouse and frustrate the female reader'.[17] While I would take issue with Halpern's assumption about the implied gender of the reader, as I noted above in my own description of the poem's form, I certainly agree that one of the ways the poem works is in its refusal of closure. I would suggest that it is from its tantalization of the reader, its joyful insistence on contradiction and multiplicity, that the poem derives much of its energy.

THE READER AND THE NARRATOR

We clearly cannot draw definitive conclusions about *Venus and Adonis* from this history of conflicting readings, but it might be possible for us to learn something from the poem's own assumptions about the nature of its readership. According to Halpern, while the poem 'poses as an offering to a male, aristocratic readership, it actually appealed to a broadly popular and (to judge by contemporary accounts) a largely if not predominantly female audience'.[18] Cousins, on the other hand, thinks that 'the assumed readership for the poem would seem to be primarily male', on the grounds that its characters are subjected to a 'male gaze'.[19] Cousins seems to be wrong, for Halpern discusses a number of early references that suggest that women were indeed frequent readers of the poem. The problem Cousins perceives can be resolved if we accept that the poem's 'male gaze', generated by what I think is unquestionably a male narrative voice, does not necessarily imply a male reader. There is sufficient room for irony in the making of the narrative voice to allow the poem both to construct a male gaze and to provide a subtle criticism of it.

In writing *Venus and Adonis* Shakespeare was attempting something quite different from what he had done before, and he must have been acutely conscious of the need to acknowledge the sophistica-tion of the readers to whom he hoped to appeal. He fashioned for them a narrative voice that gives an impression of control, balance and refined knowingness. Like Marlowe, whose *Hero and Leander* possibly provided a model, Shakespeare was reshaping and enlarg-ing the urbane, ironic Ovidian pose for the tastes of his own time. His narrator is not a so much a 'character' as a device that allows for a differentiation between the narrator's perspective and the poem's. This is an important element in the blending of the tragic with the comic in the poem and also in its critique of masculine values. The components of the narrative – the baffled desire of Venus and the loss of the object of her love, the embarrassed irritation of Adonis and his violent death – are unrelievedly painful for the participants, and yet they are frequently interpreted by the narrator with cool play-fulness. Consider, for example, his deflating comment at the end of Venus's first lengthy seduction speech: 'By this, the lovesick queen

began to sweat' (175); the picture of a sweating Venus is quite enough
to undermine what is in many ways a powerful piece of argumentation. Or consider the crucial moment when the goddess of love
discovers that the object of her desire is more interested in a boar:
'She's Love, she loves, and yet she is not loved' (610). The paradox
of an embodiment of love who cannot make herself loved is presented with witty economy as the repetition slides and shifts along
the line.

   The sophistication of the narrator is presented in other ways. In
describing Adonis's horse, for example, he exhibits his knowledge of
aesthetic issues (as well as of how to judge horse-flesh) by reference
to the debates concerning the connections between art and nature,
directing the reader's attention to the manner in which a painter
would depict a horse:

> Look when a painter would surpass the life
> In limning out a well proportioned steed,
> His art with nature's workmanship at strife,
> As if the dead the living should exceed:
> So did this horse excel a common one
> In shape, in courage, colour, pace, and bone.
>
> Round-hoofed, short-jointed, fetlocks shag and long,
> Broad breast, full eye, small head, and nostril wide,
> High crest, short ears, straight legs, and passing strong,
> Thin mane, thick tail, broad buttock, tender hide–
> Look what a horse should have he did not lack,
> Save a proud rider on so proud a back.
>
> (289–300)

Indeed, on a number of occasions the narrator draws the reader's
attention to his cleverness at creating analogies with the 'Look
when...' kind of construction. When Venus first overwhelms
Adonis, the narrator says 'Look how a bird lies tangled in a net, /
So fastened in her arms Adonis lies' (67–8). When she tries to deduce
Adonis's fate from the wounded state of his hounds, the narrator
shows his awareness of and superiority to the superstitions of
common people:

> Look how the world's poor people are amazed
> At apparitions, signs, and prodigies,
> Whereon with fearful eyes they long have gazed,

Infusing them with dreadful prophecies:
So she at these sad signs draws up her breath,
And, sighing it again, exclaims on death.

(925–30)

He is inviting the reader to share and admire his detached knowingness.

This sense that the narrator is interested in drawing attention to
himself is also apparent in his use of rhetoric. His description of the
horse and jennet reflects the Aristotelian definition of *mimesis* or
'imitation', which was understood by Renaissance theorists to mean
that poetry is a matter of creating a resemblance to something in the
outside world. This idea was further encouraged by a phrase in
Horace's *Ars Poetica*, '*ut pictura poesis*' ('poetry is like painting'). Sidney
reflects this strain of thought: 'Poesy therefore is an art of imitation,
for so Aristotle termeth it in his word '*mimesis*', that is to say, a representing, counterfeiting, or figuring forth: to speak metaphorically,
a speaking picture'. (*Apology*, p. 223). Such poetic picture-making led
to displays of rhetorical virtuosity, and Shakespeare's narration has
many of them. Not only in his large scale descriptions, but particularly in his descriptions of Venus (when he is not insisting on her
comic incongruity), he is fond of the exquisite pictorial moment:
'Her two blue windows faintly she upheaveth' (482); 'Her eye seen
in the tears, tears in her eye, / Both crystals, where they viewed each
other's sorrow' (962–3). This sort of writing can lead to widely
diverging responses. Take, for instance, the description of Venus
holding Adonis's hand: 'A lily prisoned in a jail of snow' (362).
According to Sandra Clark this is one of those lines that 'astound us
with their beauty,' while Robert Ellrodt dismissively calls it 'pre-
cious'.[20] The modern reader might be inclined to agree with Ellrodt,
but I suspect that Shakespeare was giving the poem's original readers
what they wanted.

For of course, the self-consciously exhibitionist art that is being
offered up for the reader's admiration is Shakespeare's own, and
I am not saying that the narrator cannot in any way be identified
with the author. But his voice is carefully calculated to speak to the
cultivated reader, and that calculation should be examined with
great care. Indeed, there is a division in the narrative perspective that
accounts for many of the apparent contradictions and paradoxes in
the poem, for narrator and author do not necessarily see the events
in the same way. The amused detachment of the narrator is, in the

end, a limited response to the painful events. His exhibitionism is ironically close to the manly narcissism of Adonis, and his misogyny is part of his inadequacy. By his limitation the poem hints at the limitation of the masculine courtly ethos that he reflects. This can be seen more clearly through a broader examination of his treatment of Venus, to which I shall return shortly.

MYTH AND ANTI-MYTH

One thing that is apparent in the history of critical reception that I outlined above is that many readers have attempted to find consistent meaning in the poem by finding a rigid pattern in what is, in fact, unruly material – hence the attraction of moralizing allegorical readings. As my discussion of the ambiguity of the narrative voice suggests, however, such readings cannot account for the poem's effects, which seem to depend on misdirection and indeterminacy. Consider the poem as myth. Classical myths were stories that attempted to explain phenomena in the world in terms of the actions or experiences of supernatural beings, and were not necessarily concerned with moral issues. Shakespeare uses the myth of *Venus and Adonis* to explain why human love is such a painful business. At the end of the poem, the suffering Venus lays a lengthy curse upon the world (1135–64) that can be summed up in its opening words: 'here I prophesy / Sorrow on love hereafter shall attend' (1135–6). And yet her own experience is that love is already a matter of sorrow. Venus, that is, is from the outset confused about the nature of love, and since she *is* Love, she is confused about her own identity. This is not surprising, since a perennial difficulty with the word 'love' is that it is attached to a vast and often incompatible range of experiences, from altruistic spiritual love to animal desire. The poem's comedy arises in part from having at its centre a Venus who does not understand her own mythic meaning. This comedy is augmented by other incongruous elements.

The myth of *Venus and Adonis* is tragic, and it was treated as such in most Renaissance accounts. It was a popular subject for painters as well as poets, and Shakespeare was apparently familiar with pictures of the story; in the Induction to *The Taming of the Shrew* Christopher Sly is offered 'Adonis painted by a running brook' (Ind. 2. 48). Most painters took the story seriously, giving Venus the dignity that the goddess of love might be expected to possess, and it was rare to have Adonis reject Venus. Titian is an exception; in his painting of 1554, he portrays a desperate Venus, observed from behind, clinging to a notably reluctant Adonis who is youthful but not childish. Physically he is more than a match for her, and there is nothing comic about the depiction. Erwin Panofsky has suggested that Titian's painting might have been a source for Shakespeare's poem, though I think this is improbable.[21] Still, it is understandable that scholars have wanted to read Shakespeare's narrative poems in terms of paintings. Clark Hulse has demonstrated the force of Shakespeare's pictorial imagination in the two narrative poems, which he describes as 'a painter's poems, founded on a subtle understanding of the creation and interpretation of visual images'.[22]

What happens, though, if we take a static representative moment in Shakespeare's *Venus and Adonis* and visualize it as if it were a painting? One result is that the tragic story shifts into a comic mode. From information we are given in the early stanzas of the poem we have to generate an image of Venus from what she does and says rather than from description of her. She is golden-haired, we are told, but apart from this what we learn is that she is physically powerful, large enough to pluck Adonis from his horse and carry him under her arm. In the opening stanza she is pictured as 'a bold-faced suitor' (6), appropriating what in Shakespeare's time would certainly have been a masculine role. Her attitude in the opening section is informed by aggressive passion or enraged desire, her face 'red and hot as coals of glowing fire' (35). When she kisses Adonis she does so as if she were an eagle devouring its quarry, 'Till either gorge be stuffed or prey be gone' (58). At the same time, his refusal of her advances makes her a pathetic victim of her own appetite, begging in vain for what she wants: '"O pity," gan she cry, "flint-hearted boy! / 'Tis but a kiss I beg – why art thou coy?"' (95–6). Our painting of the poem's opening, therefore, would depict a Venus who, however beautiful, is also muscular; her posture would be of baffled aggression, her face expressing blazing but frustrated lust. Adonis, in clear contrast, would have to be much smaller, a mere boy, and a rather effeminate one at that, since the poem presents him in terms that were conventionally applied to feminine beauty (as they are insistently applied to Lucrece in the later poem): 'More white and red than doves or roses are' (10). The damasked red and white of his cheeks is increased by the fact that his bashful blushing is mixed with scorn and disdain, ''Twixt crimson shame and anger ashy-pale' (76).

Our painting will necessarily be distinguished by the incongruity in the role-reversal of the two figures. We can see in it an inversion of the conventional Petrarchan relationship, familiar to all readers of Elizabethan sonnets, in which the man is aggressive but disappointed, the woman passive and reluctant. Whatever posture we give to them, Venus will be dominant, expressing manipulative desire mixed with the pain of frustration; the tender Adonis will show shame or scorn or a mixture of the two, but perhaps also a determination in his resistance that will subvert the power of Venus. The pathos of emotional distress will be blended with the burlesque comedy produced by the physical incompatibility of the two figures. The opening passage of the poem does not give us much evidence upon which to build a setting for our encounter between Venus and Adonis, but as it progresses we can see English woodland rather than any kind of mythic or allegorical scene, emphasizing the earthliness (and earthiness?) of the two. This would be an unorthodox painting of Venus and Adonis, complicating and interrogating the issues raised by the original tragic story, which are made troublesome by the insistence on their comic potential.

Shakespeare's Ovidian epigraph ('*Vilia Miretur vulgus; mihi flavus Apollo / Pocula Castalia plena ministret aqua*') is apparently making a claim for the poetic seriousness or elevation of *Venus and Adonis*, but the treatment of the material mingles gravity with levity in a manner that is sometimes so broadly comic that it subverts the potential seriousness of the story. Consider the opening stanza:

> Even as the sun with purple-coloured face
> Had ta'en his last leave of the weeping morn,
> Rose-cheeked Adonis hied him to the chase.
> Hunting he loved, but love he laughed to scorn.
> Sick-thoughted Venus makes amain unto him,
> And like a bold-faced suitor 'gins to woo him.

(1–6)

There is an epic sonorousness to the first two lines, and the metaphor in them foreshadows the events of the narrative. The sun is personified as a lover leaving behind a weeping woman, and his 'purple-coloured face' is immediately reflected, though in a diminished sense, in the 'Rose-cheeked' face of Adonis. The repetition of 'love' in the fourth line shifts the meaning of the word: the youth's masculine passion for hunting is set against his impatient contempt

for the effeminacy of erotic love, and the harshness of the word
'scorn' indicates the futility of Venus's desire. She herself is 'Sick-
thoughted' – love-sick, evidently, but perhaps also with a sense of
the hopelessness of her desire; nevertheless, she approaches him
with apparent confidence, 'bold-faced'. The stanza is brought to an
incongruous end by the jingling rhyme of the last two lines.

There is nothing particularly problematic in this until we consider
the implications of a bold-faced Venus who has taken on the normally
masculine role of suitor, and a rosy-cheeked Adonis, perhaps not
quite as masculine as he wants to believe himself to be. This reversal
of gender roles is not, of course, comic in itself, but within four more
stanzas Shakespeare leaves us in no doubt about his comic intent.
Driven by passion Venus shifts into the notorious physical action
that has worried many critics:

> Being so enraged, desire doth lend her force
> Courageously to pluck him from his horse.
>
> Over one arm the lusty courser's rein,
> Under her other was the tender boy.
> Who blushed and pouted in a dull disdain
> With leaden appetite, unapt to toy.
>
> (29–34)

The visualized effect of the passage is ludicrous, and this is reinforced
by the bullying way in which she makes her amorous approach to
him: 'Backward she pushed him, as she would be thrust, / And gov-
erned him in strength' (41–2). The ambiguous suggestions implicit in
the rosy cheeks of the great hunter Adonis are now clarified: he
appears as a blushing, pouting child.

Perhaps we can understand this apparently burly Venus if we
visualize the poem in a different way, for the visual images with
which Shakespeare was most familiar were displayed on the stage
rather than on the canvas, and I think we should consider how his
theatrical experience might have a bearing on how he imagined
Venus and Adonis. With the possible exception of some sonnets, all
of Shakespeare's writing prior to the composition of this poem had
been for the public playhouses. All of his female characters were
written with the knowledge that they would be played by boys, and
the writer's consciousness that the staged 'woman's part' had an
unavoidable masculine core is apparent in many of the roles that he
wrote early in his career. Consequently, when we contemplate the

undeniable dramatic elements in Venus's character, as well as her comic physical incompatibility with Adonis, we do well to consider her as if she were a character in a play written by Shakespeare for the public theatre as it existed in 1592 rather than for the private theatre of the reader's imagination. That is, at some level Shakespeare conceived of her as a cross-dressed boy, making playful use of his theatrical experience.

In his early plays, whether because he distrusted the ability of the boy actors who embodied the female characters, or because he was intrigued by the ambiguities available in turning a boy into a woman, Shakespeare frequently stressed the 'masculine' element in at least one (usually the leading) female role. This is done most obviously for Julia in *The Two Gentlemen of Verona*, who spends most of that play disguised as a young man. In *1 Henry VI* Joan La Pucelle spends much of her time in armour, and on her first appearance her manlike vigour is pointedly stressed when she is identified as 'an Amazon' (1.3.83). This is a term rarely used by Shakespeare, but he uses it on two other occasions in the *Henry VI* plays, both with reference to Queen Margaret. In *3 Henry VI* she is called 'an Amazonian trull' by York (1.4.115); later, it is reported to King Edward that she is ready to put on armour, to which he replies 'Belike she minds to play the Amazon' (4.1.104). In *2 Henry VI*, in a line that compares the Queen's masculine nature to the effeminacy of her husband, it is said of their marriage that 'in this place most master wear no breeches' (1.3.150). This is immediately after she has given the Duchess of Gloucester a box on the ear.

One might think that the move to narrative poetry in *Venus and Adonis* would have liberated the writer from the necessity of incorporating Amazon elements into the women he constructed. It seems, however, that he decided to make comic use of his theatrical experience. He conceived the poem in part as if it were a play, a two-hander to be performed by two apprentices, one large and beefy, the other small and barely adolescent. He then gave them the wrong parts. The obvious incongruousness of writing aggressive masculinity into Venus, goddess of love and feminine sexual beauty, is compounded by the outrageous inflation of that masculinity. One of its consequences is to drain virility out of Adonis, who is constantly mastered by her. No wonder he blushes and pouts: not only is his role inferior, but as things turn out it is also shorter. The effect is of burlesque (or perhaps more accurately travesty), a comic treatment of material normally treated seriously through a distortion and deflation of the characters akin to the later, much more ferocious deflation of mythic archetypes in *Troilus and Cressida*.

VENUS

Venus is at the centre of the poem (much of it consists of dialogue, and the larger part of that comes from the mouth of Venus, who speaks 537 of the 1194 lines; Adonis speaks only 88), and she is at the centre of the problems that so many critics have found with it. Not the least of these has arisen from the reversal of gender-roles and the effect this has on the representation of Venus, which for some has presented a (literally and metaphorically) large problem. Notoriously, C.S. Lewis compared Venus to childhood memories of 'voluminous female relatives': 'this flushed, panting, perspiring, suffocating, loquacious creature is supposed to be the goddess of love herself, the golden Aphrodite. It will not do. If the poem is not meant to arouse disgust it was very foolishly written'.[23] Lewis should have known better, but his response has been echoed by many sub-sequent readers. The word 'grotesque' is one that has frequently come to mind for the representation of the goddess of love as a woman sufficiently brawny to pluck the object of her affections from his horse and tuck him under her arm. Gordon Williams, for example, finds that in these actions she appears 'too grotesque to command either [Adonis's] or the reader's wholehearted sympathy,' although he goes on to defend her developing role in the poem.[24] Robert Ellrodt suggests that this grotesquery might have been handled successfully 'in a Cervantic manner but the contrast between the actions of the characters and the prevailing prettiness of the descriptive style creates in the reader an unresolved conflict of impressions'.[25] Heather Dubrow, while acknowledging the ways in which Venus's behaviour is mimetic of the actions of real people, draws a line at this improbable act: 'Few women could literally tuck a young man, however slim and "hairless" he might be, under their arms'.[26]

However, the role-reversal that gives us an apparently masculine Venus is not a simple matter of distorting conventional gender demarcations. Shakespeare unsettles our expectations even further by locating Venus's muscular assertiveness within a body that he also depicts as an extreme of feminine fertility and lushness, both motherly and erotic, so that we respond to her in conflicting ways. In her fears of the boar's threat to Adonis she clearly exhibits maternal concern; she runs through the bushes 'Like a milch doe, whose swelling dugs do ache, / Hasting to feed her fawn hid in some brake' (875–6). Earlier her concern for Adonis is rather different: 'My flesh is soft and plump' (142), she tells him, and makes him an offer that most of Shakespeare's male readers would have found it difficult to refuse:

Graze on my lips, and if those hills be dry,
Stray lower, where the pleasant fountains lie.

Within this limit is relief enough,
Sweet bottom-grass and high delightful plain,
Round rising hillocks, brakes obscure and rough,
To shelter thee from tempest and from rain.

(233–8)

Elsewhere Venus asserts the supernatural lightness of her body:

Witness this primrose bank whereon I lie:
These forceless flowers like sturdy trees support me.
Two strengthless doves will draw me through the sky
From morn till night.

(151–4)

What can we make of this contradiction? Part of it arises from the fact that the poem presents Venus simultaneously as a goddess and as an all-too-human being. More significant, however, is the fact that one version of Venus is her self-presentation and the other is the narrator's version of her. Venus is a site of conflicting energies, both goddess and woman, temptress and mother, predator and victim. But in all of these divisions the intervention of the narrative voice plays some part: that is, for every account Venus gives of herself, her experience, or her attitude the narrative voice provides a competing and usually adverse interpretation.

Let us consider some of the contradictions. We might expect that as a goddess Venus would have supernatural power, and yet in the poem her desire for the mortal Adonis has made her vulnerable, transforming her from goddess to mortal, and she is rendered powerless, or, at the least, powerless to awaken a reciprocal desire in him. As a goddess she is the embodiment of love, essentially an abstract entity, but as a mortal she is victimized by love, being made to experience its painfully perplexed human reality. She is thus apparently confused about what love is, or at any rate, about how

mortals respond to it. In part this confusion reflects competing tradi-
tions of mythic interpretation, in some of which Venus has been
idealized into a principle of fecundity and nurturing, while in others
she has been demonized into a figure of aggression and domination.
This is not a sufficient explanation, however. When she chides
Adonis for his narcissistic focus upon himself, she points out that he
is denying nature and that to live in accordance with the order of
nature is a moral duty:

> Torches are made to light, jewels to wear,
> Dainties to taste, fresh beauty for the use,
> Herbs for their smell, and sappy plants to bear.
> Things growing to themselves, are growth's abuse,
> Seeds spring from seeds, and beauty breedeth beauty:
> Thou wast begot; to get it is thy duty.
>
> (163–8)

This is, surely a healthy, positive view of nature. However, the nature
that she herself is said to inhabit is much more savage than the
benign landscape she evokes here. In this other nature she is presented figuratively as a bird of prey an embodiment of devouring
appetite:

> Even as an empty eagle, sharp by fast,
> Tires with her beak on feathers, flesh and bone,
> Shaking her wings, devouring all in haste,
> Till either gorge be stuffed or prey be gone;
> Even so she kissed his brow, his cheek, his chin,
> And where she ends she doth anew begin.
>
> (55–60)

There is an almost identical description later, but this time the eagle
is replaced by a vulture that feeds 'glutton-like' upon its yielding
prey' (547–52). The important point to bear in mind is that the representation of Venus as predatory appetite, as eagle or vulture, is in
both cases provided by the narrator.

The narrator often disguises actual animosity under a veneer
of cleverness. As presented through her own speeches, Venus's idea
of love is conflicted and often selfish, but it is not so malignant as
the narrative voice would have us believe. Take as an example the
opening lines of her first speech:

'Thrice fairer then my self,' thus she began,
'The fields' chief flower, sweet above compare,
Stain to all nymphs, more lovely then a man,
More white and red than doves or roses are –
Nature that made thee with her self at strife
Saith that the world hath ending with thy life.

(7–12)

Her focus here is firmly on Adonis. Her language, mixing images
from pastoral and Petrarchan conventions, is hyperbolic, reflecting
the ways in which the sonnet lover attempted to seduce his mistress, but what would have concerned (and almost certainly
amused) an Elizabethan reader is the role-reversal implied in
a woman's using this kind of rhetoric to a man. If there is anything
threatening to be found in the Petrarchan gaze it surely derives
from the conventions, and not from the way in which Venus is
using them.

Venus goes on to present sensual pleasure as a kind of paradise:

Here come and sit where never serpent hisses;
And being sat, I'll smother thee with kisses,

And yet not cloy thy lips with loathed satiety,
But rather famish them amid their plenty,
Making them red, and pale, with fresh variety;
Ten kisses short as one, one long as twenty.

(17–22)

Her reference to the absent serpent sets up positive echoes of an
unfallen Eden, but what she fails to see is that the insatiable hunger
she offers is anything but Edenic. The image of a man famished in
the midst of plenty invokes the figure of Tantalus, condemned to have
his appetite eternally deprived of satisfaction – later in the poem the
narrator makes explicit allusion to that myth, saying of Venus's own
sexual frustration 'That worse than Tantalus' is her annoy' (599).
One of the poem's many ironies is that what Venus offers to Adonis
is what she alone suffers:

Never did passenger in summer's heat
More thirst for drink than she for this good turn.
Her help she sees, but help she cannot get;
She bathes in water, yet her fire must burn.

(91–4)

The poem's entire elaboration of Venus generates contradiction: her presentation of herself offers pleasure, but the narrator's presentation of her interprets the pleasure as pain, and he enjoys the ironies of her suffering: 'Poor queen of love, in thine own law forlorn, / To love a cheek that smiles at thee in scorn' (251–2).

The narrator's insistent subversion of Venus can also be seen in his treatment of Venus's offer to smother Adonis with kisses (18). The figure of speech is a commonplace, and in spite of the literal meaning of the word 'smother' it is harmless. However, a few lines later when Adonis tries to speak, the narrator distorts the figure into sinister hyperbole when he says that she 'murders' his words with a kiss (54). This relationship between Venus and the narrative voice is a crucial one, for it is in the hyperbole of his readings of her, and rarely in her own words, that the 'grotesque' Venus is to be found. For example, when she kisses Adonis the narrator says, 'Her face doth reek and smoke' (555). This is a stock element of traditional allegorical descriptions of lust, but it is preposterous given the essentially literal presentation here. The narrator, as the reader's guide, offers a consistently cynical interpretation of Venus-as-love, one shaped by Elizabethan misogyny. But I think that the poem wants us to see through his response to a different version of Venus.

Since so many readers have accepted the narrator's 'grotesque' interpretation of Venus, it is refreshing to read the dissenting response of Katherine Duncan-Jones, who writes: 'It is almost as if twentieth-century, male, critics feel threatened by the overwhelming physicality of Venus – her fleshy strength, her hot breath, her ardour, and her verbal brilliance – the very features that Elizabethan readers evidently found irresistible'.[27] If we are to locate a version of Venus different from that of the narrator it will presumably be in her 'verbal brilliance', in the account of herself that she renders in her own words. This, too, I think, should be observed with some scepticism. Venus is, like Marlowe's Leander, a self-conscious rhetorician. She tries to subdue her object with a seductive language that reproduces her own seductive body; indeed, her first action in the poem is her attempt to subdue Adonis with her body, but when he resists her she mounts her lengthy rhetorical assault. From the outset, however, we see that she misjudges the implications, and therefore the effects, of her words. She begins by telling Adonis the story of her subjection of Mars:

Over my altars hath he hung his lance,
His battered shield, his uncontrolled crest,

And for my sake hath learned to sport and dance,
To toy, to wanton, dally, smile, and jest,
Scorning his churlish drum, and ensign red,
Making my arms his field, his tent my bed.

(103–8)

The story of Venus overcoming Mars can be interpreted in opposed ways: it can be understood as a story about the emasculation of military might by erotic weakness, or as a story about the civilizing influence of love over male savagery. Venus clearly thinks that Adonis will want to follow the lead of the great warrior god; it does not occur to her that the prospect of being led 'prisoner in a red-rose chain' (110) might not be appealing to the immature hunter.

Perhaps the main flaw in her rhetorical campaign lies here. The youthful Adonis is seeking an adult identity: he wants to be a man, and his desire for the boar is a desire for manhood. Venus wants to create an identity for him, and to do this she insistently emphasizes his effeminacy. The image of himself that she presents to Adonis is far distant from what he wants to see. She is a subtle rhetorician, but she makes a fundamental error: the purpose of rhetoric is to persuade or seduce, but to do that the rhetorician needs more than fine language and must understand his or her audience; Venus grossly misjudges Adonis. Yet, as we have seen, the words she speaks offer what is natural, fruitful, life-giving: 'having no defects, why dost abhor me?' (138) Why indeed? The fact is that Adonis is impervious to her rhetoric because he believes it to be lies:

If love have lent you twenty thousand tongues,
And every tongue more moving then your own,
Bewitching like the wanton mermaid's songs,
Yet from mine ear the tempting tune is blown;
For know, my heart stands armed in mine ear,
And will not let a false sound enter there.

(775–80)

'Bewitching', 'tempting', 'false': not because she is telling him lies, but because she is attempting to exert power over him.

Is the reader, subjected to the same display of rhetorical devices and arguments, expected to judge her in the same way? Shakespeare does write another response into the poem. At the end of the first lengthy rhetorical attack on Adonis, the sun-god Titan, who watches over them, wishes that he could change places with Adonis,

'So he were like him, and by Venus' side' (180). A more natural response, we might think, but we should remember that Titan himself appears as a seducer in the poem's opening lines, as he forsakes the 'weeping morn' Aurora. Perhaps we are expected to see both responses to Venus as deficient. I shall consider this question further in discussing Adonis.

Before moving on to Adonis, I want to address one further aspect of Venus as she appears in the poem. As a representation of woman she is freed from the social and moral constraints that were imposed upon Elizabethan women and is thus enabled to behave like a man. In this she clearly reflects the position of Queen Elizabeth herself, and it would have been impossible for a contemporary reader to avoid the allusion. Venus figured as part of the mixture of myth and pseudo-myth that underpinned the cult of Elizabeth. In his address to the queen in *The Arte of English Poesie* Puttenham says she is '*Venus* in countenance, in life *Diana, Pallas* for government, and *Juno* in all honour and regal magnificence' (*Arte*, p. 5). The juxtaposition of erotic appearance and chaste life that here sets Venus beside Diana was a source of constant unease for writers concerned with the cult of Elizabeth, though the interpretation of Venus had a complex history and most writers struggled to isolate the positive elements of the goddess.[28] Nevertheless, there was frequently an undertone of animosity in such treatments of Elizabeth as a trespasser into patriarchal privilege. The hostile presentation of Venus in Shakespeare's poem has clear subversive possibilities; Heather Dubrow has suggested that 'Venus' assertions of power may well reflect resentment of Elizabeth herself'.[29] Certainly, the narrator's hostility to Venus could be read as hostility to Elizabeth, though the complex treatment of the figure makes it impossible to say that the resentment is the author's rather than the reflected resentment of his implied reader. The poem, I think, is careful to obscure its aims.

ADONIS

Venus is a 'large' character in more ways than the fleshly, and Adonis is inevitably cast into shadow by her. It is clear, however, that what Venus finds attractive in him must be entirely his physical beauty, since his responses to her are for the most part sullen, petulant and self-regarding. Some critics have tried to see in him a kind of moral counterweight to Venus's carnality, an idealistic defender of the principle of chastity. The main support for such a reading comes from his late, major denial of what Venus represents:

> Call it not love, for love to heaven is fled
> Since sweating lust on earth usurped his name,
> Under whose simple semblance he hath fed
> Upon fresh beauty, blotting it with blame;
> Which the hot tyrant stains, and soon bereaves,
> As caterpillars do the tender leaves.
>
> Love comforteth like sunshine after rain,
> But lust's effect is tempest after sun.
> Love's gentle spring doth always fresh remain;
> Lust's winter comes ere summer half be done.
> Love surfeits not; lust like a glutton dies.
> Love is all truth, lust full of forged lies.

> (793–804)

This is certainly a powerful passage, in part because of its Biblical echoes. There cannot be much doubt about its intended application to Venus: the image of 'sweating lust' recalls the sweating Venus of line 175; the image of devouring lust evokes the glutton-like Venus feeding on Adonis's lips in line 548. Robert P. Miller praises Adonis, who he says exhibits here 'sound Renaissance morality when he somewhat coldly chides Venus', while Ted Hughes goes so far as to call him the 'new Christ'.[30] Such moral force can only be given to Adonis by making the poem an allegory, but it does not fit with other aspects of what we see of him.

The passage is clearly significant, but I think it is rather difficult to justify using it to make Adonis into a figure of positive moral authority, since his responses to Venus's advances mainly reflect his self-absorption rather than any thought-out ethical position. When she plucks him from his horse, 'He saith she is immodest, blames her miss' (53). This certainly sounds like moral reproach, but its effect is blunted by the fact that it is reported indirectly by the narrator. The first words we hear directly from Adonis are 'The sun doth burn my face; I must remove' (186), reflecting concern more for his own comfort than for moral rectitude. He is more interested in his horse than he is in Venus: he is understandably angry when it runs off with the jennet, but it is childish of him to blame Venus: '"For shame," he cries, "let go, and let me go! / My day's delight is past; my horse is gone, / And 'tis your fault I am bereft him so"'

(379–81). His single-minded concern with the hunt leaves him no time for love:

> 'I know not love,' quoth he, 'nor will not know it,
> Unless it be a boar, and then I chase it.
> 'Tis much to borrow, and I will not owe it.
> My love to love is love but to disgrace it,
> For I have heard it is a life in death,
> That laughs and weeps, and all but with a breath'.
>
> (409–14)

Perhaps there is something attractive in his forthright presentation of his priorities here, but it is based, paradoxically, on a refusal of experience. 'I *will not* know it', he says of love, and 'I *will not* owe it', but his determination is founded on rumour, not on something that he understands: '*I have heard* it is a life in death'. His rejection of erotic desire is the articulation not of moral idealism, but of a perspective limited by his youthfulness. This somewhat undercuts the authority of the later passage.

One could argue that in so forcefully rejecting love, even as it is embodied in the worrying figure of Venus, Adonis is rejecting life. Early in the poem Venus points out to him the dangers of love of self: 'Narcissus so himself himself forsook, / And died to kiss his shadow in the brook' (161–2). Denial of the natural need to procreate is a denial of life itself:

> Upon the earth's increase why shouldst thou feed
> Unless the earth with thy increase be fed?
> By law of nature thou art bound to breed,
> That thine may live when thou thy self art dead;
> And so in spite of death thou dost survive,
> In that thy likeness still is left alive.
>
> (169–74)

While this might be seen simply as a part of Venus's arsenal of rhetorical persuasions, it also contains a clear human truth, and in the case of Adonis it is prophetic. The speaker of the *Sonnets* makes a similar point in trying to persuade his young friend to marry:

> who is he so fond will be the tomb
> Of his self-love to stop posterity? . . .

But if thou live remembered not to be,
Die single, and thine image dies with thee.

(Sonnet 3)

Any argument that tries to present Adonis as a figure of moral rectitude can be countered by one that presents him as childishly and narcissistically life-denying, and the poem insists on such a complication of motives.

Let us look at Adonis from another perspective. I have noted that one of the errors that Venus makes in her attempt to seduce him is to dwell on the effeminacy of his appearance, but the narrator too uses language that in the context of poetic convention foregrounds his femininity: his dimples are 'lovely caves', 'round, enchanting pits' (247), his mouth is a 'ruby-coloured portal' (451) and a 'sweet coral mouth' (542). Cousins notes that Adonis 'is pervasively and primarily subjected throughout to the male gaze of the implied reader'.[31] I have stated my own view of the complex ironic relations between poet, narrative voice and reader, but I would agree that Adonis is subjected to a male gaze. Much could be made of the homoerotic potential of this, especially if we compare it with Marlowe's treatment of Leander, but the point appears to be that, as a result of the poem's reversal of Petrarchan gender roles, Adonis is the true bearer of female experience, and it is in this that the poem invites sympathy for him. His comparative silence in the poem reflects the silence of the woman within the Petrarchan structure, and if we consider the reversed-role implications of Venus's physical attacks on him we can see them as attempted rape. Thus the poem lays bare the disturbing underside of Petrarchism, and by implication of courtly fashion and mores. Through his travesty, that is, Shakespeare contrives to provide a comic situation that reveals serious issues.

CONCLUSIONS

The conclusion to the poem is provided by the boar. What does it 'mean'? Like the poem itself it has invited a range of interpretations, mythic, allegorical and symbolic. It has been understood as a figure of winter in a vegetation cycle; as a figure for masculine aggression, both military and sexual; as the embodiment of lust; as an illustration of the irrationality of evil. No simple explanation of how it is to be interpreted seems adequate, though the temptation to perceive it as a representation of death or destructiveness, the antithesis of the fertile figure of Venus, has been great. Venus herself at first seems to see it thus, falling to the ground at Adonis's mere mention of it. For her the boar is a 'mortal butcher, bent to kill' (618); 'Being moved, he strikes whate'er is in his way, / And whom he strikes his crooked tushes slay' (623–4). Her fears for Adonis are in the event well-founded. To Adonis, on the other hand, the boar is not an object to fear, but rather it is an obsession, the sum of his desires, and stands for all that matters in his conception of life: 'I know not love,' he says, 'unless it be a boar, and then I chase it' (409–10)

His heedless identification of the boar with love here is important and is more than just a joke. Almost all of what the poem tells us about the animal comes from Venus herself, first in her attempt to dissuade Adonis from hunting (614–42), then in her lament over his lacerated body (1105–16). In the latter passage she offers an astonishing eroticization of the moment of his death. The boar, like her, must have been enslaved by Adonis's beauty: 'If he did see his face, why then I know / He thought to kiss him, and hath killed him so' (1109–10). The boar's act thus becomes an act of copulation: 'nuzzling in his flank the loving swine / Sheathed unaware the tusk in his soft groin' (1115–16). The logical end of this progression is for Venus to identify herself with the boar in this act: 'Had I been toothed like him, I must confess, / With kissing him I should have killed him first' (1117–18). Venus's acknowledgement here marks quite a shift from her initial fearful revulsion, almost as if she had come to understand the boar as a kindred spirit: it both is and is not her antithesis.

At only one point is the boar presented from a different perspective; when Venus suddenly comes upon the bloodied creature the narrator describes its 'frothy mouth, bepainted all with red, / Like milk and blood being mingled both together' (901–2). He is reporting what Venus sees, but the figurative language is his own, and its implications are significant. The word 'milk' applied to the enraged foaming of the beast provides a jolt to the reader because of the incongruousness in this context of its associations with nurturing and fecundity. Like Adonis thinking of love as a boar, like Venus imagining the boar as Adonis's lover, the narrator forces together images of life and death within the single object, and the reader is compelled to question his own response to the boar, which perhaps is merely fulfilling its own nature – after all, if it had not killed Adonis he would have killed it.

The mingling of white and red here links the boar to a larger pattern of images, a powerful figurative motif that recurs so frequently in *Venus and Adonis* (as well as in *The Rape of Lucrece*) that one critic has called it an 'obsession' of Shakespeare's.[32] The traditional association of red and white has a long and complex history, encompassing the mystical or spiritual (the blood and body of Christ) and the political (the red and white roses of Lancaster and York) as well as the pagan erotic in which the colours symbolized two aspects of the feminine: red was associated with passion or desire, white with chastity or purity. Broadly speaking, through Petrarchism red and white had become for Renaissance writers conventional terms in the description of feminine beauty as, for example, when the narrator describes in Venus 'the fighting conflict of her hue, / How white and red each other did destroy' (345–6). However, the poem carefully establishes from the outset that red and white are the colours of rose-cheeked Adonis, 'More white and red than doves or roses are' (10). Instances of the poem's use of these colours are too numerous to mention, but their tendency is to dissolve conventional demarcations, not just of gender but of emotions too. Thus, red is usually associated with rage and white with shame, but we are told that Adonis frets ''Twixt crimson shame and anger ashy-pale' (76).

These images of red and white find their resolution in the poem's final moments, when a purple anemone springs from Adonis's blood, 'chequered with white, / Resembling well his pale cheeks, and the blood / Which in round drops upon their whiteness stood' (1168–70). The flower is all that Venus retains of Adonis, but it also offers some measure of hope in implying the continuity of nature. The pattern of red and white thus embraces Venus and Adonis, the boar and the flower, tragedy and comedy. It forms a design somewhat different from those offered by symbolic or allegorical readings of the poem in that it suggests inclusion rather than division. The allegorical potential of the mythic story of *Venus and Adonis* allows for the projection of a whole range of meanings in which the two figures represent binaries or paired opposites that could be set in motion as the two sides of a debate. Shakespeare's poem certainly uses such opposites, but it insistently complicates them, denying the reader the possibility of any simple response or experience. Just as red and white exchange places and functions, so should the reader's response shift about, recognizing that no human experience is simple, that Venus can be a comic figure and a suffering woman at the same time, that Adonis can be a callow youth and a tragic victim at the same time, and that we all have our own boars to confront.

6

The Rape of Lucrece

In 1594 Shakespeare published *The Rape of Lucrece,* also dedicated to the Earl of Southampton, and, presumably, the 'graver labour' mentioned in the dedication of *Venus and Adonis.* Like that earlier poem, *The Rape of Lucrece* is concerned with erotic desire as it manifests itself in a struggle to exert power over its object. However, whereas *Venus and Adonis* finds comedy in a tragic situation as it gleefully reverses and parodies conventional sex-roles, this 'graver' poem contemplates the effects of masculine violence and of institutionalized attitudes to feminine chastity and the 'shame' of its loss. Furthermore, it connects these subjects to larger political issues of tyranny, for the violation of Lucrece is an image of the violation of the state and a motivating factor in the expulsion of the Roman monarchy and the foundation of the Roman Republic.

The Rape of Lucrece consists of 1855 lines of iambic pentameter, divided into 265 seven-line stanzas (septets) rhyming *ababbcc.* This stanza form, known as 'rhyme royal', appears to have been introduced into English poetry by Chaucer, most notably in *Troilus and Criseyde,* but also in *The Parliament of Foules.* The form was also used by Chaucer's contemporary, John Gower. It subsequently became popular for courtly poetry (its name arises from its use for *The Kingis Quair,* a fifteenth-century poem attributed to James I of Scotland). It was not especially popular as a form amongst Renaissance poets, though Sir Thomas Wyatt used it for his tragic song 'They flee from me'. The form had, however, become associated with solemn or tragic matter, and it no doubt seemed to Shakespeare appropriate for the disturbing story of Lucrece. He used it again for 'A Lover's Complaint', the lament appended to the *Sonnets.* Rhyme royal is a flexible stanza form, essentially a quatrain overlapping with a pair of couplets.

The story of the rape of Lucretia, wife of Collatinus, by Tarquinius Sextus, son of the Roman king Tarquinius Superbus, was history rather than myth. It had been re-told many times before it came into Shakespeare's hands, but his main sources for it were Livy,

96

(*Historia* 1. 57–60) and Ovid (*Fasti* 2. 721–852), which as we know he would have encountered at his grammar school. He appears also to have been familiar with Chaucer's version in *The Legend of Good Women* (lines 1680–885), and with William Painter's translation of Livy's account in *The Palace of Pleasure*. Most versions of the story agree on the main details; Livy is the earliest recorder of it, and his might stand for all. The story began one night in 509 BC, during the Roman siege of Ardea. A group of noblemen were arguing over the virtue of their wives, and Collatinus, who boasted insistently about the superior beauty and virtue of his wife Lucretia, persuaded them to return immediately to Rome to check on how their wives behaved when their husbands were away. All the wives except Lucretia were found carousing; Lucretia sat virtuously at her spinning. Sextus Tarquinius was fired with lust at her beauty and chastity, and resolved to possess her. Going alone to her house, he was courteously welcomed by her as a guest, but at night he came with unsheathed sword to her bedchamber, and attempted to seduce her. When she repulsed his overtures he threatened her with death, and when this also failed he said that not only would he kill her but he would also leave her body next to that of a slave. Fearing the posthumous disgrace that this would bring upon her name and that of her husband, she submitted to him. After he left, Lucretia, overcome with shame, summoned her husband and father, who arrived with their kinsmen Publius Valerius and Lucius Junius Brutus. She told them what had happened, and made them promise to take revenge, and then stabbed herself to death because of her lost chastity and to free her family from shame. Brutus took the bloody dagger from her breast, and he and her kinsmen bore her body through the streets, stirring up the people to drive the Tarquin family out of Rome, thus opening the way for the foundation of the Roman republic, of which Brutus and Publius Valerius became the first consuls.

Shakespeare's version of this narrative opens in a burst of violent energy: 'Lust breathed Tarquin' (3), excited by a description of the 'unmatched red and white' (11) of Collatine's wife Lucrece, races from Ardea to Collatium. The narrator claims not to know what exactly motivated Tarquin, but chides Collatine for boasting about something that should have been kept secret: 'why is Collatine the publisher / Of that rich jewel he should keep unknown / From thievish ears because it is his own?' (33–5). Arriving in Collatium, Tarquin finds Lucrece far superior in beauty and chastity to her husband's 'niggard' account. Innocent Lucrece, whose 'unstained thoughts do seldom dream on evil' (87), has no suspicion of him or ability to 'moralize his wanton sight' (104), and entertains him as his rank demands, joyfully listening to his praise of her husband.

At night Tarquin is brought to his bed, and in a lengthy sequence (120–280) we are presented with the conflict in him between will on the one hand, and conscience and the material dangers of what he desires on the other, though the narrator notes that he is 'ever to obtain his will resolving' (149). The narrator points out that what Tarquin has to lose is beyond 'honour, wealth, and ease in waning age' (142), encompassing all that he is and represents: 'for himself himself he must forsake' (157). We then shift to Tarquin's inner monologue, as he thinks of the 'dangers of his loathsome enterprise' (184). He considers the dishonour to his rank, his profession, his family name, and that his own posterity will curse him. He acknowledges the vileness of his intent, noting that Collatine would be justified in taking revenge against him, especially as Collatine has done no harm to him, but then dismisses these objections: 'My will is strong past reason's weak removing. / Who fears a sentence or an old man's saw / Shall by a painted cloth be kept in awe' (243–5).

Tarquin proceeds to Lucrece's chamber, undeterred by obstacles he finds in his way, and opens her bed-curtains. There follows a blazon or catalogue of Lucrece's beauty (386–413), each element feeding Tarquin's lust until, like a military conqueror, he places his hand on her breast. So rudely awakened the terrified Lucrece prays to know 'Under what colour he commits this ill' (476), to which he replies that she herself is to blame for arousing him: 'The fault is thine, / For those thine eyes betray thee unto mine' (482–3). He tells her he has thought of all the objections to his actions, but 'will is deaf' (495). He asserts that if she does not give herself to him he will force her, and leave her to bring shame to her family; but if she yields herself it will be their secret, for a 'fault unknown is as a thought unacted' (527). In a lengthy reply (575–644) Lucrece reiterates many of the objections that Tarquin has himself considered, but her fundamental argument is that his actions are a betrayal of himself: 'Thou art not what thou seem'st, and if the same, / Thou seem'st not what thou art, a god, a king, / For kings like gods should govern everything' (600–2). When Lucrece continues to plead he silences her with a threat to put her ravished body in the bed of a servant to increase the shame that will fall on her family. He then extinguishes the light, gags her with her nightdress, and accomplishes his deed of darkness. It is a moment in which both are losers, for while she 'hath lost a dearer thing than life' (687), he is 'A captive victor that hath lost in gain, / Bearing away the wound that nothing healeth, / The scar that will, despite of cure, remain' (730–2). He departs, too late a 'heavy convertite' (743), leaving Lucrece to pray never to see the day.

Lucrece embarks on her long complaint. She begins by attacking personified figures of the conditions of her victimization: Night (764–812), Opportunity (876–924), and Time (925–1001). Night's connection with hell, chaos, death is a commonplace, and Lucrece accuses Night of being Tarquin's accomplice; to make amends Night should smother day and light to conceal Lucrece: 'Make me not object to the tell-tale day: / The light will show charactered in my brow / The story of sweet chastity's decay' (806–8). This leads her to thinking about the shame that light will bring; her concern is with what she thinks she has done to her husband, yet she wonders how she might have avoided it:

> Yet am I guilty of thy honour's wrack;
> Yet for thy honour did I entertain him.
> Coming from thee, I could not put him back,
> For it had been dishonour to disdain him.
>
> (841–4)

She then chides Opportunity for giving occasion only to corruption and never to truth or virtue. Finally, she turns upon Time the great destroyer. Since Time has taken so much from her, she asks that it now curse Tarquin with calamitous effects: 'Devise extremes beyond extremity / To make him curse this cursed crimeful night' (969–70). In the end, however, she recognizes the vanity of her words, seeing suicide as the only way open to her: 'The remedy indeed to do me good / Is to let forth my foul defiled blood' (1028–9).

As she seeks means of suicide her thoughts about her state strengthen her resolve to be active to protect Collatine from shame, insisting 'I am the mistress of my fate' (1069). But at daybreak grief returns, and 'cloudy Lucrece shames herself to see' (1084); the nightingale's song reminds her of the rape of Philomel by Tereus. She also considers the spiritual risks of suicide: '"To kill myself," quoth she, 'alack, what were it / But with my body my poor soul's pollution?"' (1156–7). She finally resolves not to die until she has told all to Collatine and made him promise to take revenge on Tarquin – this will be her 'legacy'. She then calls her maid who, sensing her mistress's grief, joins her in weeping, 'the poor counterfeit of her complaining' (1269). Lucrece takes control of herself and, learning that Tarquin is gone, writes a letter summoning her husband, but does not explain the cause of her woe, 'Lest he should hold it her own gross abuse, / Ere she with blood had stained her stain's excuse' (1315–16). Indeed her sensitivity to (mis)interpretation is such that she thinks the messenger to whom she entrusts the letter has penetrated her guilt, because 'they whose guilt within their bosoms lie / Imagine every eye beholds their blame, / For Lucrece thought he blushed to see her shame' (1242–4).

Lucrece's attention is now absorbed by a painting of the fall of Troy that presents a general picture of the crowded turmoil of the doomed city and the major participants on each side of the conflict (1366–1582). She seeks in it a face that might reflect her own distress, and finds 'despairing Hecuba' (1447) staring at the bleeding body of her husband: 'On this sad shadow Lucrece spends her eyes, / And shapes her sorrow to the beldam's woes' (1457–8). She then looks for Helen to mutilate the beauty that provoked the lust that led to all this carnage; failing to find her she laments for each forlorn figure she sees. Finally her gaze falls upon a 'wretched image bound' (1501); this is Sinon, betrayer of Troy. At first she can see no guile in him and thinks the painter must have erred in showing him so mild, but this inevitably recalls Tarquin to her mind and 'She tears the senseless Sinon with her nails, / Comparing him to that unhappy guest / Whose deed hath made herself herself detest' (1564–6). She finally calms herself, but while the knowledge that others have suffered like her can ease her grief, it cannot cure it.

Collatine returns with his followers and, shocked by her appearance of misery, asks Lucrece its cause. She briefly tells of her rape, identifying Tarquin only as a 'stranger' (1619), and insisting on her own innocence: 'Though my gross blood be stained with this abuse, / Immaculate and spotless is my mind' (1655–6). Collatine responds with 'speechless woe' (1674), and Lucrece then urges him to swear revenge before she will reveal the identity of her attacker. She then asks what will clear the stain on her, and in spite of the response that 'Her body's stain her mind untainted clears' (1710) she utters his name and stabs herself with his dagger at the same moment. At first all are dumbfounded, then Brutus takes the dagger from her wound, while her father Lucretius and Collatine compete over who has the greater claim to woe and to Lucrece. Brutus, who has played the part of a fool in Rome, now reveals his true self and silences the

lamentation with encouragement to vow revenge, to parade the
bleeding body through Rome, and to drive the Tarquin family to
'everlasting banishment' (1855).

READERS AND ISSUES

During Shakespeare's lifetime and for some years after, *The Rape of
Lucrece* was very popular, as is evidenced by the number of editions
published. There are numerous references to it by contemporary
versifiers like Richard Barnfield, who in 1605, praised the poet,
'Whose Venus, and whose Lucrece (sweet, and chaste) / Thy name
in Fame's immortal book have placed'.[1] Many other writers imitated
or adapted striking passages from the poem. Gabriel Harvey's comment in 1598, noted earlier, that 'the wiser sort' were pleased by
'Lucrece, & his tragedy of Hamlet, Prince of Denmark', shows that
the poem was understood to be a serious work. While no one today
would rank it with *Hamlet* we cannot assume that Harvey's linking
of the two works as if they were equals was unusual for the time.
Indeed, the comparatively small number of printed editions of the
plays indicates that readers, if not playgoers, preferred the poems.
In spite of its erotic content *The Rape of Lucrece* never achieved the
notoriety of *Venus and Adonis*, perhaps because its erotic elements
are submerged into Lucrece's disturbing experience.

After Shakespeare's death three more editions of *The Rape of
Lucrece* were issued before the end of the century. In the third of
these, a quarto of 1655, an oddly modified version of the poem was
printed along with a kind of appendix by John Quarles, entitled
'The Banishment of Tarquin: Or the Reward of Lust', perhaps
implying that readers were no longer quite satisfied with the poem
as it stood, or that those parts of its political implications that concerned the overthrowing of a king were no longer consonant with
the general mood at that late stage in the Cromwellian Common-
wealth. Whatever the reason, like *Venus and Adonis*, the poem appears
to have fallen out of any favour, and there are almost no more
recorded comments on it until the end of the eighteenth century,
when Edmond Malone's editions revived interest in the narrative
poems. Oddly, Malone himself had numerous reservations about
both poems: 'Their great defect is the wearisome circumlocution
with which the tale in each of them is told, particularly that before
us'.[2] 'That before us' is, of course, *The Rape of Lucrece*.

The late eighteenth-century editions nevertheless fired some Romantic interest in the narrative poems. Coleridge, as we have seen, found great poetic power in *Venus and Adonis*, although he thought that both narrative poems were immature. *The Rape of Lucrece*, he said, showed the same positive qualities as the earlier poem, 'with a yet larger display, a yet wider range of knowledge and reflection; and lastly, with the same dominion, often *domination*, over the whole world of language'.[3] Recent scholarship has shown that Keats too had a deep interest in the poem, reflected particularly in 'The Eve of St Agnes'.[4] However, in the twentieth century, with the vast increase in the number of professional Shakespeare scholars, *The Rape of Lucrece* has received something of the attention it deserves. While some critics have treated the poem with flat hostility, there have been thoughtful attempts to find merit in it, though few have wanted to call it a masterpiece. Perhaps the best that could be said is Ian Donaldson's measured assessment of it as 'a poem of remarkable yet sporadic brilliance'.[5] Investigations of its aesthetic qualities have concentrated on a number of areas: the character of its rhetoric; its use of generic conventions and source materials; its resolution or integration of conflicts within its materials; and its place in the development of Shakespeare's career, especially its relationship to his plays. More recent historicist and feminist criticism has been less interested in the poem's artistic success or failure than in what it reflects of contemporary anxieties and tensions, or what it suggests about power and the construction of identity.

What some have perceived as the poem's linguistic immoderation and self-consciousness has been a frequent cause of criticism. F.T. Prince, editor of the first, prestigious, Arden edition, made no attempt to conceal his hostility to the poem and its 'excesses in rhetoric'; while Robert Ellrodt, who, we will remember, had little good to say about the language of *Venus and Adonis*, thought that 'wordiness grew worse in *Lucrece*'.[6] J.W. Lever suggested that 'the opportunities for conscious eloquence tempted Shakespeare's facility and led to a piling up of tropes'.[7] While it is indubitably true that Shakespeare was showing off, in the sense that he was demonstrating his superior skill at a kind of elaborate writing that was popular in his time, there is need to find better justification of the poem's 'excesses' if it is to be shown to have aesthetic validity. Some readers have tried to give a functional explanation of them. Richard Lanham focused on the way the characters themselves employ language, arguing that both Lucrece and Tarquin are victims of rhetoric who mistake the language of feeling for feeling itself.[8] Katharine Eisaman Maus argued that the poem is about the dangers of misunderstanding metaphor and that 'the obtrusiveness and unreliability of language in *The Rape of Lucrece* is not evidence of Shakespeare's incompetence, but rather of an acute and profoundly uneasy self-consciousness about poetic techniques and resources'.[9] Heather Dubrow considered the relation of rhetoric and identity as part of a reading of the poem that starts with its use of rhetorical devices such as syneciosis and oxymoron, devices that dissolve the differences between opposed objects, and leads into a very complex examination of its concern with the shaping of stories and the writing of history.[10]

To decide upon the poem's generic success or failure it is necessary to understand what its genre is intended to be, and because the Elizabethan erotic narrative is a somewhat amorphous and inclusive form this has not been an easy task. The work of William Keach and Clark Hulse has gone some way towards locating *The Rape of Lucrece* within the developing Elizabethan fashion, especially in relating the Ovidian erotic to epic concerns. Jonathan Bate has argued that the significance of the Ovidian influence is poetic rather than political, related to the poem's rhetoric of desire and its interest in how 'art is instrumental in the pursuit of sexual satisfaction'.[11] Part of the difficulty of definition arises from the fact that with Lucrece's lengthy complaint the poem incorporates material of a quite different genre, and this raises questions about the effectiveness of its integration, but some critics have argued for the positive effects of this expansion of the genre's limits.[12] Interesting questions have also been raised about the long description of the picture of the Fall of Troy. The term *ekphrasis* is used to refer to poetry that is concerned with the depiction of works of art, or that attempts to mimic the techniques of such art; amongst Renaissance theorists the relationship between poetry and visual arts was a frequent topic. Critics who have considered the *ekphrasis* of *The Rape of Lucrece* have tended to explain its use in terms of the poem's thematic concern with questions of the relationship between art and life or illusion and reality, or have studied connections between sight and voice.[13]

Some critics have attempted to evaluate the poem's place in Shakespeare's development, a line certainly worth following in relation to the tragedies and to the Roman plays. However, such comparison raises questions about the quality of the poem as tragedy, and once again we might turn to F.T. Prince: 'if *Lucrece* is a tragedy, it is of course a tragedy by the author of *Titus Andronicus*, and not by the author of *Lear* or *Othello*'.[14] In a single statement Prince manages to question whether *Lucrece* succeeds as tragedy and to imply a dismissive judgement of the early Shakespeare, but the statement is fundamentally obtuse. *Lucrece* was written at about the same time as *Titus Andronicus*, so the argument that connects the two is a truism, as is the corollary that these works are inferior to *Lear* and *Othello*. Others have looked more sympathetically at the poem's embryonic traces of the greater tragedies. The parallels between Tarquin's and Macbeth's moral struggle have been broadly examined, and so has the potential of Lucrece herself as a tragic protagonist.

Recent critics concerned with the role of Lucrece have often been less concerned with evaluation than with seeing what the poem reflects of its time. Its connections between language, meaning and power, especially as they relate to the construction of gender, have been particularly open to feminist analysis. The use of poetic language for the objectification of the female body was fundamental to the Petrarchan tradition, which had become rather stale by 1594, and some recent writers have looked at the relationship between language and identity, and particularly how the female is constructed as an object of male rhetoric. Other important work on the poem's sexual politics has considered Lucrece's resistance to victimhood, the meaning of rape, the connections between literary publication and sexual shame, and the analogy between the female body and the state.[15] This latter issue connects the poem to broader political issues. The poem (like the play *Titus Andronicus*, which is related to it in a number of ways) clearly presents an analogy between the female body and the body of the state in the patriarchal or tyrannical oppression of both.

There has also been much critical interest in the poem's more overt political concerns. One of the earliest attempts to find political purpose was that of E.P. Kuhl, who sought historical substance in it and argued that is was written as a warning to its dedicatee Southampton of the dangers of abusing power.[16] Others have taken up Kuhl's initiative, but the problem with it is that it assumes that the commoner Shakespeare would have dared in so public a manner to tell the aristocrat Southampton how to behave, and no matter how cordial one believes the relationship between the two to have been, this seems improbable. Nevertheless, I think that the poem does provide a political lesson for the powerful amongst its readers; Shakespeare's choice of this particular story about the conditions that led in Rome to the shift from monarchy to republic, suggests a concern with issues of authority and legitimacy as they related to the Tudor monarchy.[17] That he might have written seriously subversive ideas into his poem is certainly possible, but he clearly would have had to do so in very oblique ways, which creates inevitable difficulties for interpretation. Linda Woodbridge interpreted topical issues in a different way, seeing in the poem's treatment of Lucrece's threatened body a link with Elizabethan anxieties about the threat of siege warfare.[18]

MYTH AND ITS USES

The problematic centre of Shakespeare's poem concerns the question of how Lucrece's suicide is to be understood, because the history on which Shakespeare drew contained two incompatible interpretations of the act. For the Roman authors Ovid and, especially, Livy the story of the rape of Lucretia was a story about Roman virtue, but it was only a component of the larger, more important story of the excesses and consequent fall of the tyrannical Tarquins. It took on significance not as a story of personal suffering, but as a political myth. Lucretia's self-sacrificing suicide to protect her family from shame was understood as a courageous act in itself, though as Stephanie Jed has pointed out, her rape was thus transformed into an injury done to the honour of her male relatives.[19] The importance of Lucretia's action went beyond this, however, because it motivated Lucius Junius Brutus to stir up resistance to the tyranny of the Tarquins and led to the foundation of the republic. The effect of this understanding of the story was inextricably to intertwine private and public experience by shifting the focus from Lucretia to Brutus and from moral to political application.

Shakespeare was well aware of the Roman attitude to suicide; in *Antony and Cleopatra* he has Cleopatra say, on envisioning her own suicide, 'what's brave, what's noble, / Let's do it after the high Roman fashion, / And make death proud to take us' (5.1.88–90). Christian conviction is rather different; as Hamlet reminds himself, God has 'fixed / His canon 'gainst self-slaughter' (1.2.131–2). Suicide is an act of despair, ensuring the death of the soul along with that of the body. Chastity inheres in the will, not in the body, and the 'virtue' that prompted the suicide must have been misguided. St Augustine was the first to provide a Christian reinterpretation of the story, in *The City of God*, refusing to allow Lucretia's action to be construed as heroic. He asked what crime she had committed that deserved death. If a woman suffers rape unwillingly, why should she punish herself for an act of which she is not guilty? She makes herself guilty in a different sense by so doing:

> If there is no unchastity when a woman is ravished against her will, then there is no justice in the punishment of the chaste. I appeal to Roman laws and Roman judges. To execute a criminal without trial was, according to you, a punishable offence. If anyone was charged in your courts with having put to death a woman not merely uncondemned but chaste and innocent, and this charge had been proved, would you not have chastised the culprit with appropriate severity?
>
> That is what Lucretia did. That highly extolled Lucretia also did away with the innocent, chaste, outraged Lucretia.[20]

This is without doubt a harsh judgement: Lucretia condemned herself for the loss of her chastity, but Augustine must condemn her act of self-murder. He also brings the focus back from political to moral issues and to Lucretia and her private experience. In using this material, Shakespeare was obliged to embrace the essentially irreconcilable pagan and Christian readings.

Shakespeare returned the focus to Lucrece, and at first sight it might appear that he chose to minimize the political aspects of the story, since the involvement of Brutus and the banishment of Tarquin are detailed only very briefly at the end of the poem. However, I think the poem can be seen in a different light when we consider the prose 'Argument' that prefaced the text of *The Rape of Lucrece* in the first quarto edition. The term 'Argument' here means 'plot' or 'synopsis', and this one presents a brief version of the narrative that is to follow in the poem. This version is close to those of Ovid and Livy, but it contains significant differences from the poem itself. Some critics have contended that Shakespeare did not write the Argument, pointing out that its style is not what we might expect from him (though it is wise to remember that he has no easily identifiable prose style, since the prose in his plays functions to create dramatic character). Whether or not he wrote it, however, he clearly intended it to be a part of the reader's experience of the poem; the absences in the poem that are filled in by the Argument are integral to the poem's potential meanings. I shall therefore quote the Argument in its entirety:

> Lucius Tarquinius (for his excessive pride surnamed Superbus), after he had caused his own father-in-law Servius Tullius to be cruelly murdered,

and, contrary to the Roman laws and customs, not requiring or staying for the people's suffrages had possessed himself of the kingdom, went accompanied with his sons and other noblemen of Rome to besiege Ardea, during which siege the principal men of the army meeting one evening at the tent of Sextus Tarquinius, the King's son, in their discourses after supper everyone commended the virtues of his own wife, among whom Collatinus extolled the incomparable chastity of his wife Lucretia. In that pleasant humour they all posted to Rome, and intending by their secret and sudden arrival to make trial of that which everyone had before avouched, only Collatinus finds his wife (though it were late in the night) spinning amongst her maids. The other ladies were all found dancing, and revelling, or in several disports. Whereupon the noblemen yielded Collatinus the victory and his wife the fame. At that time Sextus Tarquinius, being enflamed with Lucrece' beauty, yet smothering his passions for the present, departed with the rest back to the camp, from whence he shortly after privily withdrew himself and was, according to his estate, royally entertained and lodged by Lucrece at Collatium. The same night he treacherously stealeth into her chamber, violently ravished her, and early in the morning speedeth away. Lucrece, in this lamentable plight, hastily dispatcheth messengers–one to Rome for her father, another to the camp for Collatine. They come, the one accompanied with Junius Brutus, the other with Publius Valerius, and, finding Lucrece attired in mourning habit, demanded the cause of her sorrow. She, first taking an oath of them for her revenge, revealed the actor and whole manner of his dealing, and withal suddenly stabbed herself. Which done, with one consent they all vowed to root out the whole hated family of the Tarquins, and, bearing the dead body to Rome, Brutus acquainted the people with the doer and manner of the vile deed, with a bitter invective against the tyranny of the King; wherewith the people were so moved that with one consent and a general acclamation the Tarquins were all exiled and the state government changed from kings to consuls.

There are at least two major points of significance arising from this Argument and its relation to the poem. First, at the outset it places a strong emphasis upon the political significance of the story, which appears muted in the poem. The poem has nothing to say about the murder by Tarquinius Superbus of his father-in-law, nor about his illegitimate seizure of power. The two events, linked within the first sentence of the Argument, connect domestic violence with the imposition of tyranny, as well as indicating the endemic cruelty of the Tarquin family. The equation of the father's acts of private and public terror allows the reader of the Argument to consider the implications in the poem of the public meaning of the son's apparently private act of rape. The reader will not miss the connection between tyranny as the rape of the state, and the literal rape of Lucrece. Indeed, as I noted earlier, the poem's figurative language often presents the subjected female body as an analogy for the subjected body of the state. In addition, the end of the Argument is much more explicit about the political consequences of Tarquin's act: whereas the poem tells us only that on seeing the evidence of Tarquin's crime 'The Romans plausibly did give consent / To Tarquin's everlasting banishment' (1854–5), the Argument reminds us that the crime led to the expulsion of the 'whole hated family of the Tarquins', and to the replacement of kings by consuls, of monarchy by republic. Thus the poet is able to submerge the political commentary of the poem beneath the sensational surface of the narrative while ensuring that it is there to be decoded.

This brings us to the second intriguing difference between Argument and poem, which concerns the manner in which Tarquin's lust for Lucrece is aroused. In the Argument, as in Shakespeare's main sources, Tarquin hears Collatine's account of Lucrece's virtue and beauty, but it is only when he sees her that he is overwhelmed by desire for her. In the poem, however, Tarquin is aroused simply by the description, and the narrator can only speculate on why he goes on to act as he does:

> Perchance that envy of so rich a thing,
> Braving compare, disdainfully did sting
> His high-pitched thoughts, that meaner men should vaunt
> That golden hap which their superiors want.
>
> (39–42)

The prerogative of power, to have more than one's inferiors have, conflates sexual and political desire as it conflates lover and tyrant. Tarquin is already 'lust-breathed' before he has even seen Lucrece; that is, he is inflamed by the imaginary picture of her that Collatine's words have created. His lust is self-created, before Lucrece becomes the actual victim of it, and ultimately it is self-destructive. I think that Shakespeare intended Tarquin to be something more than a villain and, indeed, that there is something potentially tragic in him. The fact that his lust for Lucrece is in the first place a kind of abstract lust, generated, it is true, by Collatine's description of her, but originating in his own tyrannical fancy, makes him the victim of himself or of something uncontrollable within him. This complication of the character and the concealment of the political elements of the story allow for an almost claustrophobic concentration on the private moment of the act itself and the responses to it of the two participants, as well as on the potential of both characters for tragedy.

I would also suggest that the differences in Shakespeare's version of the story exist precisely to distinguish it as his, for they set his individual stamp on the story. His poem is, of course, a vast expansion of what he found in his sources. His interest is not so much in the action, and his amplification of the material is mainly in detailing the disturbed state of mind of each of his main characters. Tarquin argues at length with himself as he acknowledges all the objections to his intended action while at the same time justifying it to himself. The violated Lucrece attempts at even greater length to deal with the personal and social shame that overwhelms her. Shakespeare the dramatist provides his characters with extensive monologues that minutely detail the processes through which each arrives at a justification for violent action, Tarquin to rape Lucrece, Lucrece to kill herself. He also, however, explores the public or communal ramifications of private action.

THE NARRATOR AND PATRIARCHAL VALUES

Although clearly male, the narrator of *The Rape of Lucrece*, like the narrator of *Venus and Adonis*, should not be simply equated with the poet himself, although he seems less obtrusive than the earlier narrator in his attempts to interpret scenes and events for the reader. In the opening passage of the poem there seems to be an intention to establish the appearance of tentativeness as he hedges his suggestions about Tarquin's motivation by the use of 'haply' (8) and 'perchance' (36, 39), words that do not figure again in the poem. We might be tempted by this apparent honesty about the limits of his knowledge to trust his judgement, particularly as he offers common-sense opinion about the folly of the boastful Collatine, the viciousness of 'this false lord' Tarquin (50), and the unarguable moral difference between the 'earthly saint' and 'the devil' (85). If we look, however, at the poem's construction of Lucrece's 'value', we might wish to modify this conclusion.

It is hardly possible to read *The Rape of Lucrece* without regarding it as a disclosure of patriarchal self-regard and irresponsibility. Tarquin is undeniably a villain, but most of the other male characters, even those who are indirectly victimized by Tarquin's crime, are more than a little suspect in their behaviour and attitudes. Consider the way in which Collatine's account of Lucrece's value is presented at the outset of the poem:

> For he the night before in Tarquin's tent
> Unlocked the treasure of his happy state,
> What priceless wealth the heavens had him lent
> In the possession of his beauteous mate,
> Reck'ning his fortune at such high-proud rate
> That kings might be espoused to more fame,
>
> But king nor peer to such a peerless dame.
>
> (15–21)

At first sight this might seem admirable: Collatine is grateful to the heavens for what he has, a treasure like the Biblical pearl of great price, which makes him more content than kings or peers. However, there is a repeated association of Lucrece with material possession in 'treasure', 'priceless wealth', and the ambiguous 'fortune' ('fortune' could mean something like 'good luck', but the word 'reck'ning' implies a fortune that can be counted). Furthermore, there is a significant shift from the word 'lent' to the word 'possession'. The idea that our loved ones are only lent to us by heaven and must eventually be returned was a commonplace of Christian consolation. Ben Jonson, for example, in trying to console himself over the death of his son at the age of seven, wrote: 'Seven years tho'wert lent to me, and I thee pay, / Exacted by thy fate, on the just day'.[21] Collatine, however, fails to understand the difference between being lent and being given, a sign of spiritual arrogance.

There is more to be said about this. In describing Lucrece's virtues Collatine 'unlocks' his treasure. Later in the poem, when Tarquin approaches Lucrece's chamber, much is made of locks: 'The locks between her chamber and his will, / Each one by him enforced, retires his ward' (302–3). Tarquin's forcing of the locks is clearly an analogue of his later physical act of rape. When Collatine unlocks his treasure, he is in effect opening up Lucrece, presenting her naked to his audience (which includes Tarquin) in a symbolic moment of defilement that foreshadows Tarquin's actions. It is hardly surprising that when Collatine boasts of having something that kings do not have, Tarquin should respond by thinking that he, as the son of a king, should take what his inferior has:

Perchance that envy of so rich a thing,
Braving compare, disdainfully did sting
His high-pitched thoughts, that meaner men should vaunt
That golden hap which their superiors want.

                                              (39–42)

Not only does the childish argument that lies behind this confirm
Lucrece as an object ('so rich a thing'), but it makes Collatine
complicit with Tarquin, verbally, if unwittingly, offering his wife for
defilement.

After Collatine has unveiled his wife in this way, the narrator asks
'why is Collatine the publisher / Of that rich jewel he should keep
unknown / From thievish ears, because it is his own?' (33–5) This is
an interesting moment. The narrator again speaks common sense:
Collatine's boasting has made public what should be private, opening
himself and his wife to 'thievish ears'. Behind the narrator's common sense, however, is an attitude that is not very different from
Collatine's: Lucrece is a jewel that is Collatine's own, a possession,
an object, not a person. The poem's opening sets up a situation in
which all male perspectives deny the female subject any autonomy;
she is a treasure, an object to be locked away.

Even in death Lucrece remains an object to be possessed by men
as her father Lucretius and her husband Collatine, bordering on the
comic in spite of their grief, argue over her body about whose
she was:

'O,' quoth Lucretius, 'I did give that life
Which she too early and too late hath spilled'.
'Woe, woe,' quoth Collatine, 'she was my wife.
I owed her, and 'tis mine that she hath killed'.
'My daughter' and 'my wife' with clamours filled
The dispersed air, who, holding Lucrece' life,
Answered their cries, 'my daughter' and 'my wife'.

                                              (1800–6)

Brutus, in seizing this opportunity to channel private grief into
public, political action, might seem to be giving dignity to her death.
However, the spectacle he creates when he persuades them to 'show
her bleeding body thorough Rome / And so to publish Tarquin's foul
offence' (1851–2), acts as an uneasy reminder that it was Collatine's
foolish act of making himself the 'publisher' of his rich jewel that led
in the first place to Tarquin's foul offence. The poem begins and

ends, that is, with Lucrece's private body opened up to a voyeuristic public gaze. Consequently, while it is not possible to justify Tarquin's violation of Lucrece's body, his denial of her personal freedom and identity, it is possible to argue that his willingness to do so arises out of a larger context of such denial.

The implication of the narrator in this voyeurism might be understood as implicating the reader too. Consider what the 'foul usurper' Tarquin sees when he enters Lucrece's chamber (386–413). Immediately before this blazon of her beauty the narrator calls her 'holy thoughted', but he then sets her out 'To be admired of lewd unhallowed eyes' (392), not just the eyes of Tarquin, but also the eyes of the reader. He goes on to ask, 'What could he see but mightily he noted? / What did he note but strongly he desired?' (414–15). Tarquin, narrator and reader, as well as the poet who provided the scene, are united in gazing on the objectified Lucrece, desiring the pleasure she seems to offer, whether as sexual object or as textual object. This does not mean that the reader condones *The Rape of Lucrece*; rather, a situation of contradictory responses is produced. As Jonathan Hart puts it, 'The pleasure of the text creates a tension with the moral of the story'.[22]

TARQUIN

The focus of the first 750 lines or so of *The Rape of Lucrece* is on Tarquin, who in the poem's opening is presented in a manner both complex and ambiguous. The poem begins in a brilliant burst of energy:

> From the besieged Ardea all in post,
> Borne by the trustless wings of false desire,
> Lust-breathed Tarquin leaves the Roman host
> And to Collatium bears the lightless fire
> Which, in pale embers hid, lurks to aspire
> And girdle with embracing flames the waist
> Of Collatine's fair love, Lucrece the chaste.

> (1–7)

There are a number of questions we might wish to ask about this. We should consider, for example, the meaning of 'false desire'. Tarquin's desire is surely real enough, since it drives him to his terrible action. Is it false because it is directed to an illegitimate end?

Is it false because it is generated by his imagination working on
Collatine's description of Lucrece? Is the phrase a generalization
about desire itself, false because it mis-values its object, and therefore always 'trustless'? Can we read the stanza in a manner that
allows us to understand the phrase in all these ways? Certainly,
part of the poem's concern is to plot the catastrophic delusions of
desire.

There is a further thing we should note here, because it sets up
the conditions of the struggle of conscience that Tarquin appears
to undergo. This is the strain between on the one hand the apparent speed and energy of Tarquin's lust-driven departure, and on
the other the language used to describe his lust, which is peculiarly
muted: 'lightless fire', 'pale embers', 'lurks to aspire'. This shadows
a kind of duality of motive in Tarquin, setting him against his
conception of himself in a way that simultaneously drives him
forward and pulls him back. Later we will see that this division is
dramatized in various ways, as an inner debate between will and
conscience or between lust and honour, although there is never
much doubt that conscience and honour will be the losers, and that
he will be permanently damaged by the victory of his desire. As he
plans his campaign against Lucrece this self-division is made clear:

> Such hazard now must doting Tarquin make,
> Pawning his honour to obtain his lust,
> And for himself himself he must forsake.
> Then where is truth if there be no self-trust?
> When shall he think to find a stranger just
> When he himself himself confounds, betrays
> To sland'rous tongues and wretched hateful days?

> (155–61)

Once he has satisfied his desire he has lost all, for he has lost his self,
and he steals away in the night, 'A captive victor that hath lost in
gain, / Bearing away the wound that nothing healeth' (730–1).

We need again to consider the nature of the 'false desire' that
drives Tarquin. As I noted earlier, the poem suppresses some elements of the story that are nevertheless contained in the Argument.
One of these is the fact that Tarquin's father was a usurper who
had illegally 'possessed himself of the kingdom'. At the end of the
Argument, we are told that Brutus explained to the people the circumstances of Lucrece's death 'with a bitter invective against the

tyranny of the King;' that is, he connected the private actions of the
son to the public actions of the father as if both existed on the same
plane. The desire provoked in Tarquin, about to possess himself of
Collatine's 'kingdom', is described thus: 'These worlds in Tarquin
new ambition bred, / Who like a foul usurper went about / From this
fair throne to heave the owner out' (411–13). The simile here links
Tarquin with his father as usurper and tyrant. He is a man who uses
his power to serve only his own will. We hear a lot about Tarquin's
will. After his evening spent with Lucrece he is unable to sleep, and
lies 'revolving / The sundry dangers of his will's obtaining, / Yet ever
to obtain his will resolving' (127–9). As with any tyrant, the obstacles
to his will, however dangerous, are subordinated to that will, and
the end of apparent moral conflict is a foregone conclusion – in
other words, there is no real conflict at all between 'frozen conscience and hot-burning will' (246). So, he thinks, 'I'll beg her love –
but she is not her own. / The worst is but denial and reproving; / My
will is strong past reason's weak removing' (241–3). He goes on to
turn over in his mind all the wrong that he is doing, but always
returns to the same point. Consequently, when in her chamber
Lucrece attempts to persuade him to command his 'rebel will' (625),
he has already rehearsed all of her arguments and can brutally
silence them: 'Yield to my love. If not, enforced hate / Instead of
love's coy touch, shall rudely tear thee' (668–9).

Given the terrible aggression of the all-devouring appetite that
lies behind Tarquin's actions, we can only wonder how he can
incorporate the idea of 'love' into what he is doing, yet he uses the
word often enough to suggest that he clearly thinks of himself as
a lover. We might conclude that this is nothing more than self-
deception: his love is simple lust. There is more to it than this,
however. Readers of *A Midsummer Night's Dream* will remember
that when Bottom is assigned the role of Pyramus he asks 'What is
Pyramus? A lover or a tyrant?' (2.1.17). The joke appears to be that
in Bottom's understanding of plays there are only two roles for
a protagonist. But something more is suggested. Theseus, the main
aristocratic lover of the play, is about to marry Hippolyta, whom
he conquered in war; as he says to her, 'I wooed thee with my
sword, / And won thy love doing thee injuries' (1.1.16–17); we are
later reminded of his earlier career as rapist and abandoner of
women. The real irony is that there is not much difference between
lover and tyrant. Both are concerned with the exertion of power,
the will to dominate. As Richard Lanham has argued, 'rape in

[*Lucrece*] means *power relationship* not *sex*'.[23] This is where the poem gets its political dimension and why the private oppression of Lucrece can be used as a weapon against the public oppression of Rome. It is at this level that the body of Lucrece is equated with the body of the state.

Something else lies behind the depiction of Tarquin as lover, however. The conventions of the Petrarchan fashion that had dominated the Elizabethan literary world (particularly in sonnet sequences) in the decade before the composition of *The Rape of Lucrece* had at their centre the desire of a poet-lover for a woman who was a paragon of both beauty and chaste virtue. Her beauty aroused desire in the lover, but his desire was kept in check by her virtue. The most celebrated sonnet writer was, of course, Sir Philip Sidney, who in Sonnet 71 of his sequence *Astrophel and Stella* has his protagonist say this of Stella:

> Who will in fairest book of Nature know,
> How Virtue may best lodg'd in beauty be,
> Let him but learn of love to read in thee
> Stella, those fair lines, which true goodness show.
> There shall he find all vices' overthrow,
> Not by rude force, but sweetest sovereignty
> Of reason, from whose light those night-birds fly;
> That inward sun in thine eyes shineth so.

The idea that the woman's 'inward sun' of virtue had the power through the light of reason to control the lover's desiring will had in the late Elizabethan period been a powerful poetic myth, but the hierarchy that gave reason and virtue power over will or desire was fundamentally an idealist fantasy. As Tarquin tells himself: 'My will is strong past reason's weak removing' (243). It has been suggested that Tarquin is 'a demonic parody of the Petrarchan lover'.[24] I think, however, that Shakespeare does not so much parody Petrarchism as reveal the darker impulses that underlie it. He asks us to consider what might happen if virtue were not able to conquer the aggressive will or, indeed, if virtue itself were the provoker of the aggression.

I want to return to the opening stanza to note the emphasis given to the word 'chaste' by its position at the end of the final line. The first two lines of the next stanza repeat this emphasis: 'Haply that name of chaste unhapp'ly set / This bateless edge on his keen appetite' (8–9). Tarquin has heard Collatine praise both Lucrece's beauty and her chastity, her 'unmatched red and white', but it is the idea of her chastity as much as of her beauty that arouses his erotic interest. Some years later, in *Measure for Measure*, Shakespeare created in the apparently puritanical Angelo another figure tormented not so much by Isabella's beauty as by the desire kindled in him by her chastity. In trying to understand the sources of his lust for Isabella, Angelo, like Tarquin, finds himself transformed into a stranger to himself: 'What dost thou, or what art thou, Angelo? / Dost thou desire her foully for those things / That make her good?' (2.2.177–9). When Tarquin first sees Lucrece, he finds that Collatine's description of her has not done her justice, and he watches fascinated the flux of colour in her face. I shall return to the implications of his reading of her red and white; let it suffice to say here that the struggle that he constructs between them is a reflection of his own fractured identity. Tarquin is well aware of the evil of his actions, and as I noted earlier, what he does to Lucrece involves an alienation from his self ('for himself himself he must forsake'). Lucrece gives a more forceful account of his self-division, suggesting that the man before her cannot be Tarquin:

> In Tarquin's likeness I did entertain thee.
> Hast thou put on his shape to do him shame?
>
> To all the host of heaven I complain me.
> Thou wrong'st his honour, wound'st his princely name.
> Thou art not what thou seem'st, and if the same,
> Thou seem'st not what thou art, a god, a king,
>
> For kings like gods should govern every thing.
>
> (596–602)

The conception of self here is a social one, associating identity with rank or class. Tarquin is of a noble, warrior family, and he acknowledges that his action will stain all that he represents:

> O shame to knighthood and to shining arms!
> O foul dishonour to my household's grave!
> O impious act, including all foul harms!
> A martial man to be soft fancy's slave!
>
> (197–200)

Yet he perseveres in his destructive and self-destructive course.

Tarquin is well aware of the probable consequences to himself of the action he proposes, as is shown by the series of rhetorical questions he asks himself:

> What win I if I gain the thing I seek?
> A dream, a breath, a froth of fleeting joy.
> Who buys a minute's mirth to wail a week,
> Or sells eternity to get a toy?
>
> (211–14)

Because of his internal struggle between desire and conscience, and his wilful embracing of an action that he knows will lead to spiritual and material disaster, he has often been compared to Macbeth as a kind of prototype of the later tragic hero. The difference, I think, lies in the scope of what each desires. Macbeth risks all for a kingdom, for the utmost earthly power, and faced with certain death he resists bravely. Tarquin risks all for 'a minute's mirth', and after he has enjoyed it he slinks out of the poem, 'like a thievish dog,' 'sweating with guilty fear' (735, 740). He is neither tragic nor heroic.

LUCRECE

As in *Venus and Adonis* the colours red and white are important in this poem. As I have noted, these colours were associated in Petrarchan convention with the beauty and virtue of the idealized woman (the satirical speaker of sonnet 130 says of his only-too-real mistress, 'I have seen roses damasked, red and white, / But no such roses see I in her cheek'.). Here from the outset 'the clear unmatched red and white' (11) are the colours of Lucrece, at least as her husband boasts of her. They are also what first attracts Tarquin's gaze:

> This heraldry in Lucrece' face was seen,
> Argued by beauty's red and virtue's white.
> Of either's colour was the other queen,
> Proving from world's minority their right.
> Yet their ambition makes them still to fight,
> The sovereignty of either being so great
> That oft they interchange each other's seat.
>
> (64–70)

What Tarquin sees creates an ambiguous association between the red and white. The effect of having the white of virtue struggle against the red of beauty is to eroticise the white, and the oscillation in that final line between the red and the white undermines the protective power of virtue. In fact, the struggle between red and white is an interpretation imposed upon Lucrece by Tarquin's reading of her, as becomes clear from the ensuing lines: 'This silent war of lilies and of roses / Which Tarquin viewed in her fair face's field / In their pure ranks his traitor eye encloses' (71–3). The reading of her agitation that his 'traitor eye' desires allows him to displace on to Lucrece the guilt for what he will do to her. Immediately prior to the rape he responds to her 'vehement prayers' with this:

> The colour in thy face,
> That even for anger makes the lily pale
> And the red rose blush at her own disgrace,
> Shall plead for me and tell my loving tale.
> Under that colour am I come to scale
> Thy never-conquered fort. The fault is thine,
> For those thine eyes betray thee unto mine.
>
> Thus I forestall thee, if thou mean to chide:
> Thy beauty hath ensnared thee to this night.

(477–85)

'The fault is thine'. In attempting to conceal his aggressive desire in the confusion of her colours, he merely confirms the extent of his misogyny, turning the virtuous Lucrece into the cause of her own ruin.

There is more to it than this, however. Shakespeare was well aware of how his own culture limited women's space. The Petrarchan application of emblematic red and white to the idealized woman effectively enclosed her within a narrow definition of acceptable feminine quality and behaviour, no less than did the frequently-reiterated exhortation to Elizabethan wives to be chaste, obedient and silent. In the first part of the poem Lucrece has accepted these limiting definitions of her self (and even though she is a Roman matron she clearly reflects Elizabethan concerns). The *'silent* war of lilies and of roses' reflects her verbal silence: she is being what she has been taught to think of as a good wife. She has been constructed, that is, to take a subservient and confined place within a misogynistic hierarchy. She is not, of course, aware of this confinement, since she treats her hardly-deserving husband as if he were totally benevolent.

What the reader sees, however, is that both Collatine and Tarquin interpret her red and white in ways favourable to themselves, with no thought about what she really is.

After Lucrece has decided to commit suicide she and her maid weep together, and the (male) narrator attempts to explain this outflow of emotion in terms of the difference between men and women. He says:

> For men have marble, women waxen minds,
> And therefore are they formed as marble will.
> The weak oppressed, th'impression of strange kinds
> Is formed in them by force, by fraud, or skill.
> Then call them not the authors of their ill,
> No more than wax shall be accounted evil
> Wherein is stamped the semblance of a devil.

> (1240–6)

In *A Midsummer Night's Dream* the authoritarian Theseus responds to Hermia's reluctance to obey her father by saying that she should treat her father as a god, 'To whom you are but as a form in wax, / By him imprinted, and within his power / To leave the figure or disfigure it' (1.1.49–51). The metaphor in both passages presents a clear hierarchy between masculine hardness and power and feminine weakness or pliability. It also suggests a kind of nullity of moral essence in women, who are only what men make of them and cannot be blamed for any evil that is stamped on to them. The narrator attempts to show compassion for Lucrece, who has sought her own culpability in what has happened to her, but he does so by offering a belittling image of feminine passivity. I think, however, that we might reverse this hierarchy by suggesting that there is a virtue of subtlety in the warm pliancy of wax that is lacking in the masculine marble will. It is the positive potential of this feminine resilience that Shakespeare seeks to explore in Lucrece.

As we have seen, *The Rape of Lucrece* is brought about by Collatine's act of publication and Tarquin's reading of her as both men render her into an object. Tarquin's reading imposes meaning upon her and is thus a form of control. Lucrece, conversely, cannot read him. Her inability to see any guile in Tarquin might seem to be pathetic naivete, but her failure to penetrate his appearance is presented figuratively as an inability to read:

> But she, that never coped with stranger eyes
> Could pick no meaning from their parling looks,

Nor read the subtle shining secrecies
Writ in the glassy margins of such books.

(99–102)

After the rape she sees herself as a book, with her shame written for
all, even the illiterate, to read:

The light will show charactered in my brow
The story of sweet chastity's decay . . .
Yea, the illiterate, that know not how
To 'cipher what is writ in learned books
Will quote my loathsome trespass in my looks.

(807–8, 810–12)

Her fears are proved true, at least to her, by the messenger to whom
she entrusts her letter summoning Collatine. This servant blushes in
her presence; he is simply nervous, but she assumes he has seen her
shame, thus misreading his inability to read her. She failed to
perceive Tarquin's evil and now she fails to perceive the servant's
innocence. Lucrece's ordeal has changed everything for her. The
world that she had thought empty of guile has now become a place
of misleading surfaces. As she seeks meaning for her experience in
the painting of the Fall of Troy she is led to the figure of the betrayer
Sinon (1501–61). He seems so mild, so lacking in deceit, that she at
first thinks that the painter must have made a mistake: 'So fair
a form lodged not a mind so ill' (1530). But this thought brings
Tarquin's shape to mind, and the rage with which she tears the
image of Sinon hints that she is now indeed learning to see through
surfaces.

The rape changes her in other ways. There has been a degree of
critical hostility to Lucrece because she talks too much, yet in the
first part of the poem we do not hear her speak at all. She listens
joyfully to Tarquin's praise of her husband, but responds with
'wordless' gestures of prayer (112). When Tarquin appears in her
chamber she does speak: we are told of her 'vehement prayers'
(475), but not what she says. Tarquin's account to her of his inner
conflict is presented to us in direct speech (477–539) and at length;
she does struggle to articulate a response (563–7), but we do not hear
her voice until 575. Her ordeal, however, gives her a voice, and after
Tarquin has left she certainly uses it: the bulk of the remainder of the
poem is her lament. This, I think, is important. Lucrece learns to
refuse the silence that was part of the concept of duty insistently

imposed upon the Elizabethan wife. Her vocal suffering is carefully placed in a history of suffering women who were made to be silent. The song of the nightingale makes her think of the story of Philomel whose sister's husband Tereus raped her and tore out her tongue to prevent her from accusing him. When she looks at the painting she finds the figure of Hecuba silently weeping over the body of Priam and thinks that the painter 'did her wrong / To give her so much grief, and not a tongue' (1462–3). Lucrece resolves to make up the deficiency with her own 'lamenting tongue' (1465). The excesses of her voice may indeed be tiresome, as some critics think; her lengthy, rhetorical speeches are essentially undramatic, but they are a serious attempt on Shakespeare's part to follow the course of her response to suffering, to an understanding of the actions that lead from it.

Lucrece's decision to commit suicide is the most problematic aspect of the poem. To a modern reader it is hardly acceptable that she should consider herself in any sense responsible for the ordeal she has undergone (although rape victims often do precisely that), especially as this seems to support Tarquin's pernicious suggestion that she has brought it upon herself. What she certainly seems to feel responsible for is the shame that her 'stain' will bring to her husband; she imagines the story to be told in the future of 'How Tarquin wronged me, I Collatine' (819). Her sense of guilt is real, however, and not just a matter of what she fears will be said about her; as she considers death, she says:

> I feared by Tarquin's falchion to be slain,
> Yet for the selfsame purpose seek a knife,
> But when I feared I was a loyal wife;
> So am I now – O no, that cannot be,
> Of that true type hath Tarquin rifled me.
>
>   (1046–50)

Lucrece is apparently confusing physical and spiritual states: her violated body is not in any way a sign of her disloyalty, except in her own mind. Later she appears aware of the difference: 'Though my gross blood be stained with this abuse, / Immaculate and spotless is my mind' (1654–5), and in her death-bed moments not only does she pose a series of rhetorical questions pointing to her essential stainlessness (1702–8), but she also makes her kinsmen agree that: 'Her body's stain her mind untainted clears' (1710). And yet she kills herself.

There is a further difficulty, in that elsewhere Lucrece appears to believe that suicide is wrong: '"To kill myself," quoth she, "alack, what were it / But with my body my poor soul's pollution"' (1156–7). There is, perhaps, a collision between Roman and Augustinian attitudes to suicide here, though we can hardly blame Lucrece for not following the Christian way. The important moment comes, I think, quite early in her complaint when she says 'I am the mistress of my fate' (1069). Her roles as wife to Collatine and victim to Tarquin have been passive; now, in her refusal of passivity, she asserts a decidedly un-feminine power over her self. There might seem to be a contradiction here, since she says frequently that her intention is to protect Collatine from her stain. Her deeper purpose, however, is to remove power from Tarquin. If she continued to live he would claim that she had given herself to him willingly. She imagines him laughing at the betrayed Collatine, and the shame of the 'bastard graft' (1062), the illegitimate child he himself has fathered. In killing herself she ensures that revenge will be enacted against her betrayer. In a sense she also contrives to absolve herself of culpability for her own death. At the exact moment that she stabs herself she identifies Tarquin as the agent of her defilement (the penetration of her body with the knife re-enacting his phallic penetration of her), and she goes further: 'He, he, fair lords, 'tis he / That guides this hand to give this wound to me' (1761–2). By means of a rhetorical trick she transfers responsibility for her death from herself to Tarquin.

CONCLUSIONS

It remains, though, a rhetorical trick, and the poem does not fully resolve the problems related to Lucrece's suicide. Do we need it to resolve them? For Lucrece, Tarquin's act against her has radically changed the world, and things can never return to the way they once were. If, in her attempts to understand this, she fails to clarify all the moral or psychological issues arising from her predicament we can hardly blame her. There are other issues that the poem declines to resolve, related to what happens to her after her death, and to our response to Brutus. Lucrece's death might appear to free her from a world of masculine desire, duplicity and violence, but in fact it returns her to it. I noted earlier the response of her husband and father in their near-comic competition for ownership of her body, but her body is finally claimed by Brutus.

The historical Lucius Junius Brutus had taken on the guise of an idiot to protect himself against Tarquin's father, who had murdered Brutus's father and brother and confiscated their wealth. In this guise he was waiting for the opportunity to take revenge, and he saw it in Lucrece's suicide. Her death, that is, was only a pretext for the revenge he already intended. Shakespeare's poem has nothing to say about why Brutus had pretended to be an idiot, though many of his readers would have been well aware of the motives underlying his guile. The emphasis consequently falls on the actual act of disguising:

> He with the Romans was esteemed so
> As silly jeering idiots are with kings,
> For sportive words and utt'ring foolish things.

> But now he throws that shallow habit by
> Wherein deep policy did him disguise.

(1811–15)

What are we to make of this imposture? 'Deep policy' and 'disguise' characterize the actions of the betrayers Tarquin and Sinon, and the poem has expressed a degree of anxiety about the problems of reading them. It now appears to be asking the reader to condone deep policy in Brutus.

The poem leaves this troubling question unanswered, but it is connected to another troubling issue in the poem's conclusion, raised by the suppressed history of the injury the Tarquins had done to Brutus. In turning Lucrece's suicide into a pretext for the overthrow of the Tarquins' monarchy Brutus uses her body for the satisfaction of his own desire. In this he comes disturbingly close to Tarquin, who also used her body to satisfy his own desire. In identifying Lucrece's private body with the public body of the state Brutus rewrites her death as a noble myth of republican freedom. But it is his myth, not hers. There is deep pathos in her question 'Why should the private pleasure of some one / Become the public plague of many moe?' (1478–9). She sees her rape as a violation of her soul, which she imagines as private, protected space opened to the gaze of all: 'Her house is sacked, her quiet interrupted, / Her mansion battered by the enemy, / Her sacred

temple spotted, spoiled, corrupted' (1170–72). However changed
Lucrece is by her rape, it is difficult to imagine that she would
have wanted her private body to be used in quite the public manner
of the poem's final moments, her rape to be rewritten as a subsid-
iary part of the story of the republic's first consul.

7

Shakespeare and the Elizabethan Sonnet

THE DEVELOPMENT OF THE SONNET

When Shakespeare wrote his first sonnets, probably in the early 1590s, he was making a contribution to a genre that had existed in English for not much more than 50 years. In that time, however, the sonnet had become extraordinarily fashionable. First imported by the courtier and diplomat Sir Thomas Wyatt (1503–42), and refined and modified by Henry Howard, Earl of Surrey (1517–47), the form found a wider readership as a result of the publication in 1557 by the bookseller Richard Tottel of an anthology entitled *Songs and Sonnets written by the Right Honorable Lord Henry Howard late Earl of Surrey and other*. Better known as *Tottel's Miscellany*, this volume contained 271 poems by Wyatt, Surrey, the translator Nicholas Grimald, and a number of other unnamed writers, in a variety of forms imported from Europe and adapted to the vernacular language (it also included the earliest examples of blank verse). It would be difficult to overestimate the importance of *Tottel's Miscellany* to the early development of English lyric poetry; its publication was followed by many similar anthologies, and it initiated a process of dissemination to a broader audience of poems originally limited through manuscript circulation to an aristocratic elite.

As we saw in the opening chapter, this process of popularization of poetry, and particularly of the sonnet form, was given its strongest boost by the prestige attached to the name of Sir Philip Sidney, who between 1582–1583 wrote his sonnet sequence *Astrophil and Stella*. Sidney's sonnets were originally written for private reasons, and there is no evidence that they were circulated during his lifetime; if they were, they would have remained within his own coterie. *Astrophil and Stella* was not published until 1591, some years after his death, in an unauthorized edition. In large part because of the glamour associated with Sidney's name, *Astrophil and Stella* initiated the vogue for writing sonnets that between 1592 and 1609, the year of publication of Shakespeare's sonnets, produced more than twenty sequences. Most of the sequences, it should be noted, appeared before 1598, so the actual publication of Shakespeare's sonnets occurred well after the original vogue was ended.

As we know it today, the sonnet might seem to be a rather constricting form, with its fourteen lines of iambic pentameter (ten syllables, or five 'feet' each consisting of an unaccented syllable and an accented one) and its strict rhyming patterns. There are two major versions of the sonnet-form, differentiated by their rhyme-schemes: the Italian, or Petrarchan, and the English, or Shakespearean, though in Tudor England the term 'sonnet' was sometimes rather loosely applied to a variety of lyrical forms. The Petrarchan form is the one imported by Wyatt; Surrey anglicized it, largely by changing the rhyme-scheme. This 'English' form is the one that Shakespeare used for almost all his sonnets, and inevitably it is now closely associated with his name.

Petrarch was not the inventor of the form that has his name, though he was its greatest practitioner, and as we have seen he is associated with those conventional elements that are called 'Petrarchan'. The form appears to have originated in southern Italy a century or so before Petrarch wrote, but he made it so fashionable that it was exported to Spain in the fifteenth century, to France and England in the sixteenth, and to Germany in the seventeenth.[1] The Italian sonnet was a fourteen-line poem with eleven syllables to a line, and as Petrarch developed it, it fell into two parts, an eight-line section (now called an 'octave') with the rhyme-scheme *abbaabba*, and a six-line section (the 'sestet') *cdecde*, though there were variants of this (*cdcdcd, cdedce, cdeced*). Whatever the variant within the sestet, Italian sonnets avoided ending with a couplet. I shall return to a considera-tion of the implications of these rhyme-schemes later.

A sonnet that exhibits clearly many of the devices developed by Petrarch is number 132 of the *Canzoniere*:

S'amor non è, che dunque è quel ch'io sento?	a
ma s'egli è amor, per Dio, che cosa e quale?	b
se bona, ond'è l'effetto aspro e mortale?	b
se ria, ond'è sì dolce ogni tormento?	a
S'a mia voglia ardo, ond'è 'l pianto e lamento?	a
s'a mal miogrado, il lamentar che vale?	b
O viva morte, o dilettoso male,	b

come puoi tanto in me, s'io no 'l consento?   a
   E s'io 'l consento, a gran torto mi doglio.   c
Fra sì contrari vènti in frale barca   d
mi trovo in alto mar, senza governo,   e
   sì lieve di saver, d'error sì carca,   d
ch'i' medesmo non so quel ch'io mi voglio,   c
e tremo a mezza state, ardendo il verno.   e

A modern translation of this sonnet (without attempting a replication of the rhyme-scheme) renders it as follows:

If it's not love, then what is it I feel?
But if it's love, by God, what is this thing?
If good, why then the bitter mortal sting?
If bad, then why is every torment sweet?
If I burn willingly, why weep and grieve?
And if against my will, what good lamenting?
O living death, O pleasurable harm,
how can you rule me if I not consent?
And if I do consent, it's wrong to grieve.
Caught in contrasting winds in a frail boat
on the high seas I am without a helm,
so light of wisdom, so laden of error,
that I myself do not know what I want,
and shiver in midsummer, burn in winter.[2]

In the octave the poet attempts to understand through a series of questions the conflicted feelings aroused in him by his unattainable love; the paradoxes of the pains of love and his inexplicably willing acceptance of them are characteristically expressed though oxymoron ('O viva morte, o dilletoso male'). In the sestet the poet at first appears to accept this confusing state of being, since he embraces it freely, but the focus switches to his sense of being abandoned and without direction, and to a more general sense of alienation.

The unequal two-part structure of the Italian sonnet, which almost necessitates a dialectical movement between 'observation and conclusion, or statement and counter statement',[3] is often seen as its essential feature. The octave states and develops an idea or position, but after the eighth line there is a turn, or 'volta', and the sestet often presents a response to, or even a reversal of the octave's argument. Sir Thomas Wyatt, in importing the sonnet into England, mainly translated or adapted poems from Petrarch's *Canzoniere*. Here is his version of number 134:

I find no peace and all my war is done.	a
I fear and hope, I burn, and freeze like ice.	b
I fly above the wind yet can I not arise.	b
And nought I have and all the world I seize on,	a
That looseth nor locketh, holdeth me in prison	a
And holds me not, yet can I scape no wise;	b
Nor letteth me live nor die at my device	b
And yet of death it giveth me occasion.	a
Without eyen I see and without tongue I plain.	c
I desire to perish and yet I ask health.	d
I love another and thus I hate myself.	d
I feed me in sorrow and laugh in all my pain.	c
Likewise displeaseth me both death and life,	e
And my delight is causer of this strife.[4]	e

As with all of his adaptations, Wyatt has retained the division between octave and sestet, but he has ended the sestet with a couplet, which changes the argumentative structure of the sonnet, making it tend towards a neat conclusion in the final two lines. This is the first step in the development of the English sonnet.

The English sonnet, which has a rhyme-scheme of *abab cdcd efef gg*, was essentially the invention of the Earl of Surrey. The rhyme-scheme breaks the poem into three quatrains and a couplet (4/4/4/2), thus allowing for a different and in some ways more flexible argumentative structure from the 8/6 division of the Italian sonnet, and tending to isolate and emphasize the final couplet to make a witty point, or conclusion, or reversal of the argument. An obvious way to develop an argument within this structure is to present an idea or state of mind within the first quatrain in terms of one metaphor, restate it or develop it in terms of another metaphor in the second quatrain, do the same in the third quatrain, and provide some kind of comment on it in the couplet. There are other ways to structure an argument, however. In this sonnet Surrey treats the three quatrains as if they were a single unit, thus dividing it 12/2:

The soote season, that bud and bloom forth brings,	a
With green hath clad the hill and eke the vale;	b
The nightingale with feathers new she sings;	a
The turtle to her make hath told her tale.	b
Summer is come, for every spray now springs;	c

The hart hath hung his old head on the pale;	d
The buck in brake his winter coat he flings,	c
The fishes float with new repaired scale;	d
The adder all her slough away she slings,	e
The swift swallow pursueth the flyes small;	f
The busy bee her honey now she mings.	e
Winter is worn, that was the flowers' bale.	f
And thus I see among these pleasant things,	g
Each care decays, and yet my sorrow springs.[5]	g

The body of the sonnet presents a series of natural images expressing fruitfulness and renewal, and then the couplet presents in contrast the sorrowful state of the speaker, which turns out to be the poem's real point, though for the reader its best effects may lie in the natural description.

Why Surrey felt it desirable to modify the form is unclear; perhaps he was simply trying to make it easier by reducing the number of rhymes needed (the *abbaabba* form needs three words to rhyme with the word at the end of the first line; the *abab* form needs only one), perhaps reflecting the smaller number of rhyming words in English. John Fuller thinks that Wyatt and Surrey failed to grasp the point of the Italian sonnet,[6] but this seems rather unfair; both were experimenting, and the structure that their experiments eventually produced clearly must have satisfied Shakespeare. As to the poetic line, they chose iambic pentameter, presumably, as the closest English approximation to the eleven-syllable line of the Italian sonnets. They also used iambic pentameter for other lyrical forms, and Surrey made it the basis of his blank-verse translations of Virgil. Their work in effect initiated the establishment of iambic pentameter as the dominant line of English poetry. This is not, as it might seem, a simple matter of choosing the line that seems most 'natural' to English. As Antony Easthope has argued, the dominance of iambic pentameter is an ideological issue: 'The metre can be seen not as a neutral form of poetic necessity but a specific historical form producing certain meanings and acting to exclude others'.[7] The meanings it excludes are those related to older English verse forms, promoting instead a court culture that located its values in classical models. What is true of the line is true also of the sonnet: its initiating energies are reflective of aristocratic culture.

It is easy to see why the Petrarchan conventions of love and service produced in the sonnet should have fulfilled so completely the needs of Elizabeth's court, and why sonnet sequences should have dominated literary fashion during the last decade or so of her reign (the list of sonnet sequences at the end of this section indicates that the vogue effectively ended with her death). A female monarch governing a patriarchy, surrounded by powerful and potentially dangerous nobles, Elizabeth needed to encourage as many ideas as possible that would legitimate her rule. She fostered myths of her own divinity and initiated public ceremonies and entertainments that used a romanticized medievalism to promote models of order and service. Sidney competed in tournaments under the name 'Sir Philisides', and we can understand his sonnet sequence *Astrophil and Stella* to be at least in part an act of political courtship, for any work that attempted to win the favour of a woman who was powerful, distant and cruel, beautiful and virtuous and, above all, unattainable, clearly coded within its fictions an account of the courtier's relationship to his monarch.

Technically, the development of the sonnet sequence was in part a means of compensating for the restrictions of the individual sonnet, allowing the poet to play variations on his theme, to develop connections and contrasts from sonnet to sonnet, to build beyond the limits of a single poem. While the publication of *Astrophil and Stella* was instrumental in initiating the sonnet vogue, it was not the first sonnet sequence to be published in England. As early as 1560 a woman named Ann Lock published a series of 21 sonnets that were essentially paraphrases of psalms, prefaced by five original sonnets. This is a very interesting set of poems, but its publication was too obscure for it to have had any influence. In 1582 Thomas Watson published *Hekatompathia or Passionate Century of Love*; and in 1584 John Soowthern published a brief sequence of generally inept sonnets entitled *Pandora*. Of these two, Watson is the more significant. He referred to his poems as sonnets, though this was actually a sequence of a hundred eighteen-line poems, which gives some indication of how flexible the early idea of the sonnet was. His title-page indicates a degree of unease about the publication; the poems were, it states, 'Composed by Thomas Watson Gentleman; and published at the request of certaine Gentlemen his very frendes'.[8] Watson was a man of some distinction, a classical and legal scholar who enjoyed the patronage of the powerful aristocrat Sir Francis Walsingham and the friendship of Sidney himself. He was clearly aware of the elitist abhorrence of the idea of exhibiting themselves to a common audience that restrained aristocratic writers from publishing. Thus his insistence that he and his circle are gentlemen, and that the poems were published under pressure from his friends, with the implication that this was against his will, is a means of negotiating any potential embarrassment.

The manuscript circulation of poems amongst coteries of the powerful was not simply a matter of fastidiousness. It was a means whereby the court culture maintained its exclusiveness. Power needs secrets, and even sonnets can be secrets in this sense: they carry the values of the select group. Sidney had a keen interest in writing and in the development of a literature in English, but for him the idea of a literature could have been in no sense democratic. Apart from his seminal sonnet sequence, he wrote the most signifi-cant piece of criticism of the Elizabethan period, *An Apology for Poetry*, and the vast romance *The Arcadia*. None of this was published during his lifetime, however; it remained the possession of his clos-est friends. The printing press had no small influence on what has been called the 'crisis of the aristocracy', for it allowed the broad dissemination of their closely guarded secrets.

In order to understand the complex functioning of sonnet sequences in Shakespeare's society, it is worth looking a little more closely at *Astrophil and Stella*, a sequence of 108 sonnets interspersed with eleven songs. The very title sets up an intricate set of reson-ances. Meaning 'star-lover and star', it emphasizes the distance between the suitor and his object and the cold beauty of the woman. The name 'Astrophil' contains Sidney's own name within itself, but only in part, tantalizing the reader with the idea that the sequence is autobiographical. Astrophil is self-absorbed, however, often comically, sometimes darkly so, and the dominant experience of these sonnets is of frustration. The immediate model for Stella was Penelope Devereux, daughter of the first Earl of Essex, who in 1581 married Robert, Earl Rich, and thus became unattainable except through adultery. Obviously, the ostensible intimacy of the sequence made it potentially scandalous. But as we have seen, the relationship between poet and unattainable object had been a con-vention of sonnet sequences from Petrarch onwards, so if this work is autobiographical, it is so in a very limited sense. Without doubt, the poems reflect a keen understanding of the self-deceptions that arise from a struggle to elevate desire to something higher than mere appetite, and Sidney might well have shared much of the experience that Astrophil analyses, but he seems to stand at some distance from his creation, holding him up for judgement as much as for sympathy.

The 'narrative' of *Astrophil and Stella*, insofar as there is one, tells of the gradual growth in Astrophil of what he identifies as love. Insistently rebuffed by Stella but unwilling to take 'No' for an answer, he minutely examines his own obsessive behaviour. The closest he comes to satisfying his desire is when he steals a kiss from the sleeping woman, but the sequence ends in futility and defeat in the final sonnet:

> But soon as thought of thee breeds my delight,
> And my young soul flutters to thee his nest,
> Most rude despair my daily unbidden guest,
> Clips straight my wings, straight wraps me in his night,
> And makes me then bow down my head and say,
> Ah what doth Phoebus' gold that wretch avail
> Whom iron doors do keep from use of day?
>
> (108, 5–11)

This, like the sequence it concludes, is a fine account of sexual frustration, but if we look beneath its surface we can see that it is also a rendering of social frustration. In 1580, partly because of his opposition to the proposed marriage of Queen Elizabeth to the Duke of Alencon, Sidney went into a kind of voluntary exile at Wilton, the home of his sister, and it was there that he did much of his writing, particularly of *Astrophil and Stella*. It is difficult not to see the queen behind Stella, the real object of Astrophil's thwarted desire. Sonnet 41 is based on Sidney's own participation in a tournament in May 1581:

> Having this day my horse, my hand, my lance
> Guided so well, that I obtain'd the prize,
> Both by the judgement of the English eyes,
> And of some sent from that sweet enemy France,
> Horsemen my skill in horsemanship advance,
> Town-folks my strength: a daintier judge applies
> His praise to sleight, which from good use doth rise:
> Some lucky wits impute it but to chance:
> Others, because of both sides I do take
> My blood from them, who did excel in this,
> Think nature me a man of arms did make.
> How far they shot awry; the true cause is,
> Stella lookt on, and from her heavenly face
> Sent forth the beams which made so fair my race.

These tournaments were held for the entertainment of the queen and to win her favour, and there is an obvious, wish-fulfillment sense in which she is the beaming Stella of this poem. The sequence, from this perspective, is an oblique way of expressing the disappointments of Sidney's public career. In an influential essay, Arthur Marotti has perceived in Elizabethan sonnet sequences 'the metaphorizing of ambition as love', and we shall see that this has its significance in relation to Shakespeare too.[9]

Popular aristocrat though he was, Sidney was caught in the web of patronage. Just as the horseman puts his skills on display for favour, social or political, so the poet put his skills on display for much the same reasons. But he was unquestionably serious in his literary interests, and as he demonstrates in his *Apology for Poetry*, he had an ardent concern for the future of English poetry. In his sonnet sequence, he had to distinguish himself from his forebears, and while, as we have seen, he respected many of the Petrarchan conventions, he also sought to add something of himself. He was more of an experimenter with form than was Shakespeare, occasionally trying different line-lengths, and using a wider range of rhyme-schemes, although he tended to favour the final couplet. He gave to the voice of his poems a colloquial, even dramatic quality. Consider the first poem of his sequence:

> Loving in truth, and fain in verse my love to show,
> That the dear she might take some pleasure of my pain:
> Pleasure might cause her read, reading might make her know,
> Knowledge might pity win, and pity grace obtain,
> I sought fit words to paint the blackest face of woe,
> Studying inventions fine, her wits to entertain:
> Oft turning others' leaves, to see if thence would flow
> Some fresh and fruitful showers upon my sun-burn'd brain.
> But words came halting forth, wanting Inventions stay;
> Invention Nature's child, fled step-dame Study's blows,
> And others' feet still seem'd but strangers in my way.
> Thus, great with child to speak, and helpless in my throes,
> Biting my truand pen, beating myself for spite,
> Fool, said my Muse to me, look in thy heart, and write.

He begins with the pain/pleasure paradox familiar in Petrarchan convention, but then finds himself limited by 'others' leaves' and 'others' feet', the generic traces set up by his forebears. The last three lines of the poem resolve his problem: his Muse exhorts him to look inward, to find something of his own to set beside the conventions. This is not simply advice to be 'original'; it also moves the poet away from the externals of custom to introspection and the expression of his own subjectivity.

Sidney here confronts the crucial problem that the English sonnet had developed in its brief life: it had set up elaborate generic expectations that threatened to inhibit writing. The Petrarchan sonnet is an expression of love, but if the poet is forced to use the language and conventions implied by the genre, whose love is he expressing? Shakespeare used this dilemma to comic effect in *Love's Labour's Lost* (written at about the time when sonnet-writing would have been a preoccupation with him), in which four young noblemen attempt to woo four aristocratic ladies by writing poems for them. The young men believe themselves to be serious, but the ladies think they are playing a game. The artifice of the courtly language that the young men use actually inhibits communication, for how can conventional phrases express individual feeling? In his sonnets, Sidney did more than most of his followers to resolve this problem, though he was not always successful.

As we have seen, it was never a part of Sidney's intention to publish his writings, but after his death, interest in his public reputation encouraged curiosity about them, and after 1590 unauthorized printed versions of most of his works began to circulate, including the 1591 publication of *Astrophil and Stella*. In 1598 his sister Mary published a folio edition that collected together all his important works, presumably to reassert family control over them. The prestige of Sidney's name had a lot to do with raising the reputation of printed literature, and obviously opened up the secrets of court writing to the scrutiny of a less noble public. It took some time, nevertheless, for the sense that there was something demeaning about publication to be dissipated. Samuel Daniel, whose sequence *Delia* (1592) was the first to appear in print after Sidney's, enjoyed the patronage of the Countess of Pembroke, and in dedicating the volume to her, he wrote:

> Right honorable, although I rather desired to keep in the private passions of my youth, from the multitude, as things utterd to my selfe, and consecrated to silence: yet seeing I was betraide by the indiscretion of a greedie Printer, and had some of my secrets bewraide to the world, uncorrected: doubting the like of the rest, I am forced to publish that which I never ment. But this wrong was not onely doone to mee, but to him [Sidney] whose unmatchable lines have indured the like misfortune; Ignorance sparing not to commit sacriledge upon so holy Reliques.[10]

Twenty-eight of Daniel's sonnets were included in the first unauthorized edition of *Astrophil and Stella*, and it is possible that he is being disingenuous here, since he might well have been involved in the pirating.[11] His view of his poems as 'secrets', however, and his claim that he only published *Delia* because he was forced into it, is an indication of his discomfort about how publication might have affected his relationship with his aristocratic patron.

The explosion of sonnet sequences that followed the publication of *Astrophil and Stella* inevitably turned convention into cliché, and few of the sequences that followed Sidney's repay much attention today. The most significant of them is Edmund Spenser's *Amoretti* (1595), which tries to domesticate into Christian marriage the implicitly adulterous sexual desire that underlies Petrarchism. Although Spenser draws much from the Petrarchan model, he structures his sequence upon the cycle of the church year, and while the sequence itself follows convention by ending in disappointment, it was published along with a poem titled *Epithalamion*, which was a celebration of Spenser's own wedding. He thus wrought an uneasy fusion between the erotic and the spiritual, the conventional and the autobiographical.

This, then, was the context in which Shakespeare produced his sonnets. Introduced into England by noblemen, the sonnet's conventions were modified for the needs of an aristocratic readership, and the sonnets and sonnet sequences were only reluctantly set free into the growing middle-class market. Sonnet sequences can consequently be seen, in part, as the location of a struggle between an elite culture trying to keep hold of its privacy, which was intimately connected to the sources of its power, and an increasingly dynamic and inquisitive public culture anxious to penetrate that privacy. Sonnet sequences inevitably had an ideological weight at the point when Shakespeare intervened in their history.

Sonnet sequences printed prior to Shakespeare's

1560	Ann Lock, *A Meditation*
1582	Thomas Watson, *Hekatompathia*
1584	John Soowthern, *Pandora*
1591	Sir Philip Sidney, *Astrophil and Stella*
1592	Samuel Daniel, *Delia*
	Henry Constable, *Diana*
1593	Barnabe Barnes, *Parthenophil and Parthenophe*
	Thomas Lodge, *Phillis*
	Giles Fletcher, *Licia*

	Thomas Watson, *The Tears of Fancie*
1594	Michael Drayton, *Ideas Mirrour*
	William Percy, *Sonnets to the Fairest Coelia*
	Zepheria (anon.)
1595	Barnabe Barnes, *A Divine Centurie of Spiritual Sonnets*
	E.C., *Emaricdulfe*
	Edmund Spenser, *Amoretti*
1596	Bartholomew Griffin, *Fidessa*
	Richard Linche (?), *Diella*
	William Smith, *Chloris*
1597	Richard Barnfield, *Cynthia*
	Robert Tofte, *Laura*
	Henry Lok, 'Sundrie Sonnets' and 'Affectionate Sonnets' in *Ecclesiastic*
1598	Robert Tofte, *Alba*
1604	William Alexander, *Aurora*
1605	John Davies of Hereford, *Wittes Pilgrimage*
1609	William Shakespeare, *Shake-speare's Sonnets*

SHAKE-SPEARE'S SONNETS

Shakespeare's own sonnets were published in 1609 in a quarto volume by Thomas Thorpe, a publisher of good reputation who seems previously to have specialized mainly in the publication of plays and masques. On 20th May of that year an entry was made in the Stationers' Register on Thorpe's behalf indicating his intention to publish a book entitled *Shakespeares Sonnettes*, and later in the year the quarto volume appeared, proclaiming on its title-page that these were 'SHAKE-SPEARES SONNETS. Never before Imprinted'. Along with the sonnets the volume contained a poem entitled 'A Lover's Complaint', which for a long time a majority of scholars doubted was Shakespeare's work. The volume was printed by George Eld, and appears to have been done carelessly or in haste, though the extent of the carelessness is a debatable issue. There remain in existence thirteen known copies of the text; variant title-pages indicate that they were to be sold by two different booksellers, John Wright and William Aspley, presumably to allow broader distribution. A sign of the popularity of any publication was the frequency with which it was reprinted; the sonnets were not printed again until 1640, when a bookseller named John Benson published a volume entitled *Poems:*

Written by Wil. Shake-speare. Gent. This was a cynical attempt to fool readers into believing they were getting something new. Benson changed the order and omitted some of Shakespeare's poems, while including poems by other writers; he ran some sonnets together, making them appear to be longer poems; and he changed pronouns in some of the poems to make it appear that they were addressed to a woman. This egregious volume was unfortunately the only edition available for many years (perhaps the reason why the sonnets remained unpopular), and it was not until 1780 that Edmond Malone produced a critical edition that allowed readers to experiene the sonnets in their original form.

Following the title-page of the 1609 Quarto was this rather enigmatic dedication; the capitalization and use of points must have been intended to underscore its significance:

TO.THE.ONLY.BEGETTER.OF.
THESE.ENSUING.SONNETS.
M^r.W.H.ALL.HAPPINESS.
AND.THAT.ETERNITY.
PROMISED.
BY.
OUR.EVER-LIVING.POET.
WISHETH.
THE.WELL-WISHING.
ADVENTURER.IN.
SETTING.
FORTH.

T.T.

The peculiarity of this dedication and its potential relationship to the content of the *Sonnets*, along with the date and circumstances of publication, have raised a number of vexed issues. Among these are: the dates of composition of the individual sonnets and the circumstances surrounding their publication as a sequence; the ordering, integrity and meaning of the sequence itself; the identity of 'Mr. W.H'.; the extent to which the sequence can be understood as autobiographical and the related question of the identities of the young man, the 'dark lady' and the rival poet who figure in it. There are no certain answers to any of these questions, but important issues are raised by the kinds of speculative answers that have been given.

To take first the issues raised by the date of publication: as we have seen, the vogue for sonnet sequences was intimately connected to the last years of Elizabeth's reign and was effectively ended by her death. There was a minor revival of interest in the early years of James's reign, but the only substantial Jacobean sequences prior to Shakespeare's were Alexander's *Aurora* and Davies's *Wittes Pilgrimage*. So why did Thorpe, who was a businessman, think it would be commercially viable to publish a collection of poems which, even after revision, would have seemed to belong to an outmoded fashion? Perhaps the weight of Shakespeare's Jacobean reputation and the new uses to which he had put the sonnet conventions seemed to warrant the risk; if so, Thorpe was apparently misled, for the publication of the volume was met by what Katherine Duncan-Jones, editor of the recent Arden edition, calls a 'resounding silence'.[12] There is no contemporary record of any reader enthusiasm, and, as I noted above, the *Sonnets* was not reprinted in Shakespeare's lifetime; compare this with the reception of *Venus and Adonis*, which went into at least 16 editions.

Although Shakespeare's sonnets were not published until 1609, he must have begun writing them many years earlier, but when he began is not known, nor why he decided to try his hand at this form. Nor is the order in which they were written known, nor indeed whether Shakespeare originally intended to produce a sequence or whether he simply brought together into a semblance of order sonnets written for a number of different purposes over a number of years. Tentative dates have been proposed for a few individual sonnets; the earliest relates to sonnet 145, for which Andrew Gurr, finding in the phrase 'hate away' a possible play on 'Hathaway', the maiden name of Shakespeare's wife, has suggested the year 1582.[13] Other critics have surmised that he probably started writing them around 1592 or 1593, when he also started work on *Venus and Adonis* and *The Rape of Lucrece*. This date has been particularly attractive to scholars who believe that there is biographical information to be found in the sonnets, and especially to those who believe that the young man addressed in them is the Earl of Southampton, to whom Shakespeare had dedicated the narrative poems. This theory has claimed support from sonnet 104, which appears to make an insistently specific time reference:

> Three winters cold
> Have from the forests shook three summers' pride;
> Three beauteous springs to yellow autumn turned
> In process of the seasons I have seen,

Three April perfumes in three hot Junes burned
Since first I saw you fresh, which yet are green.

(104.3–8)

Taking this literally, supporters of the Southampton theory have suggested that the poems were composed between about 1592 and about 1596; certainly, the Elizabethan sonnet vogue was at its height in the early 1590s, and it seems probable that Shakespeare would have been interested in offering his own modifications of the fashionable form. This does not mean that he wrote all, or even most, of the sonnets at that time, however. The 'three years' of sonnet 104 could well be a conventional phrase for 'some length of time' and almost certainly should not be understood literally, but even if it is, this is a slim base upon which to build a case.

Other critics have proposed a quite different set of dates. In sonnet 107, which apparently alludes to a contemporary event, we are informed that

The mortal moon hath her eclipse endured,
And the sad augurs mock their own presage;
Incertainties now crown themselves assured,
And peace proclaims olives of endless age.

(107.5–8)

Although there are alternative interpretations, most critics take this to be a reference to the death of Elizabeth I in 1603 (the eclipsed moon); the national uncertainty this had created was dispelled by the accession of King James I. Taken in conjunction with sonnet 104, this would give a span of composition starting around 1599, and would imply a different identity for the young man. In truth, though, there is little in the sonnets that can be given a sufficiently sure and precise topical interpretation to allow dating to go beyond mere speculation. There have recently been statistical and computer-based stylometric analyses that count the use of rare words to generate a kind of evolutionary model whereby individual sonnets can be assigned a tentative date in relation to plays and to each other. This work has some potential, but the main problem with it is that the sonnets were presumably subject to revision, so such methods cannot identify a date that can certainly be accepted as the date of composition rather than of possible reworking.

The earliest reference to Shakespeare as a sonnet-writer comes in Francis Meres's *Palladis Tamia* of 1598, where Meres refers to the poet's 'sugared Sonnets among his private friends'. This is an intriguing remark, but not very helpful. Who were the private friends? Meres himself was an enthusiastic reader and playgoer, but it is not probable that he was one of them, so how did he know about the sonnets? Their circulation could not have been very private. And which sonnets were circulating? A modern reader might well be taken aback by the implications of the word 'sugared', though it is clear that Meres does not use it pejoratively; however we take the word, it does not seem appropriate as a description of many of the sonnets. It is, of course, quite possible that the sonnets to which Meres refers were not included in the 1609 quarto and that they no longer exist. Shakespeare had toyed with the form in some of his plays: the opening chorus of *Romeo and Juliet* is a sonnet and, as we have seen, in *Love's Labour's Lost* he mocked the courtly fashion of wooing in rhyme. It is generally assumed that those plays were composed between 1593 and 1595. In 1599 William Jaggard published a miscellany entitled *The Passionate Pilgrim*, which included versions of sonnets 138 and 144, along with two sonnets and a song from *Love's Labour's Lost* and a number of other poems that Jaggard tried to pass off as Shakespeare's. But if the sonnets to which Meres referred in 1598 did eventually reappear in 1609, we know nothing about how many there were, or whether they circulated as individual sonnets or as connected groups or sub-sequences.

In the absence of better evidence, a reasonable assumption would be that Shakespeare began writing sonnets seriously around 1592, after the sensation caused by the publication of *Astrophil and Stella*, and while the theatres were closed for the plague. This does not exclude the possibility that he had experimented with the form earlier than 1592. By 1598 there was a number of them circulating widely enough in manuscript for Meres to have heard about them, and no doubt Shakespeare revised and added to them over the years. Duncan-Jones has suggested that the publication of the sonnets, like the writing of his two narrative poems, was prompted by the effects of the plague, which between 1608 and 1610 caused prolonged closings of the theatres; Shakespeare's living being largely dependent on his income from the theatres, he might well have been forced by need to sell the sonnets for publication (although his financial circumstances were much better than they had been 17 years earlier).[14] This theory depends, however, on the assumption that the sonnets were published with Shakespeare's authorization, which is a view not universally held. The dominant opinion has been that the

1609 quarto edition was pirated by its publisher Thomas Thorpe, and printed without Shakespeare's permission.

This is an important issue. The case against Thorpe can be summed up in Joel Fineman's comment: 'From the many errors in Thorpe's text, it seems clear that Shakespeare did not authorize publication of his sonnets'.[15] The assumption that underlies this is that if Shakespeare had authorized Thorpe's quarto he would have supervised its composition, or at the very least checked it thoroughly. But an argument that rests largely on what is perceived as the careless state of printing of the quarto disappears if it can be shown that the printing was not, in fact, unusually bad. Duncan-Jones, in editing the text, has argued that the number and significance of the misprints has been greatly over-stated, and does not justify such skepticism about the authority of the text.[16] I might add that it seems improbable that Thorpe, who unlike Jaggard was a reputable publisher, would have risked printing without permission work by a writer as well-known as Shakespeare was by 1609. This being so, I am inclined to accept the argument that the volume was published with the poet's permission.

The reason why this issue is important is that if publication was indeed unauthorized, then we cannot be sure that the order of the poems is as Shakespeare intended them. Certainly, there appears to be no clear narrative progression to the sonnets if we take the sequence as a whole, and some critics have imagined themselves able to re-organize them into a different pattern; for example C.F. Tucker Brooke, in his edition of the *Sonnets*, proposed what he considered to be a more coherent order.[17] However, even if we assume that Shakespeare had no hand in the publication, such reorganization is not legitimate. In the absence of any other information the order in the Thorpe text has to be taken as authoritative, because any reordering has even less authority. On the other hand, it is legitimate to ask what the order in the 1609 quarto means. Does it have a coherent shape, or is it a collection of individual sonnets and groupings put together with no more than a very rough organization? It appears that the 154 sonnets make up two inter-connected sequences. The first 126 sonnets are addressed to a young man whom the speaker first urges to marry in order to project his beauty and worth into the future, but who then becomes an object of desire for the speaker himself as the sonnets explore the ambiguous joys and pains that such a relationship generates. The remaining 28 are addressed to an older woman (though the two final poems seem disconnected from the rest) who provokes lust and revulsion in the speaker. The two sequences overlap when a sexual triangle apparently develops among speaker, youth and lady, and the first sequence contains a sub-sequence starting with sonnet 78 in which the speaker is concerned with other poets who vie for the young man's attention, particularly one 'better spirit' who has become known as the 'rival poet'.

While it is generally accepted that the first 126 sonnets are addressed to the young man, it has to be acknowledged that many individual sonnets contain nothing within them to indicate the gender of the addressee. Most readers who are familiar with sonnet 18 ('Shall I compare thee to a summer's day?') only from anthologies would assume, if they have any familiarity with the conventions of love poetry of the period, that it is addressed to a woman, and there is nothing in the sonnet to suggest otherwise. But within the *Sonnets* the poem comes at the end of a series of 17 sonnets quite clearly addressed to a young man, and so it is logical to associate sonnet 18 with them. This meaning is entirely dependent on sup-positions made about its location in the context, which is why it is legitimate to ask questions about the significance of the order. Does the narrative implied in the 'plot' I gave above arise out of the sequence, or has it been imposed upon it? Heather Dubrow has recently questioned whether the order of the poems does in fact justify commonly held assumptions about the division of the sequence and the identity of the addressee.[18] This also opens up the whole question of the appropriateness of the term 'sequence' for this or indeed any of the Elizabethan sonnet collections, since its implica-tion of connectedness and progression encourages the reader to seek a narrative or thematic consistency that might not be there.

The 1609 quarto has generated other questions that have been posed so frequently (and sometimes with an obsessiveness that has turned them into 'mysteries') that I have to address them, even though I think in some ways they represent a massive misdirection of scholarly energy. These relate to the possible autobiographical element of the sonnets, and to approach them I will return to the poem's dedication. There is no complete agreement on what pre-cisely it means, but I think its phrasing can be reordered like this: THE WELL-WISHING ADVENTURER IN SETTING FORTH WISH-ETH TO Mr. W.H., THE ONLY BEGETTER OF THESE ENSUING SONNETS, ALL HAPPINESS AND THAT ETERNITY PROMISED BY OUR EVER-LIVING POET. The initials 'T.T'. at the end of the dedication are obviously Thorpe's, and presumably he composed the dedication on Shakespeare's behalf if Shakespeare authorized the volume, and on his own behalf if he did not. Thorpe is the 'adventurer in setting forth'; to 'set forth' here means to publish, and he is an adventurer because his venture involves financial risk. 'Mr. W.H.', is the only begetter of the sonnets, perhaps because they were made possible by his patronage, either in the past or, since publisher and poet are hoping to receive patronage for dedicating the volume to him, in the future. 'Begetter' might also mean 'inspirer', however, if Mr. W.H. is the young man addressed in the *Sonnets*. The 'eternity promised' by the poet refers to the claim first made in sonnet 18 and reiterated in others, that verse can confer a kind of eternity: 'So long as men can breathe or eyes can see, / So long lives this, and this gives life to thee'. The claim that the poet is 'ever-living' has been perceived as blasphemous,[19] but this is to take too seriously what is clearly playful hyperbole; it is not much different from Ben Jonson's statement that Shakespeare was 'for all time', which no one suggests is blasphemous. If verses are to immortalize their subject, the verses themselves must be immortal, and that is all that Thorpe means.

There have been numerous attempts to identify Mr. W.H., some convincing, most not. Shakespeare's brother-in-law William Hathaway has been proposed, as has his nephew William Hart, but in the early seventeenth century a volume of poems was a valuable property and no one made vanity dedications. Such candidates as these and others can be dismissed as fanciful, in spite of ingenious arguments in their support. There would not have been much sense in Shakespeare's dedicating a manuscript that had taken years to produce to a man who did not have the wealth, generosity and power to do him good, and so Mr. W.H. must have been someone from whom he could expect patronage, almost certainly an aristocrat. A reasonably strong case can be made for only two such individuals, Henry Wriothesley, third Earl of Southampton, and William Herbert, third Earl of Pembroke.

Henry Wriothesley has seemed an attractive probability to many because he was certainly Shakespeare's patron in 1593, when he was aged 19 and apparently on the verge of an illustrious career, and thus would have been the right age to be addressed as 'the world's fresh ornament' in the first sonnet. The evidence, as we have seen, suggests that the poet began writing his sonnets in the early 1590s. Shakespeare had dedicated both *Venus and Adonis* and *The Rape of Lucrece* to Southampton, and there would be a pleasing symmetry if the *Sonnets* had been dedicated to him as well. On the other hand, in 1609 Southampton was 35; he had been implicated in 1601 in Essex's failed attempt to depose Queen Elizabeth, and had spent some time imprisoned in the Tower of London; it would have seemed impolitic under the circumstances to remind him of his youthful promise. And if he *was* Mr. W.H., what purpose was there in reversing his initials? There does not seem to have been any reason to conceal an identity that Shakespeare had proudly publicized in the dedications to his narrative poems.

The case for William Herbert, in my view, is rather stronger, and not only because there is no need to manipulate his initials. The son of Sir Philip Sidney's sister Mary, Countess of Pembroke, he was, like his mother, a generous patron of writers, among them Jonson, Daniel, Donne and Chapman (any one of whom might have been the 'rival poet'). There is no evidence of any direct connection to Shakespeare, but as Lord Chamberlain for James I Herbert had much official business with Shakespeare's acting company, the King's Men, and he also had a genuine interest in the theatre, which led to a particular friendship with Richard Burbage, the company's leading actor.[20] John Heminges and Henry Condell, the editors of the 1623 folio edition of Shakespeare's plays, dedicated it to Herbert (by then Earl of Pembroke) and his brother Philip, Earl of Montgomery, claiming that the brothers had graced Shakespeare, when he was alive, 'with so much favour', which suggests that he had received some form of patronage from them and that Heminges and Condell perceived Herbert, at the very least, to be an important figure in Shakespeare's career. He was younger than Southampton, being still under 30 in 1609, and so perhaps could be seen as the more appropriate recipient of a body of sonnets addressed to a young man.

What has been a more intriguing endeavour for many scholars has been the attempt to identify Mr. W.H. not just as the poems' patron, but also as their subject. If Mr. W.H. is the young man addressed in the *Sonnets*, this clearly opens up the possibility that the speaker of the *Sonnets* can be identified as Shakespeare himself and that they encode an actual relationship; if they do, then the lady, and the rival poet who makes a brief appearance in the sequence, might also be identifiable. The desire to know more about the historical Shakespeare has led readers to rummage amongst the *Sonnets* for hints of biographical information and, very often, to find things that are not there. As with Mr. W.H. , so with the dark lady;

there have been numerous nominees for the role but few of them convincing. Perhaps the favourite candidate has been Mary Fitton, although evidence suggests she was not in fact of dark-complexion. Mary Fitton was a lady-in-waiting in Elizabeth's court with whom William Herbert had a scandalous affair for which he was briefly imprisoned in 1601. Obviously, her candidacy strengthens the case of those who believe Herbert was Mr. W.H., although it also entails a rather late date of composition for many of the sonnets. The poet Aemilia Lanyer has also been proposed as the dark lady. Born into a family of court musicians, Aemilia Bassano was of mixed English-Jewish-Italian ancestry and therefore (presumably) dark. Brought up in aristocratic households, she was for a time the mistress of Henry Carey, Lord Hunsdon, who as Lord Chamberlain was the patron of Shakespeare's acting company. She became pregnant, and was married off in 1592 to her cousin Alphonso Lanyer, who was also a court musician. She had, obviously, theatrical connections. To relate her to any proposed Mr. W.H. is, however, an impossible task.

Fitton and Lanyer are conveniently to hand (both were around at about the right time, depending on what you think the right time was; both were connected to someone who was distantly, though problematically, connected to Shakespeare; both were sexually adventurous). However, there is no compelling evidence for either case. Against both women (especially Mary Fitton) is the remoteness of the probability of a sexual triangle that would include Shakespeare. Hunsdon organized Aemilia Bassano's marriage to avoid scandal and is hardly likely to have reacted with anything but hostility if she had carried on an affair with one of his servants (which Shakespeare technically was). An affair between Shakespeare and a lady-in-waiting in Elizabeth's court is even more improbable, given the rigidity of class attitudes; the idea that he could have shared Mary Fitton with one of the most prominent young aristocrats in the country and then publicized the affair in a sonnet sequence defies credibility.

The problem that all autobiographical interpretations of the *Sonnets* share is the inherent improbability of the transgression of social boundaries that any literal reading must assume. Such assumptions fit very well into the romanticized image of Shakespeare as a universal genius whose abilities were fully appreciated in his own time, but they do not fit with the realities of a society whose government repeatedly enacted sumptuary laws in an attempt to regulate the quality of clothing that different classes of people could wear in order to make visible the social distinctions that were fundamental to its understanding of itself. There was no meritocracy and Shakespeare was a mere professional, a poet and player. Also problematically, if the 'I' of the poems is identified with Shakespeare himself, how does this affect our response to the homoerotic elements of the sonnets addressed to the young man? This is, certainly, a difficult issue no matter how we read it, but the possibility that a mere poet and playwright would parade his erotic desire for a real and identifiable aristocrat seems remote indeed.

As I wrote earlier, I think that this concentration on the auto-biographical possibilities of the sonnets has largely been a waste of scholarly energy. It has also diverted attention away from what I think is the real creative significance of the poems. If we are to understand the sonnets as art we should understand them as fiction in the same way that we understand the plays as fiction. When Hamlet says 'O that this too too solid flesh would melt' (1.2.129) we do not assume that there is a direct relationship between the speaker's words and the author's experience. It is Hamlet who is thinking about the attractions of suicide, and while it is possible that Shakespeare at some time in his life contemplated suicide and certain that he grasped imaginatively Hamlet's state of mind, we do not confuse Hamlet with Shakespeare. I think the 'I' of the sonnets must be understood in a similar way. Even if real events do lie behind the *Sonnets*, they have been fictionalized into a complex artistic structure that has a richer range of potential meanings than any autobiographical reading could provide.

First, we can see *Shake-speare's Sonnets* as a work that violently challenged the values of the genre of the sonnet sequence as they were reflected in the conventions that had developed from Petrarchan origins into the fashionable clichés of the late Elizabethan period. In the *Sonnets* the unattainable ideal woman, a romantic fiction, is replaced first by a young man who may or may not be attainable, but who generates a range of often conflicting feelings and responses in the poems' speaker; and then by a woman who certainly is attainable, and who generates both desire and loathing in the speaker. Seen from this perspective, Shakespeare's sonnet sequence can be understood as his attempt to impose a different mood upon the genre. Second, in challenging the values of the genre Shakespeare is also challenging the values of those who made it fashionable, the values of the cultural elite of late sixteenth-century England – which was, of course, also the political elite. The *Sonnets* construct a myth in which the speaker-poet attempts to assert control over the powerful and attractive youth by offering him immortality through his poems – a myth of social restructuring, in a sense, that underscores the satirical intensity of many of these 'love' sonnets.

8

Reading Shakespeare's *Sonnets*: 1

Shakespeare's sequence of sonnets has attracted a far greater volume of commentary than both of the narrative poems together. As John Kerrigan notes in the introduction to his edition, however, 'much of the literature tends to lunacy and is dispensable'.[1] This lunacy comes about not just because of the desire of many readers to find Shakespeare himself in his sonnets and thus to fashion a biography from them, but also because the poems offer so many mysteries that there has been great temptation to find bizarre solutions. And yet after all this commentary, the mysteries (if in fact it was Shakespeare who wrote the sonnets; when and for whom he wrote them; what they might have to do with his own life; if the 'characters' can be identified; if he oversaw their publication and intended them to follow the order in which they appear; if that order embodies a coherent narrative) remain virtually unresolved. Recent scholars and editors have attempted to free the sonnets from some of the lunacy in a variety of ways. Some, like Stephen Booth and Helen Vendler, have offered readings based almost entirely on the formal properties of the poems.[2] Others, such as Peter Stallybrass and Heather Dubrow, have considered some ways in which the history of editing and scholarship itself may have distorted understanding of the poems.[3] Still others, like John Kerrigan and Katherine Duncan-Jones in introducing their editions of the poems, have striven to bring about a more reliable knowledge of the facts that can be ascertained about the original writing and reading of the sonnets. I shall not attempt a broad survey of this history, but address what is relevant to my present concerns.

Figuring out how to approach a sonnet sequence is always difficult, and it is more difficult with Shakespeare's sequence than with others. The poet's apparent act of arranging the poems in a particular order (assuming that it was the poet who did the ordering) leads the reader to expect some overall coherence of direction, a kind of plot, or at any rate a thematic progression or a shift from event to event or mood to mood. The title of Sidney's *Astrophil and Stella* hints that the sequence will explore the development of the relationship between the eponymous characters, and while this is, broadly speaking, what it does, it also leads the reader who looks for uniformity into doubts and frustrations. Shakespeare's sequence simply proclaims itself as *Sonnets*, and does not even identify its central characters for us, and therefore much remains obscure. Some readers have attempted to perceive a unifying 'story', and certainly there is the shadow of a narrative about a complex love triangle, but it is difficult to discern, amongst the gaps and discontinuities, a connected set of events that fit within the story, and a reading of the sonnets in the order in which they were printed can be like moving through a maze. There are many pairs of sonnets as well as some that are grouped into longer runs, and there are sonnets that can be connected with sonnets in other parts of the sequence, but any search for continuity is continually frustrated. The intention of the sequence is further obscured by the fact that it is concluded by 'A Lover's Complaint'; if we assume that Shakespeare did authorize the publication of the volume, then we must also assume that the 'Complaint' has some significance that relates it to the sonnets that precede it.

The generally-accepted theory is that the first 126 sonnets present the relationship between the poem's speaker and a youth or young man of higher rank while the following 28 present the relationship between the same speaker and an apparently sexually passionate woman of unconventional appearance and morals – the so-called 'dark lady'. The assumptions that underlie this theory are not unquestionable, however. The first 17 sonnets, sometimes known as the 'marriage' or 'procreation' sonnets, are clearly addressed to a youth, as are many individual sonnets amongst the 109 that follow them. There are, however, many others that give no hint of the identity or even the gender of the person to whom they are addressed, so while it is not illogical to assume that the entire sub-sequence is addressed to the same youth, it is also possible that the body of the *Sonnets* was never intended as a coherently-connected unity. The belief that these poems are addressed to a young aristocrat can also be questioned, since his rank is never made explicit; however, the speaker is keenly aware of distinctions of social class, and the assumption seems reasonable. The sub-sequence of 'dark lady' sonnets is briefer and holds together more tightly, but here too there are sonnets that fit uneasily into their context, most notably 146, Shakespeare's only overtly religious poem.

A further complication is that the sequential arrangement of the sonnets encourages a linear reading; we are led to assume, that is, that the poems represent an ordered time-sequence. This assumption is wrong, however, for sonnets 41 and 42 link the speaker, the youth and the mistress in a triangle of sexual desire and jealousy:

> That thou hast her, it is not all my grief,
> And yet it may be said I loved her dearly;
> That she hath thee is of my wailing chief,
> A loss in love that touches me more nearly.

(Sonnet 42)

These same events are the subject of sonnets 133, 134 and 144:

> Two loves I have, of comfort and despair,
> Which like two spirits do suggest me still.
> The better angel is a man right fair,
> The worser spirit a woman coloured ill.

(Sonnet 144)

This means that at least some events in the two sub-sequences occur simultaneously, so that any supposition about a coherent 'narrative' must take this into account.

Comparatively few readers are familiar with the entire sequence of *Shakespeare's Sonnets*, but most people know at least some of them from anthologies. An obvious question arises, given the complications I have outlined: can individual sonnets be understood if they are detached from the context of the sequence? Let us take sonnet 18. 'Shall I compare thee to a summer's day?' as an example, since it is probably the most generally familiar of the sonnets. As I noted earlier, anyone who reads it without any knowledge of its context will quite probably and quite reasonably assume that it is addressed by a male speaker to a woman. There is nothing in the poem to indicate the gender of either speaker or addressee, and the tone, diction and figurative language are what we might expect of a love poem conventionally written by a young man to his mistress. However, if we return sonnet 18 to its context, it comes at the end of a connected series of poems in which the (male) speaker is concerned to persuade a young man to marry in order to pass on his beauty and quality through the procreation of a child, and our understanding of the poem will necessarily be different. Is the reader who understood the poem to be addressed to a woman therefore wrong? We cannot say so, since the poem, detached from its context, is clearly open to such a reading: it presents itself as a fine if conventional love-poem. Replaced in its context it is subversive of convention, and some readers will find that disturbing. Perhaps that was Shakespeare's intention.

We do not know the circumstances of the writing of any of the sonnets. While it is possible that Shakespeare had from the outset the idea of producing a sequence along the lines of *Astrophil and Stella* it is also possible (and perhaps more likely) that the poems were originally written and circulated as independent texts or groupings of texts, serving a variety of purposes, and only arranged at a later date in the sequence that we now have. If that is the case it is possible that sonnet 18 and others like it were originally intended to be read as if addressed to a woman, and only later recontextualized to give them the radically different meaning that they now seem to have. Certainly, when the sonnets are read in sequence their cumulative power and the transgressive potential of their subject-matter add to their attraction, but as we have seen, it is not even certain that the ordering of the sequence is what Shakespeare actually intended, and even if it is as Shakespeare intended it, there are enough ambiguities and obscurities to make any reading problematic and unstable.

SONNET 1: A READING

Bearing in mind these essentially insoluble questions, I will begin by suggesting how a reading of a single sonnet might work, first by intensive examination of the sonnet, then by locating it within the sequence. Since any other choice would be arbitrary, I will address sonnet 1, even though there are many better-known sonnets. In itself it is not an outstanding sonnet, but its position demands attention:

> From fairest creatures we desire increase,
> That thereby beauty's rose might never die,
> But as the riper should by time decease,
> His tender heir might bear his memory;
> But thou contracted to thine own bright eyes,
> Feed'st thy light's flame with self-substantial fuel,
> Making a famine where abundance lies,
> Thyself thy foe, to thy sweet self too cruel.
> Thou that art now the world's fresh ornament
> And only herald to the gaudy spring,

Within thine own bud buriest thy content,
And, tender churl, mak'st waste in niggarding.
Pity the world, or else this glutton be,
To eat the world's due, by the grave and thee.

Rendered to a simple prose meaning, the sonnet says that the world
(the 'we' of line 1 presumably explicating itself as 'the world' of lines
9, 13 and 14) expects individuals who possess superior qualities to
have children in order to perpetuate those qualities. It exhorts the
self-absorbed young person whom it addresses to act to reproduce
himself before his beauty goes to waste. There is a lot more to it than
this, however.

I will first consider how the form of the sonnet structures this into an
argument. The rhyme-scheme of an English sonnet (*abab cdcd efef gg*)
implies an argument that will accumulate or intensify over the first
three quatrains, to be either summed up or challenged in the closing
couplet, in a structure of 4/4/4/2 or 12/2. However, the gram-
matical structure of sonnet 1 works against this, because the sonnet
consists of three sentences, (lines 1–8, 9–12, 13–14), suggesting
a structure of 8/4/2. The actual sense of the sonnet indicates yet
another structure: lines 1–4 make a general statement about what
the world expects of beautiful creatures, lines 5–12 describe how the
young man fails to live up to this expectation, and the final couplet
makes a proposal about how the young man could satisfy the
world's desire; this falls into a structure of 4/8/2. Thus the actual
movement of the sonnet works as a matter of counterpoint and
resistance, imparting a subtle complexity to what appeared to be
a simple statement.

This complexity is reflected in the language, which brings together
a number of different and in some ways competing discourses. The
word 'increase' has clear biblical echoes of God's command to his
creatures to increase and multiply, and implies a moral authority to
this need; what 'we' desire, that is, is in accordance with God's will.
Bound to this is the language of natural fertility: 'increase' implies
natural fruitfulness, and this suggestion is picked up by many words
and images in the poem: 'rose', 'riper', 'abundance', 'fresh', 'spring'
and 'bud'. The biblical and natural connotations reinforce each
other: it is both right and natural for the addressee to produce
a 'tender heir'. The word 'increase' also has commercial connotations
of profit and loss, however, which are picked up by 'contracted' and,
in line 12, by 'mak'st waste' and 'niggarding'. This meaning of

'increase' seems to be in conflict with the other meanings: is the addressee being urged to produce an heir because it is right and natural to do so, or is it because there are good material reasons to do so? Are the former meanings being used to mask the latter?

The ambiguity here is intensified if we ask other questions. Who is the speaker, whom is he addressing, and what is their relationship? As we have already seen, we cannot assume that the poem's voice directly represents the author, but it appears that the speaker is male. The addressee also seems, from 'His' in line 4 and 'tender churl' in line 12, to be male, but if this is so, the use of the word 'rose' in connection with a male addressee's beauty is strange, since it has (and had then) feminine associations. The word is emphasized in the quarto edition of the *Sonnets* by italicization and capitalization; it appears a dozen times in the sequence, sometimes in contexts where the rose's beauty is seen to be illusory or corrupt (its next appearance is in sonnet 35, where the addressee is reminded that 'Roses have thorns, and silver fountains mud'). The rose was, of course, the emblem of the Tudor family, and associated particularly with Queen Elizabeth. It was associated with feminine beauty, but also with the female genitalia; furthermore, 'rose' was a popular word for a prostitute, and indeed the Rose playhouse, erected in 1587, was so named because it was located in the gardens of a brothel.

The attitude of the speaker to a youth to whom he attaches the word 'rose' is not easy to assess, nor is their relationship. The phrase 'tender churl' suggests an intimacy between the two, but the poem distances the speaker by reducing his identity to a part of the 'we' that embodies received opinion, the opinion of 'the world'. The word 'churl', indeed, also raises a number of questions. It could mean 'miser', and that is certainly an appropriate meaning in the context, where the youth is accused of wasting his qualities by using them too sparingly. More common use of the word, however, attached it to a low-bred, boorish fellow, and it is difficult to see how these associations could be ignored. In fact, the word is used on only two other occasions in the *Sonnets*, and in both cases it contains a measure of contempt, referring to 'that churl Death' in sonnet 32, and in sonnet 69 to the thoughts of those who slander the youth. Here the speaker is teasing the youth: if he is a churl, he is a tender one, the phrase echoing the earlier 'tender heir'. If the youth is the speaker's social equal or his inferior, such teasing is easy to understand. But what if the youth is his social superior (as is surely implied by the sonnet's characterization of him as 'the world's fresh ornament' and its insistence on the need for him to pass on his abundance)? This would certainly make their relationship problematic.

There are other troubling aspects to the sonnet. The word 'increase' at the end of line 1 leads us to expect the rhyming word 'decrease' in line 3, but instead we get 'decease' – rather more startling in that it invites the youth to contemplate his own death. This idea is picked up in the word 'buriest', and compounded by the ugliness of the 'glutton' idea in the final couplet, in which the youth's refusal to give what he owes to the world is made to link self-cannibalism to the idea of being devoured by maggots in the grave. Indeed, there is a degree of sourness in the treatment of the youth's self-absorption; the phrase 'contracted to thine own bright eyes' implies that he has signed a marriage contract with himself, but the alternative meaning of 'contracted' implies that he has thereby diminished himself. I do not want to say that the speaker is not genuinely anxious about the danger of the loss to the world of the young man's qualities, and it could easily be argued that it is his own acute awareness of mortality that provokes him into an attempt to shock the youth into a realization of his irresponsibility. Nevertheless, the ambiguities I have indicated suggest an ironic distance between the speaker and his narcissistic subject.

I have by no means exhausted the possible ideas to be found in an intensive reading of sonnet 1. However, I want to draw attention to something that becomes evident when we consider the sonnet's position at the opening of the sequence, which is that it seems to contain nothing that identifies it as the introductory poem of a sonnet sequence. It is not self-conscious about its function as is, for example, the first sonnet of Sidney's *Astrophil and Stella*, where the speaker sets out to find literary ways of expressing his love, or the first sonnet of Spenser's *Amoretti*, which is a kind of dedication of the document constituted by the sonnets to the 'Angel' who is going to read them. Shakespeare's sonnet has none of this, yet in its intimation of ambiguities and evasions, of ironies and dark double meanings, it is entirely appropriate as an introduction to all that follows.

BREEDING IMMORTALITY

What follows immediately is a series of sonnets (1–17 are usually referred to as the 'marriage' or 'procreation' sonnets) in which the pressing need for the young man to beget an heir leads the speaker to urge him to marry. The ideas proffered in sonnet 1 are expanded and complicated in a number of ways. The speaker in the *Sonnets* is obsessed with the idea of time's destructive power, its violation of youth and beauty; in sonnet 2 alone he forces the young man to think about how age will 'dig deep trenches in [his] beauty's field', when his youth will be 'a tottered weed', and his beauty will be lost in his 'deep-sunken eyes'. These are ugly images, and while they reflect the speaker's intense awareness of the ruins of time, there is something callous accompanying the urgency with which he forces the youth to observe them. These repellent ideas are countered by the suggestion that to reproduce one's own image is to achieve a kind of immortality, as if a child is less a separate entity than a continuation of its parent, and therefore literally a means of defeating time: 'This were to be new made when thou art old, / And see thy blood warm when thou feel'st it cold'. The speaker tries to reduce the youth to a state of existential terror through repeated images of an encroaching 'hideous winter', 'Sap checked with frost, and lusty leaves quite gone, / Beauty o'er-snowed, and bareness everywhere' (sonnet 5). There is a cruelty in the speaker's concentration on the ravages of time that emulates the cruelty of time itself.

The idea that the young man should reproduce his image in the child is offered as a means of overcoming time: 'This were to be made new when thou art old, / And see thy blood warm when thou feel'st it cold' (sonnet 2). To bolster the implications of this argument the speaker proffers what we might think of as an argument from nature. The images of decay with which he attempts to shock the youth are all taken from nature, and at one level the youth is being chided about his self-love because it is unnatural. Indeed, the youth's concentration upon himself, 'having traffic with [him]self alone', is seen in sonnet 4 in terms of masturbation; the speaker asks, 'why dost thou spend / Upon thyself thy beauty's legacy?' The word 'spend' picks up the language of commerce noted in the opening sonnet, but it was also an Elizabethan euphemism for ejaculation. The youth's self-love, in other words, is sterile, spent on nothing, since his seed makes no one fertile. His spending should have the purpose of producing his image. He needs a wife.

What might appear disturbing about this, however, is the fact that the youth is being encouraged to redirect his love away from himself to an image of himself in the male child he will produce, not to the wife he will marry. She, indeed, is deprived of any identity:

Now is the time that face should form another,
Whose fresh repair if now thou not renewest

> Thou dost beguile the world, unbless some mother.
> For where is she so fair whose uneared womb
> Disdains the tillage of thy husbandry?
>
> (Sonnet 3)

Fundamental to this is an ugly set of patriarchal assumptions. No doubt it was true at the time that 'some mother' would feel blessed if she could produce a child for this beautiful, noble youth, but the off-hand assumption that any appropriate woman will do, and will be overjoyed to offer her womb as a field to be ploughed, is certainly offensive to modern sensitivities. The fact is, of course, that contrary to what Shakespeare's romantic comedies might suggest, aristocratic marriage was not a matter of romantic love, but a political or economic transaction that had the purpose of ensuring the continuation of the blood-line and thus the safe passage of the family name and property. As Catherine Bates writes: 'the conjugal unit came to be regarded as the bedrock of aristocratic perpetuity, a means of uniting families, of producing and legitimizing heirs, of regulating and ensuring the trans-mission of wealth through successive generations. Every effort was therefore made to guarantee the procreation of legitimate male heirs'.[4]

The language in which the speaker challenges the youth's refusal to perpetuate his image is in sonnet 4 borrowed from the legal discourse related to the handing down of property:

> Unthrifty loveliness, why dost thou spend
> Upon thyself thy beauty's legacy?
> Nature's bequest gives nothing, but doth lend,
> And being frank, she lends to those are free.

The youth's neglect of his natural duty is represented metaphori-cally as a failure to pass on property, but the connection between propagation and property is in fact more than metaphorical:

> Who lets so fair a house fall to decay,
> Which husbandry in honour might uphold,
> Against the stormy gusts of winter's day
> And barren rage of death's eternal cold?
> O, none but unthrifts, dear my love, you know.
> You had a father; let your son say so.
>
> (Sonnet 13)

This is all about fathers and sons, not about husbands and wives, and it is about Elizabethan anxiety over the transference of name and property. These sonnets reveal a deep permeation of the language and values of morality and nature (or, more precisely, agriculture) by the language and values of commerce. The reign of Elizabeth saw the beginning of what Lawrence Stone has called a 'crisis of the aristocracy'.[5] The roles of the classes were changing, and one of the major threats to the traditional authority of the landed and propertied aristocracy and gentry came from the growing power of the merchant class. New money, that is, threatened the privilege of established power which had long been mystified as both natural and right.

The sonnets' fusion of the language of nature with the language of commerce thus sets up a contradiction and the potential for irony. The procreation sonnets state and restate the speaker's argument with an insistence that certainly implies a genuine anxiety that the youth should take the necessary steps to secure the future of his aristocratic birthright. At the same time, their use of the language of those forces that most threatened the young man's class and community might seem to mock the young man. We need, therefore, to try to assess the tone and perspective of the sonnets. What we find, I think, is that these constantly shift, and that from sonnet to sonnet an illusion of continuity and consistency is offered to us through the semblance of a narrative, while at the same time it is constantly undercut by ambiguity and indeterminacy. To address this problem we first need to try to describe the speaker.

During the first nine sonnets the speaker reveals nothing that allows us any sense of his identity; the focus is exclusively on the young man. Indeed, at the start the speaker presents himself, as we have seen, as the voice of a community: 'From fairest creatures *we* desire increase'; in the same sonnet this community seems to be defined as 'the world', and in sonnet 9 (where this phrase appears five times) he is still showing how 'the world' will respond if the young man fails to break out of his self-absorption. 'The world' here appears to have an ambiguous meaning: its obvious sense in the line 'beauty's waste hath in the world an end' refers to the natural world in which beauty flourishes and decays. However, when we consider the probable identity of those most likely to mourn the waste of the young man 'the world' might refer more narrowly to those who share the belief that the future of the propertied class must be ensured, in which case these sonnets would seem to express a conservative and impersonal view of hierarchy and hereditary right. However, in sonnet 10 the speaker suddenly emerges as an individual 'I' with an agenda of his own: 'O, change thy thought, that I may change my mind!' Public gives way to private as the speaker's own response becomes central; furthermore, he implies that his opinion might actually have some effect on the youth: 'Make thee another self for love of me / That beauty still may live in thine or thee'.

In sonnet 12 'I' appears four times, and this sudden large-scale intrusion of the first-person pronoun coincides with a number of shifts in emphasis and interest. In the earlier sonnets the speaker seeks to force the youth to acknowledge the harsh reality of the passage of time in order to disturb him into performing his duty to the world, but it now becomes clear that the poems are just as much about the speaker's own terror:

> When I do count the clock that tells the time,
> And see the brave day sunk in hideous night;
> When I behold the violet past prime,
> And sable curls ensilvered o'er with white;
> When lofty trees I see barren of leaves...
> Then of thy beauty do I question make,
> That thou among the wastes of time must go.

In this context the conventional emblem of 'Time's scythe' takes on a particularly sinister cast: that scythe appears in the *Sonnets* on three more occasions, but the personified figure of Time is much more dominant, appearing at least 30 times, and usually inflicting physical damage on objects of beauty or as the ironic mocker of man's aspirations.

As time emerges as the enemy of beauty, it also emerges as the enemy of the speaker, who begins to present himself as the preserver of beauty. Thus, in sonnet 15 the speaker sees himself in battle with time to preserve the young man: 'And all in war with time for love of you, / As he takes from you, I engraft you new'. The word 'engraft' here is pivotal. It picks up the discourse of agriculture that the speaker has used to urge the youth to 'breed', but it also suggests the act of writing, through which the speaker (now revealed as a poet) will renew the young man. Sonnets 16 and 17 focus on the act of writing; in 16 the poet speaks of his 'barren rhyme', as if it had no power of renewal, but in the couplet of 17 it is given a reproductive power equal to that of nature: 'But were some child of yours alive that time, / You should live twice: in it, and in my rhyme'. By the end of the sequence of procreation sonnets the idea of procreation has disappeared completely from the poet's programme for the young man: 'Yet do thy worst, old time; despite thy wrong / My love shall in my verse ever live young' (sonnet 19).

I have dwelt at some length on the procreation sonnets partly because they constitute the longest run of clearly connected sonnets in the sequence written to the youth, but also because they indicate some of the radical departures Shakespeare made from the sonnet conventions that developed in the last two decades of Elizabeth's reign, and because they plant the seeds of many of the difficult issues that make the *Sonnets* such a challenging text. There is little in the knotty struggle with the ideas of duty, property and procreation that the Elizabethan reader, accustomed to the tired conventions of Petrarchism, would have expected to find in a sonnet sequence. Furthermore, in the first nine sonnets the restrained voice of the poem speaks from a generalized position of social awe and, presumably, social inferiority about the young man's duty, and there is little concern with the speaker's personal feeling. In sonnet 10, however, something new emerges along with the 'I'. There is, first, an attempt by the speaker to exert control over the young man, implied in the line 'Make thee another self for love of me', for the poetic power he subsequently reveals as the means of immortalizing the young man is the only power he has to counter the young man's social power. The manner in which he exerts and expresses this power shifts a great deal of weight on to the implications of that word 'love'.

GENDER-BENDING

In sonnet 13 the speaker addresses the young man as 'love' and 'dear my love'. The most controversial question to have haunted the history of the reception of the *Sonnets* has concerned the nature of the love expressed for their youthful subject. I have already discussed some of the problems related to sonnet 18, the first in the sequence to open itself up to anything like a Petrarchan reading; its presentation of the (male) speaker's clearly 'romantic' feelings for his (in this context male) object and its location immediately after a series of sonnets that have been concerned with procreation rather than love are surely intended to unsettle the reader who is still seeking the easy certainties of Petrarchan convention. Any reader who tries to resist the implications of sonnet 18 is confronted with the full-frontal attack of sonnet 20:

> A woman's face with nature's own hand painted
> Hast thou, the master mistress of my passion;
> A woman's gentle heart, but not acquainted
> With shifting change as is false women's fashion;
> An eye more bright than theirs, less false in rolling,
> Gilding the object whereupon it gazeth;
> A man in hue all hues in his controlling,
> Which steals men's eyes and women's souls amazeth.
> And for a woman wert thou first created
> Till nature as she wrought thee fell a-doting,
> And by addition me of thee defeated
> By adding one thing to my purpose nothing.
> But since she pricked thee out for women's pleasure,
> Mine be thy love and thy love's use their treasure.

The least that can be said about this sonnet is that its treatment of sexual relationships and gender division is ambivalent, and it has been the source of an acute scholarly and critical discomfort that is a concentration of the chronic discomfort felt about the sequence as a whole.

The sonnet is equivocal in the extreme. The young man is described, fairly unambiguously, as the object of the speaker's passion, but not because he is a man, since it appears that the things about him that attract the speaker are those things that make him most like a woman: an effeminate appearance, a Petrarchan mildness of temperament and brightness of eye. The definition of these feminine qualities is somewhat negated, however, by an underlying misogyny: the young man's face is painted by nature, implying that women paint their own; the feelings of women's hearts, however gentle, are fickle, as are their eyes, constantly looking for a new object. The qualities for which he is praised, that is, are feminine qualities that women might possess if they were not women. The last five lines of the poem are, surely, a joke. We are offered the idea of inept nature bungling the job of creating a potentially ideal woman by providing 'her' with a 'thing', rendering the result sexually unattainable by the speaker. The final line draws a distinction between 'love' and 'love's use', the former being a complex mix of friendship, admiration and service, the latter being sexual union. The conclusion is, surely, a rueful acceptance that any sexual relationship between the two men is impossible. To be sure, many of the remaining sonnets addressed to the young man use the language of love, but the effect is of a radical realignment of Petrarchan conventions to serve a quite different kind of relationship. How is it to be characterized?

Starting with John Benson's pirated volume of 1640, there is a long history of editorial attempts through verbal changes, especially of pronouns, to make the sonnets to the young man appear to be addressed to a woman. This is paralleled by a scholarly history that has often struggled to downplay or explain away any suggestion of homosexual desire in the *Sonnets*, usually by offering specialized interpretations of Renaissance 'love' between men as a kind of idealized friendship. One cannot, of course, solve a problem by falsifying it, and the more liberated attitudes of the last couple of decades have made it possible to say that 'Shakespeare produced not only extraordinary amatory verse but the grand masterpiece of homoerotic poetry'; or, indeed, that Shakespeare was himself unashamedly homosexual.[6] However, while it is easier to sympathize with readers who want to enlist Shakespeare in support of a marginalized lifestyle than with those who want to suppress any indication of unorthodoxy in his writings, I do not think it is possible to derive any information at all about his sexual orientation from the *Sonnets*.

As I noted earlier, I think we have to consider the *Sonnets* to be fictions in the same way as the plays are fictions, and I do not think we can claim the homoerotic desire of the *Sonnets* as Shakespeare's own. This is not to say that Shakespeare did not understand it, because clearly he did. But he understood a great many things, and it is as illogical to say that some of his writings are unashamedly homosexual as it is to say that others are unashamedly suicidal. What we *can* say is that he understood and loved ambiguity in life as much as he loved it in language. Sonnets 1 to 17 work and rework the speaker's attempts to show the young man his duty to propagate, through a set of arguments that link duty with the ravages of time; their grim undertones are suddenly defused by the brilliant playful energies of sonnets 18 and 20. The sunny youth, presented in sonnet 18 through images that reflect the Petrarchan standard, is turned into something genuinely wonderful in sonnet 20, a living paradox or oxymoron, a near-perfect 'master-mistress' who lacks nothing, but possesses a 'thing' that baffles the speaker: his male sex makes him useless. The poem allows the speaker's desire for the young man at the same time as it mockingly denies the fulfillment of that desire.

We might compare this to Orsino's response in *Twelfth Night* to Viola disguised as Cesario.

> they shall yet belie thy happy years
> That say thou art a man. Diana's lip
> Is not more smooth and rubious; thy small pipe
> Is as the maiden's organ, shrill and sound,
> And all is semblative a woman's part.

(1.4.29–33)

Orsino is observing what he believes to be a young man, but what he sees is the femininity of Viola underneath her disguise as Cesario. Viola insists more than once on her own ambiguity: 'I am not that I play' (1.5.164); 'I am not what I am' (3.1.132). For Shakespeare's audience the puzzle was complicated by the fact that when Orsino saw the girl Viola through the boy Cesario he also saw the boy actor playing Viola playing Cesario. The first readers of the sonnets were fully aware of the wonderful and strange attractions and contradictions of this stage figure, and Shakespeare's sonnet, surely, plays with this awareness. Perhaps there is a warning here about taking too literally the implications about the speaker's love for the youth in the account in the sonnets that follow it.

IS LOVE LOVE?

The 'love' between the speaker and the young man can be understood in another way. In a very influential article Arthur Marotti has argued that the language of love in sonnet sequences is really the language of 'courtship' in its most literal sense: that the sonnet sequences encoded the poets' urgent pursuit of patronage within the demanding and competitive environment of the Elizabethan court. The sequences were, according to Marotti, 'the occasion for socially, economically and politically importunate Englishmen to express their unhappy condition in the context of a display of literary mastery'.[7] If we consider Shakespeare's *Sonnets* in this light we can see potential explanations for a number of puzzling elements. For example, much of the language of love is in them tied to the vocabulary of commerce; if we think of writing as the 'business' of the professional poet, then sonnets can be understood as a kind of currency that passes between himself and his patron. We can also grasp why the intrusion of the 'rival poet' is such a serious matter for Shakespeare's poet, since it is his living that is under threat from this interloper.

A number of sonnets do indeed seem to open themselves up to such an interpretation. Consider sonnet 29, which sees the speaker in a state of great dejection, 'in disgrace with fortune and men's eyes', that is, lacking all favour. The social envy that lies behind his 'outcast state' takes in the expectations of others ('Wishing me like to one more rich in hope'), the patronage that others enjoy ('like him with friends possessed'), even the talent of others ('Desiring this man's art, and that man's scope'). He pulls himself out of this state of anguish by thinking of his patron: 'For thy sweet love remembered such wealth brings / That then I scorn to change my state with kings'. 'Wealth' here takes on a very ambiguous resonance if we think of it in terms of patronage rather than of love. Sonnet 79, concerning the rival poet, ends with a commercial metaphor: 'Then thank him not for that which he doth say, / Since what he owes thee thou thyself dost pay'. His disappointment at being displaced from the young man's favour is seen in similar mercantile terms: 'I found – or thought I found – you did exceed / The barren favour of a poet's debt' (sonnet 83). In sonnet 87 he gives up his claim on the youth, characterizing their relationship entirely in the language of commerce and exchange:

> Farewell – thou art too dear for my possessing,
> And like enough thou know'st thy estimate.
> The charter of thy worth gives thee releasing,
> My bonds in thee are all determinate.
> For how do I hold thee but by thy granting,
> And for that riches where is my deserving?
> The cause of this fair gift in me is wanting,
> And so my patent back again is swerving.

It is a little risky to take this argument too far, since the language of love in Elizabethan poetry was often closely allied to the language of material possession; nevertheless, what Marotti revealed about sonnet sequences clearly adds an important dimension to our understanding of Shakespeare's. There is, however, another way to approach the question of what this love is.

Whatever lies behind the expression of love in the sonnets to the young man there can be no denying that they employ the discourse

of passionate, idealizing love. It is easy to multiply examples, but
the widely-admired sonnet 116 can stand for many others:

> Let me not to the marriage of true minds
> Admit impediments. Love is not love
> Which alters when it alteration finds,
> Or bends with the remover to remove.
> O no, it is an ever-fixed mark
> That looks on tempests and is never shaken;
> It is the star to every wand'ring barque,
> Whose worth's unknown although his height be taken.
> Love's not time's fool, though rosy lips and cheeks
> Within his bending sickle's compass come;
> Love alters not with his brief hours and weeks,
> But bears it out even to the edge of doom.
> If this be error and upon me proved,
> I never writ, nor no man ever loved.

The sonnet makes a powerful statement for a human love that is
transcendent, not to be changed by the vagaries of circumstance or
time, and its couplet suggests that the speaker sees his own love in
such terms, enduring and unalterable. Taken out of its context it
gives no indication of the specific relationship explored in the sonnets,
and could simply be a noble, abstract statement about the possibility
of true love. Within the sequence, however, it rings oddly false in
that it makes its claims for the value of fidelity within the context of
a relationship in which both participants have been unfaithful. The
reader will remember sonnets 33–6, in which the speaker expressed
his disappointment at the youth's infidelity in strong terms: 'No
more be grieved at that which thou hast done: / Roses have thorns
and silver fountains mud' (sonnet 35). We might also note that when
the speaker chides the youth for his affair with the woman (40–2) he
is being somewhat disingenuous, since his own relationship with
her presumably also constitutes infidelity to the youth.

However we consider it, the meaning of 'love' in the *Sonnets* is
problematic. In sonnet 144 the speaker begins, 'Two loves I have of
comfort and despair', referring to the 'man right fair', and the
'female evil'. That opening statement is ambiguous: does it mean
that one love gives comfort, the other despair, or does it mean that
both give both comfort and despair? In this sonnet at least, he gets
little comfort from either, and I think that the same can be said for
the sequence as a whole. The problem lies with the word 'love' itself:

the love for the woman that he describes, as we will shortly see, is an addictive desire indistinguishable from what most (including the speaker, as he demonstrates in sonnet 129), would think of as lust, but he usually refers to it as love. He does not find a different name for his feeling for the youth. It *is* different, of course, but it is not quite what the speaker wants it to be.

In sonnets 1–17 the speaker identifies and demonstrates the youth's narcissism and tries to get him to turn outward to a socially creative marriage. In 18 and 19 he begins the open declaration of his own love. We might ask how he can love someone whose egregious self-absorption he has so clearly delineated. The answer appears to be that he deceives himself. In sonnet 14 he reads in the youth's eyes 'such art / As truth and beauty shall together thrive / If from thyself to store thou would convert'. The triumph of truth and beauty depends on the youth turning from himself to provision for the future. In sonnet 101 he presents the youth as a Platonic amalgam of truth and beauty: 'Both truth and beauty on my love depends'. This suggests that the youth has indeed turned outward from himself, but nothing in the intervening sonnets gives the reader reason to think so, for over and over the youth is revealed as dissolute and selfish. The speaker's error is to confuse beauty with truth, for if the youth is a paragon of the former, he shows little of the latter.

One can discern two opposing motions in the sonnets to the youth. Some present the love-object as glorious and gracious, as does sonnet 18, or sonnets 53 and 54, which attempt to locate a fusion of truth and beauty in the youth. Sometimes the speaker exhibits a feeling of joyful security in their relationship, as in 25, where he says 'Then happy I, that love and am beloved / Where I may not remove nor be removed'. However, many more sonnets present the speaker's experience as painful, fearful of betrayal, and conscious of his own inferiority. There are frequent attempts at denial or concealment, as he makes light of or takes responsibility for the young man's dissipated behaviour, reflected in an anxious adulatory style that serves the power, wealth and beauty of aristocracy (as in 69 and 70 where he defends the youth against the slanders of others) and yet is sometimes undercut by an irony that suggests that he knows more than he says.

Consider sonnet 34, which presents something not quite like the perfect summer's day of sonnet 18:

Why didst thou promise such a beauteous day
And make me travel forth without my cloak,

> To let base clouds o'ertake me in my way,
> Hiding thy bravery in their rotten smoke?

Some betrayal by the young man is hinted at in this poem and the one that follows it, but in the latter the speaker takes upon himself part of the responsibility for the injury done to him: 'I an accessory needs must be / To that sweet thief which sourly robs from me'. In sonnet 40, where the nature of another betrayal is made more explicit, he uses the same figure of speech: 'I do forgive thy robb'ry, gentle thief, / Although thou steal thee all my poverty'. 'Sweet thief' is an oxymoron, and while it could be considered mild teasing, the pain it obscures is real. The youth, indeed, seems rather more super- ficial than the speaker is willing to concede; in sonnets 83 and 84 the speaker defends the merits of his own plain praise of the youth in comparison to the rhetorical excesses of others, but undermines his own argument by an acknowledgement of the youth's craving for flattery: 'You to your beauteous blessings add a curse, / Being fond on praise, which makes your praises worse'.

Underlying the speaker's fear of being cut off from his love is his sense of his own social inferiority. Although the rank of the youth is never made explicit, the language frequently suggests a gulf between the two: 'Lord of my love, to whom in vassalage / Thy merit hath my duty strongly knit' (sonnet 26). To describe a love- relationship as a hierarchical one between lady and servant was a convention of Petrarchan poetry, and it could be argued that Shakespeare intends no more than that here, but the particular words he uses (lord, vassal) have strong social suggestiveness. Again, in sonnet 37, the terms he uses suggest such a distinction between the two:

> I, made lame by fortune's dearest spite,
> Take all my comfort of thy worth and truth;
> For whether beauty, birth, or wealth, or wit,
> Or any of these all, or all, or more,
> Entitled in thy parts do crowned sit,
> I make my love engrafted to this store.

Given the earlier accusations of betrayal, there is some irony in the claim about the young man's worth and truth, but they are expounded in terms of social privilege.

Which is the most characteristic element of a rose, its flower or its thorn? Since the speaker is well aware of the young man's thorns, and taking into account his many anxieties about their relationship, it would appear that he can only continue to insist on the young man's 'truth' by deceiving himself. In sonnet 57 he admits as much: 'So true a fool is love that in your will, / Though you do anything, he thinks no ill'. In fact, the speaker does not much like the idea of being the victim of deception; as he says in sonnet 92, 'Thou mayst be false, and yet I know it not,' and he goes on in the sonnet that follows it:

> So shall I live supposing thou art true
> Like a deceived husband; so love's face
> May still seem love to me, though altered new –
> Thy looks with me, thy heart in other place.

This is a hypothetical situation in which he imagines the youth deceiving him, and yet he knows that the youth has, indeed deceived him on other occasions – in other words, he colludes in his own deception. There is, I think, an increasing sourness as the sequence progresses, as if the struggle to maintain the evasions necessary to maintain the love are becoming increasingly wearying:

> O, what a mansion have those vices got
> Which for their habitation chose out thee,
> Where beauty's veil doth cover every blot
> And all things turns to fair that eyes can see!

(Sonnet 95)

It is this frustrated struggle to recognize the deceptions that are necessary to maintain the illusion of human love that most closely connects the sonnets written to the young man to those written to the 'dark lady'.

9
Reading Shakespeare's *Sonnets*: 2

THE 'BLACK' MISTRESS

Sonnet 127 initiates a new (though associated) series that concerns the speaker's relationship with a woman who has become known as the 'dark lady', though this phrase occurs nowhere in Shakespeare's poems. In fact, the phrase obscures what Shakespeare actually does say about the woman: that her beauty is 'black'. Sonnet 127 explores this idea at witty length, and it is repeated in sonnet 130 where the woman's hair is described as 'black wires', in sonnet 131 where her black is 'fairest in my judgment's place', and in sonnet 132 where the speaker is willing to 'swear beauty herself is black'. The woman's colour is mentioned only once again in the sequence, in sonnet 147, when she is pronounced 'as black as hell'. Shakespeare has made a clear effort to establish her 'blackness' early in the sequence, so it must be of some importance. What might the speaker intend by using the word 'black'?

Amongst some of those who have read the sonnets as auto-biographical there have been suggestions that the sonnet mistress was literally black-skinned (and unconvincing attempts to identify her as a London prostitute named Lucy Negro), but the more generally accepted view has been that 'black' simply means that the woman was dark-haired, dark-eyed, dark-complexioned. However, some recent criticism has treated this milder reading of 'black' as a kind of evasion, akin to the long-standing evasion of the potential homosexual content of the sonnets to the youth. Margreta de Grazia argues that editors and critics have mis-identified the true 'scandal' of these sonnets, which is that they embody Shakespeare's own desire for a black mistress; while Linda Boose asks 'Why is the sonnet woman's "black" always referred to its other connotative possibilities and never to its racial one? And why do we insistently refer to her as a "lady" when the sonnets themselves never do?'[1] These are important issues, and it is not necessary to be in complete agreement with these critics for one to recognize how frequently Shakespeare has been protected by literary history from any imputation that he might be something other than a spokesman for established values.

The question of how literally the woman's blackness should be taken is not finally answerable, but one thing about this group of sonnets appears clear from the outset: they are intended to challenge convention on a number of levels. They challenge both in attitude and content the concepts of love, beauty, virtue, will and desire associated with Petrarchan conventions. In doing so they also challenge the social and aesthetic values that underlie them – that is, they challenge the values of the Elizabethan and Jacobean elite. In this they are subversive, a fact that might well explain Shakespeare's failure to publish them at the height of the Elizabethan sonnet vogue, and the apparent lack of interest in them when they were finally published.

Whatever one takes 'black' to mean, sonnet 127 uncompromisingly proposes a contentious definition of beauty:

In the old age black was not counted fair,
Or if it were, it bore not beauty's name;
But now is black beauty's successive heir,
And beauty slandered with a bastard shame:
For since each hand hath put on nature's power,
Fairing the foul with art's false borrowed face,
Sweet beauty hath no name, no holy bower,
But is profaned, if not lives in disgrace.
Therefore my mistress' eyes are raven-black,
Her brow so suited, and they mourners seem
At such who, not born fair, no beauty lack,
Sland'ring creation with a false esteem.
   Yet so they mourn, becoming of their woe,
   That every tongue says beauty should look so.

The speaker offers up a 'modern' definition of beauty in opposition to the 'fair' beauty valued in the past. He does not tell us when 'the old age' ended, but it is interesting to note that in *Love's Labour's Lost* (1593–1595) Biron is clearly going against orthodoxy in his love of a dark lady, and the King mocks him for it: 'Black is the badge of hell, / The hue of dungeons and the style of night' (4.3.250–1). There is, indeed, an element of bravado underlying the argument in this sonnet; we are informed that 'every tongue' declares 'black beauty' triumphant, but we only have the speaker's word for it.

The poem (and thus the sub-sequence it introduces) begins with the exploration of a set of paradoxes. 'Black' is an antonym of 'fair', since 'black' refers to darkness and 'fair' refers to light, so black could not logically be counted fair in any age. But fair also contains a positive aesthetic value judgement, and therefore black must be aesthetically negative, that is, ugly. According to the poem, however, 'fair' beauty is now counted illegitimate, made suspect because it can be counterfeited with cosmetics (significantly, it is art, usurping nature's purpose, that creates the counterfeit). This means, presumably, that the real 'fair' cannot be distinguished from the counterfeit 'fair' and therefore neither has value. What, in that case, does 'fairing the foul' mean? What is the 'foul'? Like 'black', it is an antonym of 'fair', which implies a resemblance between 'black' and 'foul', but 'fairing the foul' cannot mean 'making the black fair', since 'black' has been identified as the new standard that has displaced both the fair and the foul-made-fair. The poem confuses established meanings and elevates black into the aesthetic positive. In doing so it raises a further question, since 'fair' implies moral as well as aesthetic worth, and on such a scale black must be morally negative, the 'badge of hell'. The sonnet's elaboration of the idea of blackness constitutes, in effect, an assault on received hierarchies of value, implying that their foundation is without substance.

The reader of sonnet 127 might well be led to believe that its urgent advocacy of the value of black is a statement of the strength of the speaker's love of his dark mistress. Sonnet 128 appears to warrant such a reading, representing as it does the speaker's erotic excitement as he observes her playing the virginals and imagines himself enjoying the same physical attentions as her instrument. However, there are intriguing ambiguities in this sonnet. The speaker says 'I envy those jacks that nimble leap / To kiss the tender inward of thy hand'. The jacks are the keys of the instrument the woman is playing, and the idea seems innocent enough. But, 'jacks' could refer also to young men, and this potential play in the word gives a clear double meaning to the reiteration of the idea in the poem's couplet: 'Since saucy jacks so happy are in this, / Give them thy fingers, me thy lips to kiss'. The subtle insinuation of the possibility that the woman is promiscuous imparts a further potential ambiguity to the activity of her hands on 'dead wood'. The erotic desire in this poem is problematic because it confuses the boundary between love and lust.

The sonnet that follows it is the most powerful in the sequence, and is almost terrifying as the erotic ambiguities in the two preceding sonnets clarify themselves into a kind of deep loathing:

> Th'expense of spirit in a waste of shame
> Is lust in action; and till action, lust
> Is perjured, murd'rous, bloody, full of blame,
> Savage, extreme, rude, cruel, not to trust,
> Enjoyed no sooner but despised straight,
> Past reason hunted; and no sooner had
> Past reason hated as a swallowed bait
> On purpose laid to make the taker mad;
> Mad in pursuit and in possession so,
> Had, having, and in quest to have, extreme;
> A bliss in proof and proved, a very woe;
> Before, a joy proposed; behind, a dream.
>   All this the world well knows, yet none knows well
>   To shun the heaven that leads men to this hell.

This poem clearly describes the consequence of sexual intercourse, something not encountered in earlier sonnet sequences, which were concerned with the frustration arising from the unavailability of consummation. The speaker here generalizes his own erotic appetites into a statement of universal lust locked into a horrific cycle of desire, fulfilment and despair. We are familiar with the commercial connotations of the word 'expense' from the earliest sonnets, but this poem suggests that all sexual activity is a matter of spending rather than earning, eroding physical energy as it diminishes the soul. Desire within the imagination of the lover turns him into a brute who will use any persuasion from trickery to violence to achieve his end, 'lust in action'. Consummation of his lust does not lead to satisfaction but to feelings of shame, which do not, however, prevent him from seeking climax once again. The poem's structure enacts this sexual movement, building from the violent and deceitful pressures of 'perjured' lust, to the 'possession' of lust in action, to the woe of lust 'proved'. The peculiar reverse ordering of 'had, having and in quest to have' suggests a fatal compulsion in which the having leads to the desire to have again in a shameful vicious circle. The poem's couplet, however, does not propose a solution, but accepts as inevitable the sexual imprisonment of men.

The implications of the sonnet's couplet are deeply misogynistic. The term 'hell' was at the time a common term for the female sexual organ, and feminine beauty ('heaven') is here understood as a trap. The man who penetrates that heaven finds himself in hell. In terms of traditional Christian teaching about the Fall and about human sexuality this was not new, but Shakespeare's account has a distinctive intensity to it. If we see these three sonnets as forming a sequence, the speaker has moved from a spirited defence of the unconventional nature of his mistress' beauty to a sickened suggestion that she is the cause at least of his spiritual affliction, and possibly of his damnation. Most readers will be relieved after all this to encounter sonnet 130, which combines a statement of the speaker's love for the woman with a realistic assessment of her appearance. On one level this sonnet jokes about once-fashionable Petrarchan clichés, offering a 'real' woman in place of the golden-haired rose-cheeked goddess. The woman provokes in the speaker a passionate desire that he sometimes calls love. He knows that she is not beautiful in any conventional sense, so he dismisses the conventions and redefines beauty. However the joke rebounds against the speaker, for he endures greater suffering at the hands of this hot, available woman than the Petrarchan lover ever did from his cold, distant mistress.

It is clear that these sonnets work on a number of levels: they function primarily as an analysis of the pain of erotic attraction, but they also offer a challenge to established cultural values. If we consider them first as love poems, sonnet 131 provides an interesting connection to the sonnets to the young man:

> Thou art as tyrannous so as thou art
> As those whose beauties proudly make them cruel,
> For well thou know'st to my dear doting heart
> Thou art the fairest and most precious jewel.

The opening lines refer to the cruel beauties of Petrarchan convention, but they are a reminder too of the speaker's treatment at the hands of the young man, with whom the black mistress is now equated in her power to do tyrannous harm. It is totally appropriate that the woman and the young man should have an affair (sonnets 133 and 134), in effect both betraying the speaker at the same time. The fundamental concern of the sequence as a whole can thus be seen not so much as the actions of its egocentric or cynical love-objects, as the tormented state of mind of the speaker, who is fully aware of what is happening to him, but incapable of escaping from it.

It is the sense that the speaker is trapped in what he knows to be depravity that gives these late sonnets their peculiar power. He says to the woman, 'In nothing art thou black save in thy deeds' (sonnet 131), presumably referring to her promiscuity. When she and the youth begin their affair the speaker makes her responsible for it, describes her as a predator: 'Me from myself thy cruel eye hath taken, / And my next self thou harder hast engrossed. / Of him, myself, and thee I am forsaken' (sonnet 133). The idea that she has separated him from his self (meaning both the youth and his own true nature) suggests also that his true nature ought to be in control. Why isn't it? He blames her for ensnaring him, thereby displacing his own guilt on to her – that is, her outward blackness, which he associates with her inner state, is also a reflection of his own inner darkness, his will-ful self-blinding, which he ruefully acknowledges in sonnet 137, though even here he tries to externalize the blame: 'Thou blind fool love, what dost thou to mine eyes / That they behold and see not what they see?' Sonnet 138, however, makes clear that he is fully complicit in his own corruption:

> When my love swears that she is made of truth
> I do believe her though I know she lies,
> That she might think me some untutored youth
> Unlearned in the world's false subtleties.
> Thus vainly thinking that she thinks me young,
> Although she knows my days are past the best,
> Simply I credit her false-speaking tongue;
> On both sides thus is simple truth suppressed.
> But wherefore says she not she is unjust,
> And wherefore say not I that I am old?
> O, love's best habit is in seeming trust,
> And age in love, loves not to have years told.
>   Therefore I lie with her, and she with me,
>   And in our faults by lies we flattered be.

The paradox in the opening lines, in which belief is made to contra-dict knowledge, is presented as a kind of joke, but the whole sonnet is troubled with an unease about the joke's nature. 'Simply' in line 7 means both 'absolutely' and 'like a simpleton'; the speaker is fully aware of the deception being practised, and in the sonnet's conclud-ing lines demonstrates that in their case 'love' (for a dark mistress, for an aging poet) can only be sustained by lies. However, the deception is here revealed as self-deception.

The speaker, then, is confined not by his mistress but by his own willingness to lie to himself, and he never manages to resolve that situation. The misogyny that has led him to channel his self-loathing into moral condemnation of her blinds him to other possibilities. In sonnet 144 he puts the youth and the woman into what at first appears to be an allegorical struggle between good and evil: the 'right fair' youth is characterized as a 'better angel' and a 'saint', while the ill-coloured woman is a 'worser spirit' and a 'devil'. However, what we already know of the youth's tendency to self-centredness contaminates these categories, and even the speaker fears that the youth has embraced corruption only too eagerly. The sonnet collapses into tormented suspicion as the speaker imagines the two in sexual congress ('I guess one angel in another's hell'). The full ugliness of his state of mind is well expressed in the final couplet: 'Yet this shall I ne'er know, but live in doubt / Till by bad angel fire my good one out'. The immediate meaning here, that he must wait to prove his suspicion until the woman gets tired of the youth, overlays a further meaning, that she will infect him with a venereal disease.

Presumably the speaker's state of moral horror accounts for the inclusion of sonnet 146, which is the only overtly religious poem in the sequence. As if readying himself for death, he begs his soul to relinquish the pleasures of the body ('thy fading mansion') and turn instead to spiritual riches. The poem's figurative language uses images of appetite, but it shifts their significance away from the fleshly: 'Within be fed, without be rich no more'. This, the speaker acknowledges, is the way in which death itself can be devoured and the soul freed into everlasting life: 'So shall thou feed on death, that feeds on men, / And death once dead, there's no more dying then'. This is in many ways a very powerful poem; although it relates to other sonnets that are preoccupied with age and death (63, 71, 73–4, 81) as well as to the broader concern with time in the sonnets to the youth, its specific location at this point contributes to its power. Any consolation these thoughts might appear to offer is illusory, however, because in the next sonnet the speaker is returned to his cycle of torment and the images of feeding are again attached to the body: 'My love is as a fever, longing still / For that which longer nurseth the disease, / Feeding on that which doth preserve the ill'. There is no escape; the sequence continues to move through desire, deception, doubt and disgust, and ends in frustration with the speaker still trapped inside his paradox of lying and knowledge: 'For I have sworn thee fair – more perjured eye / To swear against the truth so foul a lie (sonnet 152). The poet's 'perjured eye' is also a 'perjured I'; the speaker-as-poet acknowledges the poet's duty to see and speak the truth, and his failure to do so here makes him doubly culpable, as the pun makes clear.

The final two sonnets, 153 and 154, have sometimes been seen as detached from the body of the *Sonnets*. Both are variations of a pseudo-myth that originated in epigrams by the sixth-century Byzantine poet Marianus Scholasticus.[2] Shakespeare takes the ribald potential of the idea to develop a joke about the contracting and treatment of venereal disease. Cupid's brand has a phallic double meaning, and becomes the source of 'love's fire', which also has a double meaning: it is both passion and disease. The supposed curative powers of bathing can do nothing for this particular disease: 'Love's fire heats water, water cools not love' (sonnet 154). The source of the speaker's 'fire' is clearly identified in both poems: 'my mistress' eyes'. The cynical wit of these two sonnets might well appear to provide an appropriate ending not just to the 'dark lady' sonnets, but to the sequence as a whole, as it moves inescapably towards disillusionment and bitterness.

'WILL' AND THE POET

I have stated more than once that I do not think that the speaker of the *Sonnets* can be directly identified with the author, and I now wish to return to the question of how we can interpret the 'I'. One way to approach it might be to ask not what is the relationship between the poet and his subject, but what is the relationship between the poet, his 'voice', and the reader? If we take the *Sonnets* to be fictions, then we clearly must distinguish between poet and speaker (just as we distinguish between poet and narrator in the narrative poems), and in that case the poet's key relationship is with the reader, for whom he has created a voice that can express a new and complex range of experiences, but a voice that is like those of the narrative poems in that it should be listened through as well as listened to. I will first address this question by returning to the well-known sonnet 130.

My mistress' eyes are nothing like the sun;
Coral is far more red than her lips red.
If snow be white, why then her breasts are dun;

If hairs be wires, black wires grow on her head.
I have seen roses damasked, red and white,
But no such roses see I in her cheeks;
And in some perfumes is there more delight
Than in the breath that from my mistress reeks.
I love to hear her speak, yet well I know
That music hath a far more pleasing sound.
I grant I never saw a goddess go:
My mistress when she walks treads on the ground.
   And yet, by heaven, I think my love as rare
   As any she belied with false compare.

The first thing to be said about this sonnet is that it is an extended joke that depends on the reader's understanding of literary convention. The lady is described as the negative of what amounts to an accumulation of conventional Petrarchan similes: sun-like eyes, coral lips, snowy skin, and so on. In offering a woman who is the sum of qualities that are the antithesis of fashionable poetic beauty the speaker is making a statement that is as much about poetry as it is about the woman. Petrarchan poetic lovers are liars because they rely on a language that has been emptied of meaning because it has become mere clichés. The speaker, in offering his unillusioned account of his mistress, is presenting both a critique of poetic fashion and a statement about the woman that can be understood as 'true'. That is, one way of understanding the *Sonnets* is to see them as engaged with literature at least as much as with life.

While the poems' voice cannot be directly identified with the author, this does not prevent it from articulating something of the author's own preoccupations and anxieties, though they are distanced through the artifice of the sonnet sequence. If, as seems probable, the sequence can be understood not as a continuous whole, but rather as a set of fragments with enough inter-connections to hint at coherence, then perhaps the speaker should be similarly understood as a kind of polymorphous 'I', sufficiently coherent to give an impression of individuality, while fulfilling a range of functions. One of these is to provide a challenge to the sonneteers who preceded Shakespeare. Shakespeare was aware, at the least, of the sonnets of Sidney, Spenser and Daniel, and his own sequence offers a challenge to the established voices of these poets. Sidney, naming his protagonist 'Aristophil', a name that contains his own (Philip), teases his reader by hinting at his own presence in his sequence. Shakespeare too apparently names himself as the voice of his sequence.

Sonnets 135 and 136 play in a complicated manner on the word 'will', which appears in them a total of 20 times. In the quarto text 10 occurrences of the word are both capitalized and italicized, thus giving the impression that they refer to a proper name. Further-more, the closing couplet of 136 runs: 'Make but my name thy love, and love that still, / And then thou lov'st me for my name is Will'. For those who read the *Sonnets* as a form of autobiography the meaning of this is self-evident: Shakespeare is identifying himself as the central participant in the 'story'. However, a close reading of the two sonnets that pays particular attention to the various ways in which they pun on the word 'will' suggests something different. Apart from being a man's name, 'will' here is used with a range of meanings. As Booth lists them in his edition they are: 'what one wishes to have or do'; 'the auxiliary verb indicating futurity and/or purpose'; 'lust, carnal desire'; 'the male sexual organ'; 'the female sexual organ'; 'William'.[3] I might add that there is also 'testament', something one bequeaths to another.

Consider the word's shifting and ambiguous meanings in sonnet 135:

Whoever hath her wish, thou hast thy Will,
And Will to boot, and Will in over-plus.
More than enough am I that vex thee still,
To thy sweet will making addition thus.
Wilt thou, whose will is large and spacious,
Not once vouchsafe to hide my will in thine?
Shall will in others seem right gracious,
And in my will no fair acceptance shine?
The sea, all water, yet receives rain still,
And in abundance addeth to his store;
So thou, being rich in Will, add to thy Will
One will of mine to make thy large Will more.
  Let no unkind no fair beseechers kill;
  Think all but one, and me in that one Will.

All the non-bawdy meanings of 'will' are here contaminated by the bawdy ones. If we set aside the possibility of proper names, the meaning of the two opening lines appears to be that the woman has more than enough sexual desire and sexual activity ('Will in over-plus'), and is resisting the speaker's wish to be added to her 'sweet will'. There follows in lines 5–6 an overt image of the sexual activity the speaker is asking for: that she should allow him to hide his will (sexual organ) in her 'large and spacious' one, with the implication in this phrase that hers has been well used. There is a degree of indignation in 7–8 as he asks why she accepts the 'wills' of others and not his. The metaphor in the third quatrain suggests that her resistance is unnatural; the sea is entirely water yet can always absorb more, so she should be willing to add him to the list of those who have known her 'large Will'. The final couplet finds the speaker begging to be given this favour: after all, for a woman like this, he suggests, one man is the same as another.

The sonnet ends in a peculiar equilibrium, the speaker's contempt for this promiscuous woman balanced by his apparently irrepressible lust for her. Sonnet 136 continues in much the same vein, echoing the play upon 'will' with 'fill' and taking both into a babble of comic obscenity in lines 5–6: 'Will will fulfill the treasure of thy love, / Ay, fill it full with wills, and my will one'. The 'treasure of thy love' degrades the word 'love' into a euphemism for the woman's sexual organ, which, through lust, will be filled with male sexual organs, including the speaker's own. The sound 'ill' reverberates through the two lines, suggesting a judgement on what they contain. The lines that follow shift the language (but not the idea) from 'will' to 'thing', which was a slang term for the male sexual organ (the female sexual organ, defined by what women lack, was 'nothing'). Lines 11–12 thus contain a complicated set of suggestions: 'For nothing hold me' means 'consider me worthless', but it also implies 'hold me for your sexual organ', and this idea is extended in 'hold / That nothing me a something' or some-thing: a real penis.

The speaker is, and sees himself as, pathetic in his inability to control his desire for a woman for whom he expresses such total disgust; indeed, his contempt for her is exceeded only by his contempt for himself. The last lines of sonnet 136 surely reflect this: 'my name is Will' identifies the speaker as the embodiment of all the meanings that 'will' has accumulated in these two poems. He characterizes himself in terms of a brutal desire, driven by a lust the meaning of which he knows only too well, but which he is powerless to resist. He also, however, appears to identify himself as someone named 'William', thus raising the question of the relationship between the poet Shakespeare and the speaker of the *Sonnets*. To those who have insisted on finding Shakespeare in these poems the only response one can make is to ask why he would wish to equate himself with the pathetic figure presented here. These two poems at least, I would say, indicate precisely that this 'Will' is *not* Will. Shakespeare.

This needs elaboration. After all, the speaker of the *Sonnets* is a poet, and many of the sonnets are preoccupied with considerations of the place of the poet in his society and the powers and limitations of poetry. These, though, are questions that would exercise a mediocre poet as much as a great one, and the speaker of the *Sonnets* many times reflects on his own inferiority. As we have seen, in the group of sonnets that open the sequence written to the youth the speaker does not reveal himself as a poet until sonnet 15, and then only obscurely in the phrase 'I engraft you new'. In sonnet 17 he speaks of the inadequacy of his pen truly to present the youth for posterity, though in sonnets 18 and 19 he appears to be much more confident about the ability of his verses to overcome time. In sonnet 29, however, he is apparently attempting to deal with professional failure and his envy of those more talented than himself, 'Desiring this man's art and that man's scope'. He needs the young man's favour, but is afraid that his 'slight muse' (sonnet 38) might not merit it.

The most sustained self-criticism comes in sonnet 76 at the beginning of the 'rival poet' sequence:

> Why is my verse so barren of new pride,
> So far from variation or quick change?
> Why, with the time, do I not glance aside
> To new-found methods and to compounds strange?
> Why write I still all one, ever the same,
> And keep invention in a noted weed,
> That every word doth almost tell my name,
> Showing their birth, and where they did proceed?

The speaker depicts himself here as a writer who lags behind fashion, whose style has become distinctive in its monotony. He ascribes this to the fact that he writes only in praise of the youth, but when he faces competition his style declines even further:

> Whilst I alone did call upon thy aid,
> My verse alone had all thy gentle grace;
> But now my gracious numbers are decayed,
> And my sick muse doth give another place.
> I grant, sweet love, thy lovely argument
> Deserves the travail of a worthier pen,
> Yet what of thee thy poet doth invent
> He robs thee of, and pays it thee again.

(Sonnet 78)

The speaker claims that any poet who writes about the youth must give to the youth all credit for what is valuable in his work. When he had no rival his verse was full of the patron's 'gentle grace' as, presumably, the rival poet's work now is. One could see this as no more than a conventional compliment paid to his patron, but the self-denigration through which he demotes his 'sick muse' beneath a 'worthier pen' (called a 'better spirit' in sonnet 80) hardly reflects much professional confidence. He is, indeed, 'tongue-tied' (sonnets 80 and 85).

At no point in the *Sonnets* is there any suggestion that this poet has ever had any success. His self-pity and self-effacement, his sad willingness to give all credit for anything of value in his work to his young subject, might well reflect the realities of the patronage system, but it is hardly the sign of a powerful poetic voice. What poet could seriously wish to project himself through this figure, selling himself out to a self-absorbed young aristocrat and a promiscuous woman? There is very little in the speaker's story that reflects what we know of Shakespeare's career, even in the early-to mid-1590s. And yet, while depriving him of almost all dignity, Shakespeare does allow him to appear as the author of some very powerful lines: 'Yet do thy worst, old time; despite thy wrong / My love shall in my verse ever live young' (sonnet 19). Perhaps we need to see the speaker not as Shakespeare, but as a deeply-flawed poet-figure who is astray on terrain that Shakespeare himself had traversed so expertly – a kind of inverse of Shakespeare. Like Shakespeare, he is caught up in the necessity of making a living out of writing and of making writing relevant to life; he is concerned with the elements of his craft as well as with the circumstantial pressures that make writing difficult. But unlike Shakespeare, he has lost his way.

The effect of this distinction is to impart a kind of dualism to the character. Through the speaker Shakespeare is able to meditate on a range of subjects that are of interest to him: poetry and art, love and desire, time and decay, identity, power, social structures and distinctions, spirituality – these are only a few of the issues examined. But all of this is done within a fictional structure that allows him to treat the speaker as a poet who is quite different from himself. For the 'Will' of the *Sonnets* is a corrupt and in many ways a contemptible character, and he is so partly to the extent that he is defined by his name; 'will', as we have seen, is in these poems a semantically complex word, and it can be the antithesis of what is spiritually, socially and aesthetically healthy. This explains why the speaker as well as the two people with whom he mainly interacts are portrayed with such inconsistency: they have a dramatic function within the fiction of the sonnets, but they are also the vehicle for an examination of issues that are frequently seen from more than one perspective.

TIME'S TYRANNY AND THE POET'S PEN

One issue that preoccupies the sonnets is time and stratagems to overcome it, of which *Shakespeare's Sonnets* itself is one. When the speaker attempts in the marriage sonnets to persuade the youth to reproduce himself he repeatedly emphasizes the ravaging effects of time. Time will 'dig deep trenches' in the youth's brow, leaving his beauty 'a tattered weed' (sonnet 2); it will lead him to 'hideous winter' (sonnet 5), 'hideous night' (sonnet 12). Like all things that live, the youth will be cut down by 'time's scythe' (sonnet 12). These are, of course, commonplace ideas, but there is something obsessive about the speaker's concentration on the effects of time that endows it with a peculiar intensity beyond its function as a stimulus to the youth to copulate. The wounding physicality of time's scythe (which appears again in sonnets 60, 100 and 123, and as a 'crooked knife' in sonnet 100 and a 'bending sickle' in sonnet 116) depends upon the conventional figure of Father Time, simultaneously human and inhuman, but goes beyond the conventional.

At some moments it is time itself that appears to be the protagonist of the sonnets addressed to the youth, and then the speaker sets himself up as the antagonist; sonnet 15 provides an excellent example of this:

When I consider every thing that grows
Holds in perfection but a little moment,
That this huge stage presenteth naught but shows
Whereon the stars in secret influence comment;
When I perceive that men as plants increase,
Cheered and checked even by the selfsame sky,
Vaunt in their youthful sap, at height decrease,
And wear their brave state out of memory:
Then the conceit of this inconstant stay
Sets you most rich in youth before my sight,

Where wasteful time debateth with decay
To change your day of youth to sullied night;
  And all in war with time for love of you,
  As he takes from you, I engraft you new.

The movement of the sonnet is simple enough. The three quatrains shift from registering the decay of all things in nature, to considering the disintegration of men, to applying these eternal truths specifically to the young friend. The closing couplet reverses the movement: the poet, as if a mighty opposite to time, will renew in the youth what time has destroyed. The multiple meaning of the word 'engraft', which combines the horticultural idea of the modification and improvement of nature with the act of writing, turns the writer himself into a force of nature able to counter the work of time. This confrontational note is picked up in sonnet 19: 'Yet do thy worst, old time; despite thy wrong / My love shall in my verse ever live young'. The speaker here begins to displace the means of immortalizing the young man's beauty from the social act of marriage to the speaker's own individual act of writing.

This move could be seen as the speaker's attempt at self-empowerment, both in a social sense, as he takes control of his young friend's future, and in a more abstract sense, as he makes his claim for the power of poetry. His moves are at first tentative – in 16 he says his rhyme is 'barren' and in 17 that it is unlikely to be believed – but the closing couplet of sonnet 18 makes what appears to be a triumphant claim for the power of poetry: 'So long as men can breathe or eyes can see, / So long lives this, and this gives life to thee'. 'This' refers to the 'eternal lines' of the sonnet itself, through which the young man will be saved from wandering in death's shade – a large claim indeed. Shakespeare was not, of course, the first poet to think up this idea, which was conventional in both classical and Renaissance poetry, but he certainly exploited its paradoxes more fully than many of his predecessors.

The speaker's claim that his poetry will confer a kind of immortality on the youth recurs at intervals throughout the sequence. In sonnet 55 he contemplates the futility of attempts to avoid disintegration:

Not marble, nor the gilded monuments
Of princes shall outlive this powerful rhyme,
But you shall shine more bright in these contents
Than unswept stone besmeared with sluttish time.
When wasteful war shall statues overturn,

And broils root out the work of masonry,
Nor Mars his sword, nor war's quick fire shall burn
The living record of your memory.
'Gainst death and all oblivious enmity
Shall you pace forth; your praise shall still find room
Even in the eyes of all posterity
That wear this world out to the ending doom.
  So, till the judgment that yourself arise,
  You live in this, and dwell in lovers' eyes.

The poem indicates that the very materiality of monuments or statues will make inevitable their eventual destruction, but it makes the same self-referential statement as sonnet 18, that 'this', the poem, will somehow outlive monuments. There is a logical gap here, because this claim erases the material nature of the poem itself; it might be true that the reproducibility of a poem makes it more likely to survive than the monolithic statue, but the poem's continued existence nevertheless depends on the materiality of the paper on which it is written or the hard drive in which it is stored (or the mind in which it is memorized). Poems by many of Shakespeare's contemporaries disappeared long ago.

The problem with the claim that poetry confers a kind of immortality is that it is essentially a literary trick as, for example, John Keats acknowledges at the end of his 'Ode to a Nightingale'; having tried to intoxicate himself through imagination into believing in something that can defeat time, he is forced to admit that 'the fancy cannot cheat so well / As she is famed to do, deceiving elf'. It is only human to want to believe in the possibility of triumph over time and death, which is why powerful individuals build monuments to themselves. For them, the knowledge that something they have caused to be made will live on after them is important, but for most of us there is little consolation for the fact that death is, at least from the material perspective from which we are forced to look at it, rather final.

The *Sonnets* are ironically aware of the deception (and self-deception) they are trying to perpetrate. The speaker's claim that poetry can immortalize its subject is also an attempt to affirm his own immortality, for he 'lives' in his lines as much as does the young man. The couplet of sonnet 19 indicates this in its dual meaning: 'Yet do thy worst, old time; despite thy wrong / My love shall in my verse ever live young'. If we follow the logic of the preceding twelve lines 'My love' clearly refers to the young man, but the words also contain the meaning 'my feelings', and refer to the speaker himself. Indeed, it could be argued that the real subject of the sonnets to the youth is the dread generated in the speaker by what time can (and in fact always does) do to fragile humanity, in which case their defiance of time might sound somewhat hysterical. The 'eternal lines' of sonnet 18 are, after all, only eternal so long as men can breathe or eyes can see. Sonnet 19 begins with a picture of voracious time devouring not only wild beasts but also the supposedly immortal phoenix; in the light of this the presumed potency of the sonnet to prevent time from carving wrinkles in the young man's brow might seem unconvincing. Stephen Booth notes that this sonnet's final line 'My love shall in my verse ever live young' is 'metrically limp and thus – whether by design or not – ironically undercuts its substance'.[4] There is certainly a problem with the line, which might be fixed by the inversion of 'ever live'; I think that the limpness is 'by design' of the poet, though perhaps not the speaker, indicating the false bravado of the latter.

Shakespeare knew the truth of Keats' discovery two centuries before Keats acknowledged it. We might consider here sonnet 60, which appears to make a strong claim for the poet's art:

> Like as the waves make towards the pebbled shore,
> So do our minutes hasten to their end,
> Each changing place with that which goes before;
> In sequent toil all forwards do contend.
> Nativity, once in the main of light,
> Crawls to maturity, wherewith being crowned
> Crooked eclipses 'gainst his glory fight,
> And time that gave doth now his gift confound.
> Time doth transfix the flourish set on youth,
> And delves the parallels in beauty's brow,
> Feeds on the rarities of nature's truth,
> And nothing stands but for his scythe to mow.
>   And yet to times in hope my verse shall stand,
>   Praising thy worth despite his cruel hand.

The movement of the sonnet is by now familiar: three quatrains, each presenting through a different metaphor the destructive effects of time, reversed by the closing couplet, in which the speaker claims that his poem will overcome time. However, in this sonnet there is a sense of pessimism in its account of the struggle of nature and of human life. Optimistic readings of human life often present it in terms of the cyclical patterns of nature, but here the patterns of nature are seen in terms of the linear direction of human life. The forward motion of the waves/minutes paradoxically combines haste with toil, casting a shadow on the motion of the baby crawling towards the contorted end of his youthful beauty only to be harshly wounded by time's scythe. This surely explains the tentativeness of the claim made by the speaker that his verse will stand 'in hope' to resist time. A similar tentativeness can be found elsewhere; sonnet 65 acknowledges the fragile vulnerability, the 'sad mortality' of all things, and asks:

> Where, alack,
> Shall time's best jewel from time's chest lie hid,
> Or what strong hand can hold his swift foot back,
> Or who his spoil of beauty can forbid?

The answer implied by this question, signalled in the word 'alack', is 'nowhere', and it casts doubt on the conviction of the answer offered by the speaker, 'O none, unless this miracle have might: / That in black ink my love may still shine bright'.

CONCLUSIONS

The triumph of the poem over time, which the sonnets frequently assert, is an illusion. We might compare their stance to that of John Donne's Holy Sonnet 10, 'Death, be not proud', in which the speaker's denial of the power of death has a vehemence that borders on hysteria and makes the reader ask whether the poem's meaning is the opposite of what it says. In *Shakespeare's Sonnets* the speaker's struggle against the future decay of the youth raises similar questions. In sonnet 62, for example, the speaker suggests that he has been using the youth as a distorting mirror through which he has fooled himself into believing in his own youth and beauty; reality reflects a truth much different: ' 'Tis thee, my self, that for myself I praise, / Painting my age with beauty of thy days'. Time, which in these sonnets means decay and death, cannot be stopped. 'Spite of him I'll live in this poor rhyme', he says of death in sonnet 107, but in sonnets 71–4 he has imagined his own death with a certain finality in spite of his assertions that his spirit, inhabiting his verses, will somehow overcome it. Perhaps this accounts for sonnet 126, the final

poem in the series addressed to the youth, which is not a sonnet, but
twelve lines of rhymed couplets:

> O thou, my lovely boy, who in thy power
> Dost hold time's fickle glass, his sickle-hour;
> Who hast by waning grown, and therein show'st
> Thy lovers withering, as thy sweet self grow'st–
> If nature, sovereign mistress over wrack,
> As thou goest onwards still will pluck thee back,
> She keeps thee to this purpose: that her skill
> May time disgrace, and wretched minutes kill.
> Yet fear her, O thou minion of her pleasure!
> She may detain but not still keep her treasure.
> Her audit, though delayed, answered must be,
> And her quietus is to render thee.
> (   )
> (   )

In its suggestion of frustration, displacement and incompleteness,
emphasized by the empty brackets printed in the 1609 quarto, it
provides a strange conclusion. The power of the 'lovely boy' over
time's hourglass and sickle is negated by the inevitability of cyclical
decay imaged in lines 3 and 4; the speaker has to accept that nature
will hand the youth over to time, and the poem ends in the silence
of the empty brackets. It is not the end of *Shakespeare's Sonnets*,
which continue with the emotional cacophony of the dark lady
sonnets. In those, preoccupied with his dark obsession, the speaker
has almost no interest in time. It is difficult, however, not to see
sonnet 126 as a terminus to the *Sonnets* as a whole, a kind of tacit
acknowledgement that the power of the word cannot, in the end,
overcome the silence of death.

I think that in the *Sonnets* Shakespeare found a means of locating
himself as a sceptical voice both in relation to the conventions of
the Petrarchan sonnet sequences and to the elite values of his own
time and place. He did this through the distance he contrived
between himself and the voice of the poems. This enabled him to
use the romantic terms of Elizabethan poetry (many of the sonnets
do powerfully express a yearning for an idealized love) to write
what is essentially an anti-romantic sequence in which love is
revealed as self-centred, self-deluding appetite. It also enabled him
to express the preoccupations and anxieties of a professional poet
writing in a cultural and political context where the basis on which

he had to build his career was insecure and always liable to shift; in which he had to please an elite that was often self-regarding and ungrateful.

CODA: 'A LOVER'S COMPLAINT'

In spite of the implications of the blank at the end of sonnet 126, the rest is not quite silence. The sonnets in Thorpe's 1609 quarto are followed in the same volume by a poem of a quite different genre headed 'A Lovers Complaint by William Shake-speare'. There is a history of scholarly resistance to Thorpe's attribution of the poem's authorship to Shakespeare, and as recently as 1986 Sandra Clark could write that it is 'not now generally accepted to be by Shake-speare'.[5] Doubts have arisen partly because of the apparent generic incompatibility between the poem and the sonnets, partly because the poem has aesthetic weaknesses, though that in itself is hardly reason to deny the possibility that Shakespeare wrote it. The case against it is of course strengthened for those who believe that Thorpe's volume was not authorized by Shakespeare. For those who are persuaded by Katherine Duncan-Jones's arguments for Shakespeare's sanctioning of the volume, however, there is little reason to doubt the poem's authenticity, since Shakespeare is hardly likely to have taken credit for someone else's poem, particularly one of inferior quality. Moreover, recent studies of the poem's style, especially of its phraseology and diction, have offered strong evidence that the poem is indeed by Shakespeare.[6] Whether or not it was true in 1986 that the poem was not generally accepted as Shakespeare's, it is not true today. Even so, some recent commentators on the sonnets (Helen Vendler is the most notable example) have excluded it from their discussion. My own view is that the poem is by Shakespeare and I think that it should be read as having an essential relationship with the sonnet sequence that it accompanies.

The genre of 'A Lover's Complaint' is identified in its title. As a lyric form the complaint had been popular in the Middle Ages, usually as a monologue in which the poet-speaker moaned about his unfortunate life and/or the coldness of his mistress; such complaint could embrace a larger philosophical meditation about what the speaker perceived as a decline in the state of the world itself (in which case it took on elements of the elegy). In the Renaissance a complaint was more likely, and dramatically, to be the lament of a woman (or, frequently, the ghost of a woman) about the man who had wrought her sexual downfall (and, if she was a ghost, her consequent death). In Shakespeare's 'Complaint' a weeping woman describes her own ruined state, recounting the process of her seduction, and acknowledging both the duplicity of her seducer and her own complicity in her fall. The poem consists of 329 lines divided into 47 stanzas of rhyme royal (the same stanza-form as Shakespeare had used for *The Rape of Lucrece*, which, as we have seen, is also in part a complaint).

The primary question we need to ask concerns the poem's connection to the sonnets because this will help us to understand something of the artistic intention that might underlie it. For those who do not believe the poem is Shakespeare's the answer must be that there is no connection. If, on the other hand, Shakespeare did arrange for the poems to be published together, it is reasonable to assume that he intended some structural or thematic relationship, and it is to this possibility that much recent scholarship has directed itself. Precedents for a multiple structure in which a sonnet sequence is supplemented by a poem of a different form have long been known. Samuel Daniel first published his sonnet sequence *Delia*, consisting of 50 sonnets and a concluding ode, in 1592 and revised it in the same year with the addition of a long poem (742 lines of rhyme royal) entitled *The Complaint of Rosamund*. In Daniel's sonnets the speaker addresses the beloved Delia, exploring the pains of Petrarchan courtship familiar to Elizabethan readers from Sidney's *Astrophil and Stella*. In the 'Complaint', however, the ghost of the dead Rosamund asks to be allowed to address her own woeful story to Delia, thus creating a kind of debate about the possible deceptions through which the Neoplatonic idealism of Petrarchism might mask a destructive desire. Complaints were similarly attached to Lodge's *Phyllis* (1593) and Drayton's *Ideas Mirrour* (1594). Edmund Spenser published his sonnet sequence *Amoretti* (1595) along with the *Epithalamion*, which is not a complaint but a marriage-hymn providing a climax, rather than a corrective, to a sequence that tempers dangerous erotic desire with a more chaste Christian love. There are other sonnet collections from the period that exhibit variations of this double or multiple structure, but the differences between Daniel's and Spenser's treatment of it indicate that there were no rigid assumptions about *how* the supplementary poem should relate to the sonnets that precede it.

It is possible, perhaps even probable, that 'The Lover's Complaint' was not originally written with the intention of its forming the conclusion to a sonnet sequence. There are no contemporary references to it, and it is no easier to date it than it is to date the sonnets. Some critics have thought it a product of the early 1590s because of its affinities (both of form and of subject-matter) with *The Rape of Lucrece*. It is certainly possible that it is an early poem that was later revised, as many or most of the sonnets must have been, and recast in a form that would complete the structure of the sonnet sequence along the lines suggested above.[7] A further possibility is that it dates from around 1600, since it has stylistic affinities with plays written around that time, especially *Hamlet*.[8] In either case, it must have been revised prior to its 1609 publication, so none of the dates that have been proposed can be considered sure.

If we are properly to understand 'A Lover's Complaint' we need to find its structural and thematic relationship with the sonnets. One connection that has rarely been considered comes through its stanza form, for what is rhyme royal if not a kind of half-sonnet? Its *ababbcc* rhyme scheme provides an opening quatrain, followed by the beginning of what appears to be a second quatrain but suddenly collapses into a closing couplet. Rhyme royal echoes the structure of the sonnet while lacking its self-enclosed dialectical completeness. Consider the first stanza of the 'Complaint':

> From off a hill whose concave womb re-worded
> A plaintful story from a sist'ring vale,
> My spirits t'attend this double voice accorded,
> And down I laid to list the sad-tuned tale;
> Ere long espied a fickle maid full pale,
> Tearing of papers, breaking rings a-twain,
> Storming her world with sorrow's wind and rain.

The opening quatrain, like that of many of the sonnets, presents a complete idea, and the fifth and sixth lines begin a second, which is wrenched to an ending when the sixth line is made into a couplet by the seventh. Bear in mind that readers coming to this poem as an extension of the sonnets as, presumably, the author intended will have become accustomed to a movement that tends towards rhythmic completion with each sonnet-unit. This momentum is suddenly frustrated by the rhyme royal, which begins by hinting at the completion of the sonnet form, but then withholds it. The sense of frustration thus generated is replicated by the larger structure of the

'Complaint', which also refuses completion by denying expectations set up at its beginning.

The opening lines of the poem create expectations of a particular kind of narrative frame. The poet-speaker hears a woman lamenting and lies down to listen to her 'sad-tuned tale'. The reader might reasonably assume that this eavesdropper/voyeur will make some response to her story. This frame is then doubled with the arrival of a cow-herd, one who is nevertheless a 'reverend man, ... / Sometime a blusterer that the ruffle knew / Of court, of city' (57–9). This very specific description of the man's past, implying one who has given up a life of sophistication for the harsher attractions of the pastoral, suggests that he is here to use his experience to interpret or moralize the woman's story: 'If that from him there may be aught applied / Which may her suffering ecstasy assuage, / 'Tis promised in the charity of age' (68–70). That these multiple perspectives will be important is suggested, too, by the insistence in the opening lines on the idea of echo, or 'double voice'. The woman then begins her complaint, which is a monologue that takes up the remainder of the poem. The frame set up in the opening section is never closed: the reverend man never offers her anything to assuage her suffering ecstasy, and the poet, of whose presence she remains unaware, has nothing to say about how the story interests him. It is, of course, possible that the poem is simply unfinished, but if Shakespeare authorized its publication it seems more probable that the lack of closure was intentional, and that this double frustration in the form (of stanza and of the complaint as a whole) has some bearing on its meaning. In this it has affinities with *Venus and Adonis*.

Apart from setting up this narrative frame the opening section (1–70) locates the woman's lament in a pastoral landscape that is itself made feminine by its 'concave womb' and 'sist'ring vale'. Although the woman retains the residue of a former beauty she appears old, but she later tells the old man 'Not age, but sorrow over me hath power' (74). The ravaging of youth and beauty that in the sonnets to the young man is caused by time is here caused by grief, and so it is perhaps significant that the narrator uses an image that is familiar but, in the circumstances, unnecessary: 'Time had not scythed all that youth begun' (12). We have, that is, a situation that is and is not parallel to that of the sonnets. The woman appears to be anxious to put an end to the memory of what caused her grief, since she is in the process of destroying all the love tokens and letters given to her by the young man who has betrayed her, but the almost comic extravagance of her 'shrieking undistinguished woe / In clamours of all size, both high and low' (20–21) might make us wonder whether she can regain control of herself.

The reverend man's request that she 'divide' her sorrow with him brings some coherence to her grief, and she gives him an account of the course of her betrayal: a description of the charms of the young man (71–177); an (apparently) direct quotation of the speech he made that had such seductive success with her (177–280); and her attempt to understand her experience (281–329). Her seducer has much in common with the youth of the sonnets. He is of high rank, if we are to judge from the quality of the gifts given to him by his many mistresses. He had barely reached manhood when he seduced her, for 'Small show of man was yet upon his chin' (92), yet he already had many conquests. Like the master–mistress of sonnet 20 his attractions are androgynous, for he enchanted 'sexes both' (128). Here arises the central issue: the woman was fully aware of his history of seduction, and knew the value of her own honour, yet she asks 'who ever shunned by precedent / The destined ill she must herself assay?' (155–6), as if she were compelled by a force outside her own will. The true engineer of her downfall in this regard appears, in part, to be language:

So on the tip of his subduing tongue
All kind of arguments and question deep,
All replication prompt, and reason strong,
For his advantage still did wake and sleep.

(120–3)

Like a corrupt poet, the young man abused his medium, 'thought characters and words merely but art' (174). His will, and its language, subdued hers.

The young man's speech, at least as she reconstructs or remembers it, complicates the issue. He appears simultaneously candid and deceptive in his approach to her, admitting to a whole history of relationships with other women, while at the same time claiming that he has never loved anyone until now:

All my offences that abroad you see
Are errors of the blood, none of the mind.
Love made them not; with acture they may be,
Where neither party is nor true nor kind.

They sought their shame that so their shame did find,
And so much less of shame in me remains
By how much of me their reproach contains.

(183–9)

Through the distinction he makes between errors of the blood and errors of the mind he contrives to disconnect sexual passion from the will, suggesting that if his actions were unwilled they were innocent, and therefore he has remained pure. The women who gave themselves to him are thus themselves to blame for their downfall. He paints himself as the passive object of female sexual aggression, which is emblematized by the rich array of jewels and tokens – including 'deep-brained sonnets' (209) – that the women gave him, the 'trophies of affections hot' (218). This proclamation of his innocence appears a little disingenuous, however, when he says: 'Harm have I done to them, but ne'er was harmed' (193). Who is the agent here and who the object?

The ease with which the young man shifts responsibility for his colourful past on to the women who were the victims of it might appear to reflect a deep cynicism, particularly as his protestations of innocence, besides fudging the question of who is the victim, keep switching into a rather nasty boastfulness. He offers his innocence as if it were a kind of spiritual integrity, but he shows none of the compassion that this might lead us to expect. The story of his past, as he recounts it to the woman, has its climax when he tells her of a nun, a 'sister sanctified', who gave up all her sacred vows for him. 'My boast is true!' (246), he says, 'my parts had power to charm a sacred nun' (260). The young man's story and the attitude behind it are so transparent that we might suspect the woman of a pathetic naivete for failing to recognize that she is simply the latest of a string of women who have fallen for a rather obvious line.

The result of all of this is predictable. The woman informs her reverend listener:

> his passion, but an art of craft,
> Even there resolved my reason into tears.
> There my white stole of chastity I daffed,
> Shook off my sober guards and civil fears;
> Appear to him as he to me appears,
> All melting; though our drops this diff'rence bore:
> His poisoned me, and mine did him restore.

(295–301)

The woman, we might think, is here shifting blame back to where it rightly belongs. The young man is unquestionably a cynical predator and she, like all the other women, appears a naive but tragic victim. However, the poem's ending adds a peculiar ambiguity to the question. The woman has shown that she has a clear-eyed understanding of the deceptions to which she has fallen victim, and yet she is not sure that what she has learned is enough to prevent her from falling again: 'Ay me, I fell, and yet do question make / What I should do again for such a sake' (321–2). Knowing all that she knows about the young man's 'art of craft', she also knows her own weakness. She would repeat her fall, and thus she acknowledges that her betrayal was really a self-betrayal. But if that is so, then the young man's cynicism about female sexual appetite has more justification than at first appeared.

The woman's experience has not immunized her against a repetition of her fall, but she feels ruefulness rather than self-disgust. Her response nevertheless has affinities with the sense of doomed deficiency, of being trapped in a degrading cycle, that is manifested by the speaker of sonnet 129: 'All this the world well knows, yet none knows well / To shun the heaven that leads men to this hell'. The young man who has pursued her has been 'savage, extreme, rude, cruel, not to trust'; she knows this, and yet also knows that his charms 'Would yet again betray the fore-betrayed, / And new pervert a reconciled maid' (328–9). Perhaps the sheer ordinariness of the situation is intended as a contrast to the large obsessions of the *Sonnets*. Because the seducer is given a voice (even though it is ventriloquized by the woman) we can see both what is attractive in him and what is transparently self-serving, and in this he sheds some light on aspects of the young man that the speaker of the sonnets sought to obscure. At the same time the natural sexual desire of the maid is seen from a comparatively sympathetic perspective, in stark contrast to what is presented as a voracious appetite in the dark woman. And the voice of the 'poet', which tried to control everything in the *Sonnets*, is diminished into the voyeuristic 'I' of this poem, and is erased by the end of it.

10

Various Poems

Although the composition of Shakespeare's two narrative poems can be located, as we have seen, in a specific span of two years early in his career, the sonnets were composed and revised over a much longer time-span. It would be surprising if during that period Shakespeare had written no other non-dramatic poetry, but in fact he appears to have been able to dedicate himself more or less completely to writing plays. The number of other poems that have been attributed to him is small, and even of these not all can be said with certainty to be his. They are mainly occasional poems, and, with one exception, they are minor contributions to the canon. They are worth considering here, though, for the questions they raise about the ways in which the canon has been generated, and for what they suggest about the literary marketplace for which Shakespeare wrote.

In 1599 the printer/publisher William Jaggard published a miscellany of twenty numbered sonnets and lyrics entitled *The Passionate Pilgrim* by *W. Shakespeare*. This was a second edition of a volume that Jaggard had published shortly before, perhaps early in the same year, but which now exists in a single copy, incomplete and without a title page, in the Folger Shakespeare Library. Five of the poems in the collection are certainly by Shakespeare. Poem I ('When my love swears that she is made of truth') is a version of sonnet 138, though with a sufficient number of differences to suggest that it is an early draft. Poem II ('Two loves I have, of comfort and despair') is a version of sonnet 144. If for no other reason, *The Passionate Pilgrim* is notable in that it shows that versions of some sonnets were in existence 10 years before the publication of the *Sonnets*, raising questions pertinent to the dating, ordering and content of the sequence. The other three poems are all from *Love's Labour's Lost*: III ('Did not the heavenly rhetoric of thine eye') is Longueville's sonnet (4.3.55–68), V ('If love make me forsworn, how shall I swear to love?') is Berowne's hexameter sonnet (4.2.98–111), and XVI ('On a day – alack the day –') is Dumaine's song (4.3.97–116). Four of the remaining poems have

194

been accounted for: two (VIII and XX) are known to be by Richard Barnfield, XI is by Bartholomew Griffin, and XIX is cobbled together from Christopher Marlowe's 'The Passionate Shepherd to his Love' and Sir Walter Ralegh's 'The Nymph's Reply to the Shepherd'. No author has been identified for the remaining 11. It is not possible to say that none of the other poems in the miscellany is by Shakespeare, and some (especially XII, 'Crabbed age and youth cannot live together') have had their champions, but the issue currently remains unresolvable.

Editors of Shakespeare's poems differ on how to treat *The Passionate Pilgrim*. While the editors of the 1997 Riverside edition print it in its entirety, Bevington excludes it from his edition on the grounds that it provides 'no new poems that are convincingly [Shakespeare's]'.[1] Evans prints all of it except the four poems known for certain not to be Shakespeare's. The Oxford and Norton editors do the same, except that they print the 11 anonymous poems together and treat the five poems known to be Shakespeare's as variants of the more authoritative versions. Each of these positions can be defended, but I think that if *The Passionate Pilgrim* is to be printed at all, it should be printed as a whole. It is possible, however remotely, that Shakespeare was involved in the publication, and even that he wrote some of the orphan poems. That being the case, the five poems known to be his should be presented in the context and arrangement in which they first appeared, since that might very well affect their meaning. For example, because some of the poems (IV, VI, IX and XI) explicitly concern the romance between Venus and Adonis and others can be read as having an implicit bearing on it, some critics have argued that the collection as a whole might in some way be a response to Shakespeare's narrative poem.[2] While I do not think that the miscellany has the thematic coherence such a supposition would demand, I can see that it is a tempting idea.

A more plausible theory is that Jaggard hoped that Shakespeare's name and the implied association with his hugely popular (and commercially successful) poem would help to sell his own volume. We know from Francis Meres that some of Shakespeare's 'sugared sonnets' were in manuscript circulation in 1598, and perhaps Jaggard also had in mind the idea that his little book would be taken as a collection of these. Such suspicions are given support by subsequent events. Jaggard published a third edition in 1612 with the title *The Passionate Pilgrim. Or Certaine Amorous Sonnets, betweene Venus and Adonis, newly corrected and augmented. by W. Shakespere* and with additions which the title page describes as 'two Love-Epistles'. The clear implication was that Shakespeare was the author of these additional poems (not two, but nine), but they were, in fact, by Thomas Heywood. Jaggard had extracted them from *Troia Britannica*, a volume that he himself had published in 1609. Heywood was understandably upset by this, and if we are to believe him, so was Shakespeare. Heywood wrote to Nicholas Okes, in an epistle included in his *An Apology for Actors* (1612):

> Here likewise, I must necessarily insert a manifest injury done me in that worke, by taking the two Epistles of *Paris* to *Helen*, and *Helen* to *Paris*, and printing them in a lesse volume, under the name of another, which may put the world in opinion I might steale them from him; and hee to doe himselfe right, hath since published them in his owne name: but as I must acknowledge my lines not worthy of his patronage, under whom he hath publisht them, so the Author I know much offended with M. *Jaggard* (that altogether unknowne to him) presumed to make so bold with his name.[3]

Heywood's own anger arises partly out of fear that it is he, the actual author of the poems, rather than the author under whose name the poems were printed, who will be suspected of literary theft. Shakespeare's anger, as Heywood interprets it for us, is at the appropriation of his name.

Our information about Shakespeare's irritation rests entirely on Heywood's account, and it is possible that he exaggerated or even invented it to strengthen his own sense of injury. But assuming it was real, it is surely reasonable to ask why Shakespeare was 'much offended' by this abuse of his name in 1612 when he had apparently remained silent about the same abuse in 1599. One possible answer arises from Heywood's clear sense of the superiority of Shakespeare's name over his own: that in 1612 Shakespeare felt a weight of professional authority that he had not felt in 1599. But there are also intriguing questions of literary ownership (what we would today mean by 'copyright') here. There can be no question that when in 1599 Jaggard published *The Passionate Pilgrim* he was aware that most of the poems were not Shakespeare's. He was certainly trying to mislead potential readers, but how seriously must he have been misleading Shakespeare? After all, the injury done to the other 'contributors' was greater than that done to Shakespeare: Barnfield and Ralegh certainly, and Griffin probably, were alive in 1599. Their names did not have the selling power that Jaggard must have

believed Shakespeare's had, partly as his had just begun to appear
on the title-pages of published works (it was for the first time on the
title-page of the fifth and sixth Quartos of *Venus and Adonis* published
in that year; prior to that it had appeared only in the dedication).
The Passionate Pilgrim would have brought Shakespeare publicity
even if it did not bring him money.

As we have seen, literary property was treated rather differently
in Shakespeare's time from the way it is treated today. Authorial
rights over a text were not obvious. When a dramatist sold a play to
an acting company it ceased to be his, and any subsequent profit
made from selling it to a publisher went to the company. When
a poet dedicated a work to a patron in exchange for money he sold
at least part of his right in it. Ben Jonson spent much of his career
attempting to assert control over his writings against printers, booksellers and patrons. Some commentators have seen Jaggard as
a pirate and an unscrupulous exploiter of writers, but what had he
stolen from Shakespeare? Three of the poems had been printed in
1598 in the quarto edition of *Love's Labour's Lost*, and Shakespeare
could certainly have expected no more payment for them. The two
sonnets, to be sure, had not been published before, and since they
did not see the light of day again until 1609, Shakespeare must have
wished, for unknown reasons, to protect them from publication. We
cannot know, however, that he resented Jaggard's actions, which
were certainly devious but by no means illegal; nor were they far
outside the norms of the contemporary publishing trade. He might,
indeed, have been pleased at this demonstration of the selling
power of his name. This might also account for his different reaction
in 1612, when his reputation was such that he had no need for
spurious publicity, especially if it came from seeing his name
attached to inferior work. Whatever the case, however, the offense
he took in 1612 could not have been so great that it caused the sever-
ing of all connections with the publisher, for William Jaggard and
his son Isaac were amongst those invited a decade later to print the
First Folio of Shakespeare's plays.

In all probability Jaggard's 1599 collection adds nothing to Shakespeare's canon. A couple of years after its publication, however,
a volume appeared that contained a brief poem of great richness;
now known as 'The Phoenix and Turtle', this is almost certainly
Shakespeare's work. In 1601 a minor writer named Robert Chester,
who lived in the household of Sir John Salusbury, a distant relation of Queen Elizabeth, published a volume entitled *Loves Martyr:*

or, Rosalins Complaint. Allegorically shadowing the Truth of Love, in the constant Fate of the Phoenix and the Turtle. It contained Chester's own only intermittently interesting poem. It also contained '[s]ome new contributions, of severall modern writers', each of whom provided a poem or poems responding to the volume's title. Although the volume does not make the attribution of all of the poems clear, it appears that four were written by John Marston, four by Ben Jonson, one by George Chapman, two by a poet identified only as 'Ignoto' (but who is generally believed to have been John Donne) and an untitled poem by Shakespeare, his sole contribution. It is not known how the obscure Chester persuaded these 'severall modern writers' to contribute to his volume, but it was probably a good promotional move. Of the four who are identified, Shakespeare had, in 1601, the highest reputation.

Chester's poem is long and digressive. Much of it is spoken by Dame Nature to the (female) phoenix, to whom she narrates the patriotic pseudo-history of King Arthur, which was popular material during the Tudor period, and also gives a lengthy explanation of the mineral, vegetable and animal worlds. There follows a dialogue between the phoenix and the turtle as the two birds build a funeral pyre for the phoenix and then die together on it. The poem ends with a funeral lament and a series of prayers containing the ideal love of the turtle-dove for his phoenix. The point of the phoenix story, of course, is that it is fundamentally celebratory, since the new phoenix arises from the ashes of the old one, and the offerings of the other poets generally go along with this. Shakespeare, however, takes a different line.

The circumstances around the publication of *Loves Martyr* are unknown. Salusbury had married Ursula Stanley, illegitimate daughter of the Earl of Derby, in 1586, and it is possible that Chester originally wrote his own poem to celebrate that marriage, flattering the young couple by rendering them as the dove and the phoenix. Salusbury was knighted by the Queen in 1601; it is credible that Chester might have refurbished his poem to mark the occasion, and elicited contributions from some more illustrious writers, though why they would have been willing to respond is not clear (though Jonson is known to have had some connection with the Salusbury family), since it is hardly probable that he would have been able to offer much in the way of patronage. The complicated issues support-ing the identification of the Salusbury family as participants in the poem were expounded some years ago by Carleton Brown.[4] Much of Brown's argument is persuasive insofar as it concerns Chester's poem, but it is not necessarily the case that all the contributors to the volume had much interest in flattering the Salusburys, and I think this is particularly true of Shakespeare.

There is another historical possibility that must be considered. Amongst the complex web of mythic versions of Queen Elizabeth that were fostered throughout her reign was one that related her to the phoenix, and it has been difficult for some readers to see how, in 1601, a publication about the love between a phoenix and a turtle-dove would not be understood as referring in some way to the queen and her favourite, the Earl of Essex, who led his doomed rebellion against her in that year.[5] This was proposed by A.B. Grosart in 1878, and although there are objections to a reading of the poem that tries to find parallels that are too specific, it has had its adherents. It might well be that what drew Shakespeare, and perhaps the other poets, to Chester's project was the opportunity to write covertly about a subject far more interesting to them than Salusbury's domestic bliss could have been. It is also possible to see the queen as the phoenix without accepting Essex as the turtle; Marie Axton, for example, argues that Shakespeare's contribution is about the relationship between the queen and her subjects, the identity of interests between the body of the monarch and the body of the nation.[6]

With the current state of our knowledge, none of these possibilities can be proved, any more than can the argument of E.A.J. Honigmann that Shakespeare's poem was actually written for Salusbury's marriage in 1586.[7] Such a suggestion requires that Shakespeare began his writing career earlier than is generally accepted. Honigmann has made much of the possibility that Shakespeare lived and wrote in the household of Alexander Hoghton of Hoghton Tower in the 1580s. The Hoghtons were connected to the Stanley family; Ferdinando Stanley, Lord Strange, was Ursula's brother and it has long been thought possible that Shakespeare entered the theatrical profession through Lord Strange's company of actors. Alexander Hoghton was also Catholic, and this possible connection has been used to argue that Shakespeare himself was a Catholic, at least in his early years. The latter possibility has been given some support in a recent article by Clare Asquith, who points out the metrical similarity of 'The Phoenix and Turtle' to the *Lauda Sion*, mystical songs attributed to Thomas Aquinas. The *Lauda Sion* were translated by the Jesuit Robert Southwell, to be sung in secret celebrations of the prohibited religion. Southwell suffered lengthy imprisonment and torture for his beliefs, and was hanged in February 1595. Asquith suggests that Shakespeare's poem was a commemoration of Southwell's martyrdom.[8] These connections are, obviously, arresting, but there is need for more evidence if we are to accept an early beginning to Shakespeare's writing career or the poet's Catholicism. I assume in what follows that the poem was written in 1601.

Given all this obscurity, it is hardly surprising that Shakespeare's contribution, 'The Phoenix and Turtle', has, despite its brevity, been considered one of his most puzzling works; it has also garnered a great deal of critical praise. In 1922 John Middleton Murry called it 'the most perfect short poem in any language', while describing it as 'obscure, mystical, and strictly unintelligible' – something of a contradiction, one might think, but it reflects the general response to the poem.[9] It has been the subject of a broad range of interpretations. The claim in the subtitle of Chester's volume that the poems in it are allegorical has inevitably directed readers to find (or construct) 'hidden' meanings in 'The Phoenix and Turtle', both abstract, connecting it to beliefs about ideal love, and concrete, relating it to contemporary historical figures. While that is interesting, it is of necessity inconclusive. What, I think, is potentially more interesting is Shakespeare's treatment of his material. The myth of the phoenix was well-known: the beautiful bird, sole representative of its kind, lived for five or six centuries until, reaching the end of its span, it built a fire in its nest of spices in a tree in the Arabian desert, where it died in the flames but rose again from its own ashes, thus renewing its own life-cycle. The turtle-dove, on the other hand, was known for its constant (usually married) love for its mate. All the other poems in the volume respect the traditional reading of the phoenix myth, following Chester's version of the story which foresees the new phoenix arising out of the ashes of the phoenix and the dove; this is an essentially optimistic myth implying the permanence of both beauty and an ideal, constant love through the bird's rebirth. Shakespeare seems to undermine this idea, for in his poem both phoenix and dove are dead, with no apparent possibility of a resurrection: 'Death is now the phoenix' nest, / And the turtle's royal breast / To eternity doth rest' (56–8). It is almost as if Shakespeare conceived his poem in ironic relation not only to Chester's poem, but also to those of the other contributors, setting himself against the orthodoxies of their versions of the story.

A poem of astonishing compression and concentration, 'The Phoenix and Turtle' consists of 67 lines of trochaic tetrameter, divided into 13 quatrains (*abba*) followed by five tercets (*aaa*). The poem has a tripartite structure: an introduction or invocation of five quatrains, in which birds are called together to form a funeral procession; this is followed by an anthem of eight quatrains, apparently sung by the birds, in which the meaning of love as represented by the phoenix and the turtle, is presented in such a way as to defeat reason; the final section of five tercets is headed '*Threnos*' (a lament for the dead), performed, in spite of its defeat, by reason.

The convocation of birds in the opening section reflects a long tradition of poems in which birds were used to debate human issues, including the anonymous mediaeval poem *The Owl and the Nightingale*, Chaucer's *Parliament of Fowls*, most particularly John Skelton's *Philip Sparrow*, and even the folk rhyme 'Who Killed Cock Robin?' Here, the 'bird of loudest lay' calls together birds whose presence is appropriate to mourn the death of 'love and constancy': the royal eagle, the swan (supposed to sing its own funeral anthem just before its death), and the 'treble-dated' (long-lived) crow 'That thy sable gender mak'st / With the breath thou giv'st and tak'st' (18–19). Crows were believed to propagate by kissing rather than by sexual congress, and so the crow's presence at this 'chaste' funeral is appropriate for more than its black garb. Birds of disturbing presence, such as the screech-owl, harbinger of death, and all birds of prey except the eagle, are excluded.

This seems straightforward enough, but there is a problem in the opening lines:

> Let the bird of loudest lay
> On the sole Arabian tree
> Herald sad and trumpet be,
> To whose sound chaste wings obey.

> (1–4)

What is 'the bird of loudest lay'? Sitting on the 'sole Arabian tree', unique home of the unique bird, it ought to be the phoenix, but the poem seems insistent that the phoenix is dead: 'Death is now the phoenix' nest' (56). Some critics have questioned whether this is indeed the poem's intention; Maurice Evans, pointing out that various suggestions have been made, 'including the nightingale, the crane and even the cock', concludes that the bird is in fact the phoenix, and that although the poem is ambiguous in this, it does finally imply the bird's resurrection.[10] While I agree with Evans that the suggested birds hardly seem likely, I think the repeated stress on the idea of loss in the *Threnos* disallows his own reading. Perhaps, however, the bird of loudest lay is not a bird at all. The voice behind the voice of the poem is Shakespeare's own, after all, and it is clear that his poem sets out to distinguish itself from the others in Chester's volume. Perhaps the incomparable singer is a witty (and in the circumstances provocative) self-reference. Ben Jonson, at least, would have understood such self-preferment.

The anthem is preoccupied with wit of a different sort, though this wit too might reflect literary contestation. At its centre is a set of paradoxes or antitheses arising from and bringing together ideas about love and death. The phoenix in itself is a paradox, uniting opposed possibilities: being self-propagating it combines the functions of male and female; it is also extraordinary in that its continued life depends upon its own death. Inevitably it has been used as a figure for exploring spiritual puzzles; in its cycle of death and resurrection it is a type of Christ (the title of Chester's volume surely hints at this). Because the phoenix unites male and female functions, the turtle-dove might seem to be redundant, but it allows the poet to explore the paradox of constancy in 'married chastity', an ideal love untainted by the carnal. This chaste love is a uniting of two and one, and has affinities with the the three-in-one of the Trinity:

> So they loved as love in twain
> Had the essence but in one,
> Two distincts, division none.
> Number there in love was slain.
>
> (25–8)

The abstract language of the anthem reflects the logical explorations of mediaeval scholasticism, which attempted to resolve the mysteries of Christianity through deductive reasoning. This is combined with the idealism of Neoplatonism so that not only number, but our understanding of the nature of things is rendered meaningless by the essential perfection of the two-in-one: 'Single nature's double name / Neither two nor one was called' (37–40). Such intellectual play is characteristic of the kind of poetry that became known, misleadingly, as 'Metaphysical', and particularly of the poetry of its first great exemplar, John Donne.

Donne almost certainly contributed to *Loves Martyr* as 'Ignoto'. He had written about the paradoxes of the phoenix in terms superficially similar to Shakespeare's in his poem 'The Canonization':

> The phoenix riddle hath more wit
> By us: we two being one are it.
> So to one neutral thing both senses fit,
>   We die and rise the same, and prove
>   Mysterious by this love.
>
> (23–7)

It could well be that Donne's presence as a contributor to the volume prompted Shakespeare to demonstrate that he could out-Donne Donne, writing in a manner that reflected Donne's, though to a different end. For one aspect of Donne's phoenix image, implicit in the phrase 'die and rise', is muted in Shakespeare's. For Elizabethans, 'to die' could mean 'to achieve sexual climax', and Donne's phrase, considered blasphemous by many readers, implies the satisfaction and renewed excitement of an erotic cycle, thus wittily (and paradoxically) combining sexual and spiritual meanings. Shakespeare's lovers, on the other hand, are defined by 'married chastity', a paradox of a different sort.

Shakespeare's avian lovers too are made 'mysterious', but it is because they represent a love that cannot exist on earth – cannot, indeed, be comprehended in the terms that human wit must use. Their spiritual mutuality can only be expressed by contradiction: 'Distance and no space was seen / 'Twixt this turtle and his queen' (30–1). As the poem plays upon words, language begins to dissolve, and the concepts we use to understand our experience crack under the pressure:

> So between them love did shine
> That the turtle saw his right
> Flaming in the phoenix' sight.
> Either was the other's mine.
>
> Property was thus appalled
> That the self was not the same.
>
> (33–8)

The word 'mine' here has a number of meanings, shifting from the material to the spiritual. The phoenix and the turtle are a source of riches for each other; each is the other's possession, but each, also, is the other's self, making problematic the concept of identity. No wonder reason is confounded, admitting defeat:

> How true a twain
> Seemeth this concordant one!
> Love hath reason, reason none,
> If what parts can so remain.

$(45\text{--}8)$

The personified voice of reason here denies itself when faced with a transcendent love that cannot be understood in human terms.

Having so forcefully constructed a logical impossibility it was inevitable that Shakespeare would change the ending of the myth, for such a love cannot exist in the material world. Thus 'Phoenix and the turtle fled / In a mutual flame from hence' (23–4), 'hence' meaning this world. It is presumably intended as an irony that the defeated reason sings the funeral dirge:

> Death is now the phoenix' nest,
> And the turtle's loyal breast
> To eternity doth rest.
>
> Leaving no posterity....

$(56\text{--}9)$

There is no resurrected phoenix; phoenix and turtle rest to eternity. There is a possible double meaning here: that they are dead forever, or that they now rest in heaven. Either way, they cannot be found on earth; truth and beauty are merely illusions: 'Truth may seem but cannot be, / Beauty brag, but 'tis not she' (62–3). Shakespeare's poem insists on the unbridgeable gulf between the real and the ideal.

This is all highly abstract, and it is difficult to resist the idea that there is more to the poem than a clever reworking of a myth. I have already noted that the phoenix was one of the emblems associated with Queen Elizabeth, and the line that refers to 'this turtle and his queen' seems to me transparent in indicating her relationship with the Earl of Essex, not in a specific way, but in terms of the lost possibilities that their relationship, understood in terms of metaphor, implied. In 1601 Elizabeth was 68 years old; the possibility of her producing an heir was far in the past, and she continued to refuse to name a successor. Throughout her reign, however, she diverted attention away from the succession problem by maintaining an illusion of romance with a series of favourites and with her subjects as a body. The Earl of Essex, last of her favourites, had exploded hope of stability by his attempt at a coup in 1601. What Shakespeare marks in his poem, I think, is the loss not just of hope, but of the illusion of hope: 'Truth and beauty buried be' (64). This is the 'tragic scene', not to be taken as representing the literal deaths of the couple, but as the death of any enabling illusions about the succession, 'leaving no posterity'. Such a reading makes 'The Phoenix and Turtle' politically risky in its deeply pessimistic account of the succession issue, but its pessimism is concealed by the brilliant wit of its riddling manner.

Other brief scraps of verse have been attributed to Shakespeare over the years. Most of them are preserved in seventeenth-century manuscript miscellanies from about 1625 onwards. These were essentially commonplace book collections of whatever took the fancy of their compilers; the generally haphazard method of collection meant that poems were often misattributed or left without attribution, and they are often in a corrupt state because of careless copying. The poems attributed to Shakespeare are connected in some way to people with whom he was acquainted, so they were eagerly taken up by early biographers. In no case has it been established that he was actually the author, but there is nothing either to suggest that he could not have been. Some contain a flash of wit, but most of them are epitaphs, and are rendered unremarkable by the conventions of the form. Wells and Taylor included some of the least improbable in their Oxford edition, and since these have subsequently been included by Evans in his Penguin edition and by Greenblatt in the Norton edition, I shall briefly discuss them, as their inclusion in those editions affords them some legitimacy.[11]

Epitaphs are not, of course, usually intended as works of literature, but to be engraved on marble or gilded monuments. The Stanley tomb at Tong, Shropshire, containing the remains of Sir Edward Stanley and Sir Thomas Stanley, is just such a monument, and boasts two epitaphs (or an epitaph in two stanzas). The epitaphs appear in a number of manuscripts in which Shakespeare is identified as the author, including one appended to Sir William Dugdale's *Visitation of Shropshire* (College of Arms MS C.35, fol. 20 D, 1664). Shakespeare had a number of connections with this family and although the date of the tomb's construction is unknown it is certainly possible that he composed the epitaphs. On the east end of the tomb is the following:

Ask who lies here, but do not weep.
He is not dead; he doth but sleep.

This stony register is for his bones;
His fame is more perpetual than these stones,
And his own goodness, with himself being gone,
Shall live when earthly monument is none.

On the west end is written:

Not monumental stone preserves our fame,
Nor sky-aspiring pyramids our name.
The memory of him for whom this stands
Shall outlive marble and defacers' hands.
When all to time's consumption shall be given.
Stanley for whom this stands shall stand in heaven.

As epitaphs go these are not bad, in spite of the uneasy shift from tetrameter to pentameter in the third line of the first, and the lame, though understandable, play on 'Stanley/stand'. There is a good image in the 'stony register', and there appear to be clear echoes of the *Sonnets*, particularly sonnet 55, though this does not necessitate that Shakespeare himself wrote these lines. The 'bones/stones' rhyme comes, of course, with epitaph territory, and indeed it recurs in Shakespeare's own epitaph, carved on his tomb in Holy Trinity Church in Stratford:

Good friend, for Jesus' sake forbear
To dig the dust enclosed here.
Blessed be the man that spares these stones,
And cursed be he that moves my bones.

A number of sources have claimed that Shakespeare wrote the epitaph, the earliest being Francis Fane in a seventeenth-century manuscript miscellany compiled around 1655–6 (Folger MS V.a. 180, fol.79). While it is certainly not unknown for a man to compose his own epitaph, there is nothing much remarkable about this one beyond a grim wit.

Another pair of epitaphs said to have been written by Shakespeare was for the Stratford moneylender John Combe, with whom Shakespeare had a long-standing business relationship. The first of these is a jest, obviously concocted while Combe was alive; there are early versions of it that are not about Combe and not attributed to Shakespeare, but Fane, among others, identifies him as its author and it may be that he wrote it or it may be that he heard it and modified it for Combe:

Ten in an hundred here lies engraved
A hundred to ten his soul is not saved.
If anyone ask who lies in this tomb,
'O ho!' quoth the devil, ''tis my John-a-Combe'.

The writing of appropriately satirical epitaphs was a common game, and it is not probable that Combe was deeply offended by the idea that the charging of excessive interest was a diabolical activity, since at his death in 1614 he left 20 pounds for the poor of Stratford and five pounds to Shakespeare, who, according to a single manuscript source (Bodleian MS Ashmole 38, p. 180) wrote what was, presumably, a real epitaph:

Howe'er he lived judge not,
John Combe shall never be forgot
While poor hath memory, for he did gather
To make the poor his issue; he, their father,
As record of his tilth and seed
Did crown him on his latter deed.

Again, there is nothing much beyond the conventional here (though the pun 'engraved' in the first is rather pleasing, and could be typically Shakespearean).

A further example of a jesting epitaph supposedly arises out of an evening of drinking that Shakespeare had with Ben Jonson. Fane, once again, is one of the earliest sources of the legend. Jonson began an epitaph on himself;

Here lies Ben Jonson
That was once one.

He then gave it to Shakespeare to complete, who wrote:

Who while he lived was a slow thing,
And now, being dead, is nothing.

There is a long history of alleged rivalry between Shakespeare and Jonson, and there are many anecdotes like this one, in which Shakespeare's quick wit triumphs over Jonson's more laborious intelligence. Unfortunately, the basis of this history is untrustworthy, and this epitaph fits rather too neatly into it.

There is one more serious epitaph that was attributed to Shakespeare around 1637 (Bodleian MS Rawlinson poet. 160, fol. 41). Elias

James, a London brewer known to Shakespeare, died in 1610, and although his tomb no longer exists, his epitaph does:

> When God was pleased, the world unwilling yet,
> Elias James to nature paid his debt,
> And here reposeth. As he lived, he died,
> The saying strongly in him verified:
> 'Such life, such death'. Then, a known truth to tell,
> He lived a godly life, and died as well.

Again, this is a competent epitaph, but there is nothing in it that marks it as Shakespearean.

There is little else to report. A brief poem found in Fane's miscellany was supposedly written by Shakespeare for a Stratford schoolmaster, Alexander Aspinall, to accompany a gift of a pair of gloves to his wife:

> The gift is small,
> The will is all:
> Alexander Aspinall.

The Oxford editors point out what they see as a pun on 'will', and a parallel with lines in the play *Pericles*, but the poem is so lightweight that one might feel that the schoolmaster should have been able to do as good a job himself.[12]

Finally, the 1616 edition of the *Works* of King James I has on its frontispiece, a poem that has been attributed to Shakespeare (Folger MS V.a.160):

> Crowns have their compass; length of days, their date;
> Triumphs, their tombs; felicity, her fate.
> Of more than earth can earth make none partaker,
> But knowledge makes the king most like his maker.

Wells and Taylor point out that 'Shakespeare was the chief dramatist of the only theatrical company patronized by King James himself, and in the absence of a poet laureate might have served such a function'.[13] While this is true, it is equally true that Ben Jonson had for many years been providing masques and entertainments for the court, and was more likely than Shakespeare to have been invited to provide such patronage verse. The little poem has also been attributed to the printer Robert Barker, and it is conventional enough that it could equally easily have been by him – or by someone else entirely.

The problem with attempting to assign any of these poems to Shakespeare is that they are all relatively trivial and most of them are written to fulfil a set of conventions. Consequently they provide a very small basis for literary judgement. At the same time, the circumstances surrounding each of them make the attribution to him tempting, not least because they appear to shed light on him as a social being rather than a writer. To accept them into his canon would add nothing much to his literary reputation, but it would certainly broaden our sense of him as a man. If they are by Shakespeare the image they suggest is far from the historical construction of the immortal, myriad-minded bard, 'out-topping knowledge', as Matthew Arnold has it; it is rather of a writer willing to undertake the kind of work that most journeyman writers would have been happy to provide.

It must be clear from the foregoing that it has always been tempting for scholars to try to expand the Shakespearean canon by demonstrating that he wrote, or had a hand in, anonymous works or works of doubtful authorship, though such attention has usually been confined to plays. Recently, however, there have been controversial attempts to augment his non-dramatic works. It would not, certainly, be logical to deny the possibility that Shakespeare wrote poems other than those conventionally attributed to him, given that so much Elizabethan and Jacobean writing never progressed beyond manuscript, and that so much of it is anonymous. Nor would it be logical to claim that Shakespeare was incapable of producing inferior work. On the other hand, anyone wishing to get a poem added to the canon, especially if that poem is not particularly good, must make a strong case. Two major recent attempts at such addition have met with some degree of resistance, but they should be mentioned here because they have received strong support in some quarters.

The first of these, a song commonly known by its first line 'Shall I die?', exists in two manuscript miscellanies, the first, in which it is ascribed to Shakespeare (Bodleian MS Rawlinson poet, 160, fols.108–9), dating from 1637, the second (Yale MS Osborn b. 197) in which it is unattributed. There are variations between the two versions, both of which are corrupt. The poem was generally ignored by Shakespearean scholars until 1985, when Gary Taylor made a case for its authenticity; he and Stanley Wells subsequently printed it in the Oxford Shakespeare.[14] It has since been included in a number of other editions, though not all. Amongst editions that do not include it is John Roe's 1992 Cambridge edition of the poems; Roe excludes the poem because he is not convinced that it is Shakespeare's (pp. 2–3). Maurice Evans prints it in his 1989 Penguin edition of the narrative poems; he shares Roe's doubts but includes it because it has not been proved *not* to be Shakespeare's (p. 64). Taylor's claim was based partly on the argument that the 1637 manuscript ascription of the poem to Shakespeare should be accepted because the great majority of ascriptions in that manuscript are correct. This can hardly be said to provide convincing proof. In addition, Taylor identified stylistic and linguistic parallels, that he claimed have particular significance, to plays by Shakespeare dating from the early 1590s. Sceptics have since then used stylistic and linguistic examinations to refute Taylor's claims, and computer analyses have also been used to attempt to settle the issue.[15] Although the question has not been resolved conclusively either way, the current preponderance of opinion seems to be that Shakespeare was not the poem's author; however, as Wells and Taylor point out, generally 'objections to this cumulative external and internal evidence have been based upon personal judgements of the quality of the poem'.[16]

If Shakespeare did write 'Shall I die?' he did not do a very impressive job. It consists of nine 10-line stanzas in which a Petrarchan lover expresses the kinds of complaint that had long since become conventional. Its purpose, however, seems to be a flashy demonstration of rhyme: each stanza has eight pairs of rhyming words, some internal, some external. The opening stanza provides sufficient demonstration of its quality:

Shall I die? Shall I fly
Lovers' baits and deceits,
    Sorrow breeding?
Shall I tend? Shall I send?
Shall I sue, and not rue
    My proceeding?
    In all duty her beauty
Binds be her servant for ever.
    If she scorn, I mourn,
I retire to despair, joining never.

The poem is trapped inside its own attempted cleverness, the need to rhyme twisting its structure and undercutting its coherence. It is difficult to believe that Shakespeare could have written this at a time close to his uncompromising attack on poetic affectation in *Love's Labour's Lost*.

Another recent attempt to augment the canon concerns a poem entitled *A Funeral Elegy*, written in 1612 to commemorate the death of one William Peter, by a poet identified by the initials 'W.S.'. It was printed by George Eld for Thomas Thorpe, respectively printer and publisher of the *Sonnets*, though they had of course published texts by many other writers. The poem must have been hurriedly written (Peter was killed on 25 January, and it was entered in the Stationers' Register on 13 February 1612), which might explain some of its short-comings. In 1989 Donald Foster tentatively offered circumstantial evidence suggesting that Shakespeare might be its author, a sugges-tion that he subsequently resubmitted as a certainty, building sup-port for his claim through complex statistical and computer-based analyses of stylistic elements to show that the poem corresponds to Shakespeare's late work in many respects, and differs from the work of other contemporaries in many respects.[17] Richard Abrams argued for Shakespeare's authorship of the poem on different grounds, finding in it allusions to the acting profession and to Shakespeare himself.[18] This attribution too has met strong resistance, some scholars questioning the accuracy of Foster's statistical tests, others offering alternative possible identities for 'W.S.'. Interestingly, one of the strongest to resist has been Stanley Wells, who as joint editor of the Oxford *Works* was so welcoming to 'Shall I Die?' and the epitaphs.[19]

As a poetic exercise *A Funeral Elegy* is certainly competent, a more complex and in many ways more interesting poem than 'Shall I die?'. In 578 lines of rhyming iambic pentameter it fulfills the requirements of its genre, though it does not always manage to avoid dulness. It has been praised for its assured use of enjambment, as in the following:

> Look hither then, you that enjoy the youth
> Of your best days, and see how unexpected
> Death can betray your jollity to ruth
> When death you think is least to be respected!
>
> (483–6)[20]

The elegy has numerous echoes of the *Sonnets*, though since they had been public property for some years that is hardly conclusive, for Elizabethan and Jacobean poets often emulated each other. There are flashes of metaphorical brilliance, as in its rendering of fragile human bodies, 'those weak houses of our brittle flesh' (1890), but overall there is an absence of complex figurative language, along with a rather conventional application of Christian attitudes, which would seem to argue against Shakespeare's authorship. If we credit Foster's analysis it contains many stylistic features, linguistic and syntactical, that are to be found in Shakespeare's works, but a stylistic model would need to be very sophisticated indeed to provide certain identification of any writer. Nonetheless, if Shakespeare did write the epitaphs attributed to him he could certainly have written this.

I personally am not persuaded that either of these two poems is by Shakespeare, though of the two the *Elegy* appears the stronger candidate. The arguments that have gone on around them raise important issues, however. It is clearly possible that Shakespeare wrote more works, whether plays or poems, than those that are generally agreed to be his. There are a dozen or more plays, most of them anonymous, not all of them of high quality, that have at one time or another been claimed as at least partially Shakespeare's; the 1997 Riverside edition of the complete works includes *King Edward III*, the first ever to do so. It also includes *A Funeral Elegy*, but not 'Shall I die?'. David Bevington's recent edition includes the elegy even though Bevington thinks 'the attribution remains uncertain'.[21] The Oxford and Norton editors print 'Shall I Die?' but not the elegy. What can we make of such editorial disagreement? We might sympathise with Roe, who rejected 'Shall I die?' because he did not think it was Shakespeare's, or we might applaud the flexibility of Evans and Bevington, who, in spite of their doubts, included poems because Shakespeare's authorship of them had not been disproved. On the face of it, the more liberal approach might seem the better one: if there is a possibility that Shakespeare wrote a poem, should it not be included with his known works? But where do we draw the line? How remote a possibility will we accept? Is the earnest conviction of a scholar or two sufficient evidence, given that the general acceptance of a new Shakespearean work would be of immense value to the career of the scholar who established it?

Any additions need to satisfy rigorous criteria, and these have not yet been established. It will hardly do to scrutinize every anonymous text or every text supposed to have been written by someone with the initials 'W.S'. Nor are similarities of theme or content sufficient in themselves to demonstrate authorship: the correspondences between *A Funeral Elegy* and the *Sonnets*, for example, can be explained in ways that do not necessitate Shakespeare's authorship of the *Elegy*. Statistical and computer-based analyses of texts might seem to offer the best hope of validating new attributions, but the kinds of question that have been raised about such models as Foster's suggest that we have not got there yet. On the other hand, we cannot treat the Shakespearean canon as if it were a rigidly exclusive club that will never allow new members to join it. What we understand as the canon today has not expanded much over the past four centuries, but it has expanded, and it would be foolish to argue that it cannot grow any further. What is needed is for scholars and critics to be open-minded while adhering to strict and widely accepted standards – obvious enough but, as the quarrels over these two poems suggest, a difficult balancing-act to maintain.[22]

Conclusion

When Shakespeare turned to writing poetry, he did not have the luxury that we assume modern poets have of writing to please himself. He wrote for a living and so he wrote for a patron, a man who shared and in some ways directed the values and tastes of the Elizabethan courtly elite. When he dedicated his two narrative poems to Southampton, Shakespeare had to hope that what pleased his patron would please other powerful courtiers, and beyond them the growing merchant/middle-class audience whose curiosity about high fashion would lead them to buy volumes of his poems. One might assume that whatever Shakespeare's own views might have been, he could not have afforded to jeopardize his livelihood by going against the establishment grain. Nevertheless, an underlying assumption of this book has been that Shakespeare was in many ways sceptical of elite values.

However great his artistic and commercial success might have been, Shakespeare was kept by both his class and his profession on the margins of the circles of power in Elizabethan society. Common sense would seem to suggest that a degree of resentment must have been a component of his attitude to those he had to serve through his poetry. When the Poet in *Timon of Athens* complains: 'When we for recompense have praised the vile, / It stains the glory in that happy verse / Which aptly sings the good' (1.1.15–17), he surely articulates feelings akin to those that Shakespeare must have had 15 years before when his living depended on pleasing a patron. We do not have to believe that Shakespeare was as embittered as the Poet or that he thought that his patron was 'vile', to appreciate that he might have fretted at the constraints imposed upon him by the need to gratify his privileged readers. Something, at any rate, persuaded him to withdraw from this literary servitude in spite of his conspicuous success at it. It might well have been this same concern that inhibited him from publishing his anti-romantic *Sonnets* at a time when sonnets were still in vogue.

The needs of the Elizabethan poet and the needs of his readers were, then, sometimes in conflict, and the disruptions caused by that conflict must be reflected in the poems, though it would be difficult, perhaps impossible, to locate all of them. For the modern reader seeking to identify the poet's intentions there is a further complication. This is the fact that Renaissance poets, however 'experimental' they might appear, were writing within the conventions of genres. That is, what sounds like the poet's voice is often actually the genre's voice or the voice of a broader convention. We see this in sonnet 55, in which the poem's speaker claims that 'these contents', that is, this specific poem, will ensure that the young man's memory will not die. However, the sonnet itself echoes passages from Ovid (*Metamorphoses* XV, 871–9) and Horace (*Odes* III, xxx). Not only that, but those passages were so frequently echoed by Renaissance poets that they were, in effect, commonplace. What does that say about the 'sincerity' of 'this powerful rhyme'? The poem's claim to be able to bestow immortality depends upon the claims of other poems to do the same thing. It is, in the strictest sense, simply a variation on a theme. In the same way, the anti-Petrarchism of the sonnets depends upon the speaker taking a Petrarchan stance in many of them. Even the narrative poems work within a set of conventional assumptions, and while the poet works to impose his own mark upon them, he is in many ways controlled by them.

What all of this suggests is that what we seek to identify in the poems as Shakespeare's voice is unstable, because what we are hearing is only in part the voice of the poet; it is also in part the voice of his time, in that it incorporates the perspective that he constructed for his contemporary readers, and it is in part the voice of the tradition in which he was writing. Perhaps we should think of it as the voice of the poems rather than the voice of the poet. This is why there are no final answers to the question of what Shakespeare 'means', and why the poems remain rich for modern readers. It also suggests that looking for Shakespeare's biography in the poems does not help much in our understanding of them, any more than does applying to them the biography we know about. Suppose we could resolve some of the speculation that has arisen from the mystery of the lost years (whether Shakespeare was a schoolteacher, whether he was a soldier, whether he was a lawyer's clerk, whether he was a Catholic, whether he travelled abroad, and so on). These might be interesting ideas to consider, but how much would they illuminate the texts? The voice of Shakespeare's poems is powerful and unique, but 'Shakespeare the man' is not to be found in them. Perhaps we should think of it as the voice of a culture, not the voice of an individual.

Notes

Chapter 1

1. The best sources of biographical material on Shakespeare are two books by S. Schoenbaum: *William Shakespeare: A Documentary Life* (Oxford: The Clarendon Press, 1975); and *Shakespeare's Lives* (Oxford: The Clarendon Press, 1991).
2. D. Palliser, *The Age of Elizabeth: England under the Later Tudors, 1547–1603*, 2nd edn. (London and New York: Longman, 1992) p. 83.
3. E.M.W. Tillyard, *The Elizabethan World Picture* (1943; rpt. Harmondsworth, Penguin Books, 1970) p. 18.
4. T. Eagleton, *William Shakespeare* (Oxford, Blackwell, 1986) p. 1.
5. L. Tennenhouse, *Power on Display: The Politics of Shakespeare's Genres.* New York: Methuen, 1986, p. 38.
6. A. Patterson, *Shakespeare and the Popular Voice* (Oxford, Blackwell, 1989) pp. 1, 25.
7. C. Burrow, The Sixteenth Century, in A.F. Kinney (ed.), *The Cambridge Companion to English Literature, 1500–1600* (Cambridge: Cambridge University Press, 2000) p. 16.
8. *Greene's Groats-worth of Wit* (1592), reprinted in E.K. Chambers, *William Shakespeare: A Study of Facts and Problems*, vol. 2 (Oxford: Oxford University Press, 1930) p. 188.
9. G. Parfitt (ed.) *Ben Jonson: The Complete Poems* (Harmondsworth: Penguin Books, 1975) p. 476.
10. D. Kay, *Shakespeare: His Life, Work, and Era* (New York: Quill) 1992, p. 156.
11. Sir Philip Sidney. *An Apology for Poetry*, in D. Kalstone (ed.), *The Selected Poetry and Prose of Sidney* (New York: New American Library, 1970) p. 260.
12. M. Francis, *Palladis Tamia* (1589), reprinted in R. McDonald, *The Bedford Companion to Shakespeare: An Introduction with Documents* (Boston and New York: Bedford Books, 1996) p. 32.

Chapter 2

1. P. Sheavyn, *The Literary Profession in the Elizabethan Age* (2nd edn. Revised by J.W. Saunders; New York: Manchester University Press, 1967) p. 101.
2. H. Love, 'Scribal Publication in Seventeenth-Century England', *Transactions of the Cambridge Bibliographical Society*. 9(2) (1987) p. 146.
3. A.F. Marotti, 'John Donne and the Rewards of Patronage', in G.F. Lytle and S. Orgel (eds), *Patronage in the Renaissance* (Princeton, NJ: Princeton University Press, 1981) p. 209.
4. M. Brennan, *Literary Patronage in the English Renaissance: The Pembroke Family* (London and New York: Routledge, 1988) p. 4.

5. G. Kipling, 'Henry VII and the Origins of Tudor Patronage', in G.F. Lytle and S. Orgel, *Patronage in the Renaissance*, p. 118.
6. Brennan, *Literary Patronage*, p. xii.
7. L. Stone, *The Crisis of the Aristocracy, 1558–1641* (Oxford: Clarendon Press, 1965) p. 703.
8. G. Taylor, *Cultural Selection* (New York: Basic Books, 1996) p. 53.
9. Quotations from Spenser are from *Spenser: Poetical Works*, J.C. Smith and E. De. Selincourt (eds) (London: Oxford University Press, 1912).
10. E. Faas, *Shakespeare's Poetics* (Cambridge: Cambridge University Press, 1986) p. xii.
11. K. Duncan-Jones (ed.) *Shakespeare's Sonnets* (London: Thomas Nelson and Sons Ltd, 1997) p. 45.

Chapter 3

1. See A.C. Baugh and T. Cable, *A History of the English Language*, 3rd edn. (Englewood Cliffs, NJ: Prentice-Hall Inc., 1978) pp. 237–40.
2. S. John, *Philip Sparrow*, in D. Damrosch (ed.), *The Longman Anthology of British Literature*, vol. 1 (New York: Longman, 1999) pp. 590–619.
3. P. George, *The Arte of English Poesie*, G.D. Willcock and A. Walker (eds) (Cambridge: Cambridge University Press, 1936) p. 84.
4. For an extensive account of the influence of Castiglione, see D. Javitch, *Poetry and Courtliness in Renaissance England* (Princeton: Princeton University Press, 1978).
5. Sheavyn, *Literary Profession*, pp. 210–38.
6. A. Easthope, *Poetry as Discourse*. London and New York: Methuen, 1983, pp. 61–5.
7. J. Ben, *Volpone or, The Fox*, (ed.) R.B. Parker (Manchester: Manchester University Press, 1983) p. 70.
8. Cicero, *De Optimo Genere Oratorum*, 3. Quoted in P. Dixon, *Rhetoric* (London: Methuen, 1971) p. 51.

Chapter 4

1. M. Christopher, *Hero and Leander*, in S. Orgel (ed.), *Christopher Marlowe: The Complete Poems and Translations* (Harmondsworth: Penguin, 1971).
2. D. Kay, *William Shakespeare: Sonnets and Poems* (New York: Twayne, 1998) p. 20.
3. Meres, *Palladis Tamia*, p. 32.
4. D.W. Robertson, Jr. *A Preface to Chaucer: Studies in Medieval Perspectives* (Princeton: Princeton University Press, 1962) p. 356.
5. J. Bate, *Shakespeare and Ovid* (Oxford: The Clarendon Press, 1993) pp. 21–3.
6. W.H.D. Rouse (ed.), *Shakespeare's Ovid, Being Arthur Golding's Translation of the Metamorphoses* (London: Centaur Press, 1961) p. iii.
7. S. Greenblatt, *Renaissance Self-Fashioning* (Chicago: University of Chicago Press, 1980) p. 2.

8. Part of a longer note in Harvey's copy of Speght's 1598 edition of Chaucer. It is reprinted in the *Norton Shakespeare*, p. 3329.
9. See Schoenbaum, *Documentary Life*, pp. 130–1.

Chapter 5

1. C. Belsey, 'Love as Trompe-l'oeil: Taxonomies of Desire in *Venus and Adonis*', in P.C. Kolin (ed.), *Venus And Adonis: Critical Essays* (New York: Garland, 1997) pp. 261–85, 262.
2. M. Thomas, *A Mad World, My Masters*, in D.L. Frost (ed.), *The Selected Plays of Thomas Middleton* (Cambridge, Cambridge University Press, 1978).
3. Quoted in C.M. Ingleby, *The Shakspere Allusion-Book: A Collection of Allusions to Shakspere from 1591–1700*, vol. 1 (London: Oxford University Press, 1932) p. 220.
4. B. Vickers (ed.) *Shakespeare: The Critical Heritage*, vol. 1 (London: Routledge and Kegan Paul, 1981) p. 286.
5. S.T. Coleridge, *Biographia Literaria*, vol. 2, J. Shawcross (ed.) (Oxford: Oxford University Press, 1954) p. 16.
6. L.E. Pearson, *Elizabethan Love Conventions. Shakespeare Studies* (Berkeley: University of California Press, 1933) p. 285.
7. T.W. Baldwin, *On the Literary Genetics of Shakespeare's Poems and Sonnets* (Urbana: University of Illinois Press, 1950) pp. 83–4.
8. N. Rabkin, *Shakespeare and the Common Understanding* (New York: The Free Press, 1967) p. 162.
9. K. Muir, '*Venus and Adonis*: Tragedy or Comedy?', in A. Thaler and N. Sanders (eds), *Shakespearean Essays* (Knoxville: University of Tennessee Press, 1964) p. 13.
10. E.B. Cantelupe, 'An Iconographical Interpretation of *Venus and Adonis*: Shakespeare's Ovidian Comedy', *Shakespeare Quarterly*. 14 (1963) pp. 141–51.
11. R. Putney, '*Venus and Adonis*: Amour with Humour', *Philological Quarterly*. 20 (1941) 533–48, p. 546.
12. Muir, 'Tragedy or Comedy?', pp. 4, 12.
13. J. Buxton, *Elizabethan Taste* (1963; repr. Sussex: Harvester Press, 1983) p. 298.
14. R.A. Lanham, *The Motives of Eloquence: Literary Rhetoric in the Renaissance* (New Haven: Yale University Press) 1976.
15. H. Dubrow, *Captive Victors: Shakespeare's Narrative Poems and Sonnets* (Ithaca and London: Cornell University Press, 1987) p. 19; A.D. Cousins, *Shakespeare's Sonnets and Narrative Poems* (London: Longman, 2000) p. 29.
16. A. Mortimer, *Variable Passions: A Reading of Shakespeare's VENUS AND ADONIS* (New York: AMS, 2000) p. 15.
17. R. Halpern, '"Pining Their Maws": Female Readers and the Erotic Ontology of the Text in Shakespeare's *Venus and Adonis*', in Kolin (ed.), *Venus and Adonis*. 377–88, p. 381.
18. Halpern, 'Female Readers', p. 379.

19. Cousins, *Poems*, p. 46, n. 67.
20. S. Clark, *The Hutchinson Shakespeare Dictionary* (London: Arrow Books, 1986) p. 47; R. Ellrodt, 'Shakespeare the Non-Dramatic Poet', in S. Wells (ed.), *The Cambridge Companion to Shakespeare Studies* (Cambridge: Cambridge University Press, 1986) p. 45.
21. E. Panofsky, *Problems in Titian, Mostly Iconographic* (New York: New York University Press, 1969) pp. 150–54.
22. C. Hulse, *Metamorphic Verse: The Elizabethan Minor Epic* (Princeton, Princeton University Press, 1981) p. 143.
23. C.S. Lewis, *English Literature in the Sixteenth Century, Excluding Drama* (Oxford, Oxford University Press, 1954) p. 498.
24. G. Williams, 'The Coming of Age of Shakespeare's Adonis', *The Modern Language Review.* 78 (1983) p. 770.
25. Ellrodt, 'Shakespeare the Non-Dramatic Poet', p. 45.
26. Dubrow, *Captive Victors*, p. 25.
27. K. Duncan-Jones, 'Much Ado with Red and White: The Earliest Readers of Shakespeare's *Venus and Adonis*', *Review of English Studies.* 44 (1993) 479–501, p. 500.
28. For an account of the involvement of writers in the construction of the cult of Elizabeth see P. Berry, *Of Chastity and Power: Elizabethan Literature and the Unmarried Queen* (London: Routledge, 1989).
29. Dubrow, *Captive Victors*, p. 34.
30. R.P. Miller, 'Venus, Adonis and the Horses', *ELH,* 19 (1952) 249–64, p. 263; T. Hughes, *Shakespeare and the Goddess of Complete Being* (New York: Farrar Straus Giroux, 1992) p. 57.
31. Cousins, *Poems*, p. 34.
32. E. Maurice (ed.), *Shakespeare: The Narrative Poems* (Harmondsworth: Penguin, 1989) p. 20.

Chapter 6

1. B. Richard, 'Remembrance of some English Poets', *Shakspere Allusion Book,* vol. 1, p. 51.
2. Quoted in *The Critical Heritage*, vol. 6, p. 550.
3. Coleridge, *Biographia Literaria*, vol. 2, p. 19.
4. J. Kerrigan, 'Keats and *Lucrece*', *Shakespeare Survey.* 41 (1989) pp. 103–18.
5. I. Donaldson, *The Rapes of Lucretia: A Myth and Its Transformations* (Oxford: The Clarendon Press, 1982) p. 55.
6. F.T. Prince (ed.), *The Poems*, New Arden Shakespeare (London: Methuen, 1961) p. xxxv; Elrodt, 'The Non-dramatic Poet', p. 46.
7. J.W. Lever, 'Shakespeare's Narrative Poems', in K. Muir and S. Schoenbaum (eds), *A New Companion to Shakespeare Studies* (Cambridge: Cambridge University Press, 1971) p. 125.
8. Lanham, *Motives of Eloquence*, p. 100.
9. Katherine Eisaman Maus, 'Taking Tropes Seriously: Language and Violence in Shakespeare's *Rape of Lucrece*', *Shakespeare Quarterly.* 37 (1986) 66–82, p. 82.
10. Dubrow, *Captive Victors*, pp. 80–168.

11. Bate, *Shakespeare and Ovid*, p. 66.
12. G. Schmitz, *The Fall of Women in Early English Narrative Verse* (Cambridge, Cambridge University Press, 1990) pp. 88–98.
13. See, for example, J. Dundas, 'Mocking the Mind: The Role of Art in Shakespeare's *Rape of Lucrece*', *Sixteenth Century Journal*. 14, 1 (1983) 134–22; E. Freund, '"I see a voice": The Desire for Representation and the Rape of Voice', in Avrahan Oz (ed.), *Strands Afar Remote: Israeli Perspectives On Shakespeare* (London: Associated University Presses, 1998) pp. 62–86.
14. Prince, *Poems*, pp. xxxiv–xxxv.
15. See especially the work of C. Kahn, J.O. Newman, N. Vickers, W. Wall and L. Woodbridge.
16. E.P. Kuhl, 'Shakespeare's *Rape of Lucrece*', *Philological Quarterly*. 20 (1941) 352–60. This initiative was followed up extensively by G.P.V. Akrigg, *Shakespeare and the Earl of Southampton* (Cambridge: Harvard University Press, 1968).
17. See B. Nass, 'The Law and Politics of Treason in Shakespeare's *Lucrece*', *Shakespeare Yearbook*. 7 (1996) 292–311.
18. L. Woodbridge, 'Palisading the Elizabethan Body Politic', *Texas Studies in Literature and Language*. 33 (1991) 327–54.
19. S. Jed, *Chaste Thinking: The Rape of Lucretia and the Birth of Humanism* (Bloomington, Indiana University Press, 1989) p. 10.
20. St. Augustine. *The City of God* (tr.) Henry Bettenson, (ed.) David Knowles (Harmondsworth, Penguin, 1972) p. 29.
21. Ben Jonson, 'Epigram XLV, On My First Son', in C.H. Herford and P. E. Simpson (eds), *Ben Jonson*, vol. 8 (Oxford: The Clarendon Press, 1925–52) p. 41.
22. J. Hart, 'Narratorial Strategies in *The Rape of Lucrece*', *Studies in English Literature*, 32 (1992) 59–77, p. 75.
23. R. Lanham, 'The Politics of *Lucrece*', *Hebrew University Studies in Literature*. 8 (1980) 66–67, p. 71.
24. Cousins, *Poems*, p. 63.

Chapter 7

1. For a good account of the early history of the sonnet, see M.R.G. Spiller, *The Development of the Sonnet: An Introduction* (London and New York: Routledge, 1992).
2. Francesco Petrarca, *Canzoniere*, commento di G. Leopardi (Milan: Feltrinelli economica, 1979); translation by M. Musa, in J. Conway Bondanella and M. Musa (eds), *The Italian Renaissance Reader* (New York: New American Library, 1987).
3. J. Fuller, *The Sonnet* (London: Methuen, 1972) p. 2.
4. Sir Thomas Wyatt, *The Complete Poems*, in R.A. Rebholz (ed.) (Harmondsworth: Penguin Books, 1978).
5. *The Poems of Henry Howard, Earl of Surrey*, in Frederick M. Padelford (ed.) (Seattle, University of Washington Press, 1928).
6. Fuller, *The Sonnet*, p. 14.

7. A. Easthope, *Poetry as Discourse* (London and New York: Methuen, 1983) p. 64.
8. W. Thomas, *The Hekatompathia: or, Passionate Centurie of Love*. A facsimile reproduction with introd. by S.K. Heninger, Jr. (Gainesville, Fla.: Scholars' Facsimiles & Reprints, 1964).
9. A. Marotti, '"Love Is Not Love": Elizabethan Sonnet Sequences and the Social Order', *ELH*, 49 (1982) pp. 396–428.
10. D. Samuel, *Poems and a Defence of Ryme*, in A.C. Sprague (ed.) (Chicago: University of Chicago Press, 1965).
11. For a full account of the murky circumstances surrounding the publication of *Astrophil and Stella*, see H.R. Woudhuysen, *Sir Philip Sidney and the Circulation of Manuscripts, 1558–1640* (Oxford: Clarendon Press, 1996) especially Chapter 11.
12. Duncan-Jones, *Shakespeare's Sonnets*, p. 7.
13. A. Gurr, 'Shakespeare's First Poem: Sonnet 145', *Essays in Criticism*. 21 (1971) pp. 221–6.
14. Duncan-Jones, *Shakespeare's Sonnets*, pp. 10–13.
15. J. Fineman, *Shakespeare's Perjured Eye: The Invention of Poetic Subjectivity in the Sonnets* (Berkeley: University of California Press, 1986) p. 319, n. 6.
16. Duncan-Jones, *Shakespeare's Sonnets*, pp. 38–40.
17. C.F. Tucker Brooke (ed.), *Shakespeare's Sonnets* (London: Oxford UP, 1936). See also B. Stirling, *The Shakespeare Sonnet Order: Poems and Groups* (Berkeley: University of California Press, 1968).
18. H. Dubrow, '"Incertainties now crown themselves assur'd": The Politics of Plotting Shakespeare's Sonnets', *Shakespeare Quarterly*, 47 (1996) 291–305.
19. Noted in Kay, *Sonnets and Poems*, p. 108.
20. L. Barroll, *Politics, Plague, and Shakespeare's Theatre* (Ithaca and London: Cornell University Press, 1991) pp. 38–41.

Chapter 8

1. J. Kerrigan, (ed.) *The Sonnets and A Lover's Complaint* (Harmondsworth: Penguin, 1986) p. 65.
2. S. Booth, *An Essay on Shakespeare's Sonnets* (New Haven and London: Yale University Press, 1969); H. Vendler, *The Art of Shakespeare's Sonnets* (Cambridge and London: Harvard University Press, 1997).
3. P. Stallybrass, 'Editing as Cultural Formation: The Sexing of Shakespeare's Sonnets', *Modern Language Quarterly*. 54 (1993) 91–103; H. Dubrow, '"Incertainties now crown themselves assur'd": The Politics of Plotting Shakespeare's Sonnets', *Shakespeare Quarterly*, 47 (1996) 291–305.
4. C. Bates, *The Rhetoric of Courtship in Elizabethan Language and Literature* (Cambridge: Cambridge University Press, 1992) p. 18.
5. Stone, *The Crisis of the Aristocracy*.
6. J. Pequigney, *Such Is My Love: A Study of Shakespeare's Sonnets* (Chicago: University of Chicago Press, 1985) p. 1; D. Middlebrook, *Sweet My Love: A Study of Shakespeare's Sonnets* (Adelaide: New World Press, 1980).
7. A. Marotti, '"Love Is Not Love": Elizabethan Sonnet Sequences and the Social Order', *ELH*. 49 (1982) 396–428, p. 408.

Chapter 9

1. M. De Grazia, 'The Scandal of Shakespeare's Sonnets', *Shakespeare Survey*. 46 (1994) pp. 35–49; L. Boose, '"The Getting of a Lawful Race": Racial Discourse in Early Modern England and the Unrepresentable Black Woman', in M. Hendricks and P. Parker (eds), *Women, 'Race' and Writing in the Early Modern Period* (London and New York: Routledge, 1994) 35–54, p. 49.
2. See James Hutton, 'Analogues of Shakespeare's Sonnets 153–54: Contributions to the History of a Theme', *Modern Philology*. 38 (1941) pp. 385–403.
3. Booth, *Shakespeare's Sonnets*, pp. 466–7.
4. Booth, *Shakespeare's Sonnets*, p. 162.
5. Clark, *Shakespeare Dictionary*, p. 60.
6. See, for example, MacD.P. Jackson, 'Shakespeare's *A Lover's Complaint*: Its Date and Authenticity', *University of Auckland Bulletin*. 72 (1978); Eliot Slater, Shakespeare: 'Word Links between Poems and Plays', *Notes & Queries*. 220 (1975) 157–63. Further support is given by Kerrigan in his edition (pp. 389–94).
7. This answer is suggested by the research of A. K. Heiatt, C.W. Heiatt and A. L. Prescott, 'When Did Shakespeare Write *Sonnets 1609?*', *Studies in Philology*, 88, 1 (1991) pp. 68–109.
8. J. Roe (ed.), *The New Cambridge Shakespeare: The Poems* (Cambridge: Cambridge University Press, 1992) pp. 61–2.

Chapter 10

1. D. Bevington (ed.), *The Complete Works of Shakespeare* (New York: Longman, 1997) p. v.
2. Roe, in the introduction to his *New Cambridge* edition (56–8) makes a strong case that the collection does have such coherence.
3. Quoted in S. Schoenbaum, *Documentary Life*, p. 219.
4. C. Brown (ed.), *Poems by Sir John Salusbury and Robert Chester* (*EETS*, Extra Series, no. 113, 1914).
5. A.B. Grosart (ed.), *The Poems of Robert Chester, 1601–1611. With verse contributions by Shakespeare, Ben Jonson, George Chapman, John Marston, etc.* (1879).
6. M. Axton, *The Queen's Two Bodies: Drama and the Elizabethan Succession* (London: The Royal Historical Society, 1977) p. 119.
7. E.A.J. Honigmann, *Shakespeare: The Lost Years* (Manchester: Manchester University Press, 1985) pp. 90–113.
8. Clare Asquith, 'A Phoenix for Palm Sunday: Was Shakespeare's poem a requiem for Catholic martyrs?', *Times Literary Supplement* (April 13, 2001) pp. 14–15.
9. Quoted in G. Taylor, *Reinventing Shakespeare: A Cultural History from the Restoration to the Present* (London: The Hogarth Press, 1989) p. 251.
10. Evans, *The Narrative Poems*, pp. 53, 58.

11. For each of the epitaphs I have provided a commonly-used source, but for any reader who is interested in tracing the poems to their manuscript origins, all sources are given in S. Wells and G. Taylor (eds), *William Shakespeare: A Textual Companion* (London and New York: W.W. Norton, 1997) pp. 449–60.

12. Wells and Taylor, *Textual Companion*, p. 455.

13. Wells and Taylor, *Textual Companion*, p. 459.

14. Taylor's claim first appeared in the *Times Literary Supplement*, 20 December 1985. It met strong resistance in subsequent correspondence.

15. T.A. Pendleton, 'The Non Shakespearean Language of "Shall I Die"', *Review of English Studies*. 40 (1989) pp. 323–51, argues that an examination of the poem's language shows that Shakespeare could not have been its author. W.E.Y. Elliott and R.J. Valenza, 'A Touchstone for the Bard', *Computers and the Humanities*. 25 (1991) pp. 199–209, use modal analysis to support the same conclusion.

16. Wells and Taylor, *Textual Companion*, p. 451.

17. D.W. Foster, *Elegy by W.S.: A Study in Attribution* (Newark: University of Delaware Press, 1989); 'A Funeral Elegy: W[illiam] S[hakespeare]'s "Best-speaking Witnesses"', *PMLA*. 111 (1996) pp. 1080–1105.

18. R. Abrams, 'W[illiam] S[hakespeare]'s *Funeral Elegy* and the Turn from the Theatrical', *Studies in English Literature*. 36 (1996) pp. 435–60.

19. S. Wells, 'A Funeral Elegy: Obstacles to Belief', *Shakespeare Studies*. 25 (1997) pp. 186–91.

20. W[illiam] S[hakespeare,] *A Funeral Elegy in Memory of the Late Virtuous Master William Peter of Whipton near Exeter*, D.W. Foster (ed.), *The Shakespeare Newsletter*. 46 (1996) pp. 35–39.

21. Bevington, *Complete Works*, p. 1698.

22. After this book was written, G.D. Monsarrat, in a scholarly article ('A Funeral Elegy: Ford, W.S., and Shakespeare', *The Review of English Studies*, 53 (2002), pp. 186–202), presented an argument so persuasive that it seems conclusive, in support of John Ford as author of the poem. Immediately both Donald Foster and Richard Abrams, in messages to the electronic discussion group SHAKSPER (SHK 13.1514, 13 June 2002), conceded that the poem is not by Shakespeare, a concession subsequently reported widely. Since the affair illustrates so clearly the issues and dangers involved in any attempt to expand Shakespeare's canon, I decided to leave my discussion of it as it stands.

Suggested Reading

The editions listed below are recent, either collected editions of Shakespeare's complete works or single-volume editions of poems. All have useful introductions and notes. For secondary reading I have listed only books. These provide appropriate background material for the context in which Shakespeare wrote, or locate his poems in relation to the work of his contemporaries, or concentrate on the poems themselves. There are many other useful books and journal articles, however, some of which are cited in the Notes.

Editions

Bevington D. (ed.) *The Complete Works of Shakespeare*. New York: Longman, 1997.

Evans G.B. (ed.) *The Riverside Shakespeare*. Boston: Houghton Mifflin, 1997.

Greenblatt S. (ed.) *The Norton Shakespeare*. New York: W.W. Norton, 1997.

Wells S. and Taylor G. (eds) *Shakespeare: The Complete Works*. Oxford: Oxford University Press, 1986.

Booth S. (ed.) *Shakespeare's Sonnets*. New Haven: Yale University Press, 1977.

Duncan-Jones K. (ed.) *Shakespeare's Sonnets*. The Arden Shakespeare, Third Series. London: Thomas Nelson and Sons, 1997.

Evans G.B. (ed.) *The Sonnets*. Cambridge: Cambridge University Press, 1996.

Evans M. (ed.) *Shakespeare: The Narrative Poems*. Harmondsworth: Penguin, 1989.

Foster D.W. (ed.) W[illiam] S[hakespeare,] *A Funeral Elegy in Memory of the Late Virtuous Master William Peter of Whipton near Exeter*. The Shakespeare Newsletter, 46 (1996) 35–39.

Kerrigan J. (ed.) *The Sonnets and A Lover's Complaint*. Harmondsworth: Penguin, 1986.

Roe J. (ed.) *The New Cambridge Shakespeare: The Poems*. Cambridge: Cambridge University Press, 1992.

Secondary Reading

Akrigg G.P.V. *Shakespeare and the Earl of Southampton*. Cambridge: Harvard University Press, 1968.

Axton M. *The Queen's Two Bodies: Drama and the Elizabethan Succession*. London: The Royal Historical Society, 1977.

Baldwin T.W. *On the Literary Genetics of Shakespeare's Poems and Sonnets*. Urbana, University of Illinois Press, 1950.

Bate J. *Shakespeare and Ovid*. Oxford: The Clarendon Press, 1993.

Bates C. *The Rhetoric of Courtship in Elizabethan Language and Literature*. Cambridge: Cambridge University Press, 1992.

Bermann S. *The Sonnet over Time: A Study in the Sonnets of Petrarch, Shakespeare, and Baudelaire.* Chapel Hill: University of North Carolina Press, 1988.

Berry P. *Of Chastity and Power: Elizabethan Literature and the Unmarried Queen.* London: Routledge, 1989.

Bloom H. (ed.) *Shakespeare's Sonnets: Modern Critical Interpretations.* New York: Chelsea House, 1987.

Booth S. *An Essay on Shakespeare's Sonnets.* New Haven and London: Yale University Press, 1969.

Bray A. *Homosexuality in Renaissance England.* London: Gay Men's Press, 1982.

Brennan M. *Literary Patronage in the English Renaissance: The Pembroke Family.* London and New York: Routledge, 1988.

Cousins A.D. *Shakespeare's Sonnets and Narrative Poems.* London: Longman, 2000.

Desmet C. *Reading Shakespeare's Characters: Rhetoric, Ethics, and Identity.* Amherst: University of Massachusetts Press, 1992.

Donaldson I. *The Rapes of Lucretia: A Myth and Its Transformations.* Oxford: The Clarendon Press, 1982.

Dubrow H. *Captive Victors: Shakespeare's Narrative Poems and Sonnets.* Ithaca and London: Cornell University Press, 1987.

Dubrow H. *Echoes of Desire: English Petrarchism and Its Counterdiscourses.* Ithaca and London: Cornell University Press, 1995.

Easthope A. *Poetry as Discourse.* London and New York: Methuen, 1983.

Faas E. *Shakespeare's Poetics.* Cambridge: Cambridge University Press, 1986.

Ferry A. *The 'Inward' Language: Sonnets of Wyatt, Sidney, Shakespeare, Donne.* Cambridge: Harvard University Press, 1983.

Fineman J. *Shakespeare's Perjured Eye: The Invention of Poetic Subjectivity in the Sonnets.* Berkeley: University of California Press, 1986.

Foster D.W. *Elegy by William Shakespeare: A Study in Attribution.* Newark: University of Delaware Press, 1989.

Fuller J. *The Sonnet.* London: Methuen, 1972.

Giroux R. *The Book Known as Q: A Consideration of Shakespeare's Sonnets.* New York: Atheneum, 1982.

Greenblatt S. *Renaissance Self-Fashioning.* Chicago: University of Chicago Press, 1980.

Greene T.M. *The Vulnerable Text: Essays on Renaissance Literature.* New York: Columbia University Press, 1986.

Hammond G. *The Reader and Shakespeare's Young Man Sonnets.* Totowa, New Jersey: Barnes and Noble Books, 1981.

Hardison O.B. *The Enduring Monument: A Study of the Idea of Praise in Renaissance Literary Theory and Practice.* Chapel Hill: University of California Press, 1962.

Helgerson R. *Self-Crowned Laureates: Spenser, Jonson, Milton and the Literary System.* Berkeley: University of California Press, 1983.

Honigmann E.A.J. *Shakespeare: The 'Lost' Years.* Manchester: Manchester University Press, 1985.

Hubler E. (ed.) *The Riddle of Shakespeare's Sonnets.* New York: Basic Books, 1962.

Hulse C. *Metamorphic Verse: The Elizabethan Minor Epic.* Princeton, Princeton University Press, 1981.

Hyland P. *An Introduction to Shakespeare: The Dramatist in Context*. London: Macmillan, 1996.

Innes P. *Shakespeare and the English Renaissance Sonnet*. London: Macmillan, 1997.

Javitch D. *Poetry and Courtliness in Renaissance England*. Princeton, Princeton University Press, 1978.

Jed S.H. *Chaste Thinking: The Rape of Lucretia and the Birth of Humanism*. Bloomington: Indiana University Press, 1989.

Kastan D.S. (ed.) *A Companion to Shakespeare*. Oxford: Blackwell, 1999.

Kay D. *William Shakespeare: Sonnets and Poems*. New York: Twayne, 1998.

Keach W. *Elizabethan Erotic Narratives*. New Brunswick, N.J.: Rutgers University Press, 1977.

Kerrigan J. (ed.) *Motives of Woe: Shakespeare and 'Female Complaint': A Critical Anthology*. Oxford: The Clarendon Press, 1991.

Kinney A.F. (ed.) *The Cambridge Companion to English Literature, 1500–1600*. Cambridge: Cambridge University Press, 2000.

Kolin P.C. (ed.) *Venus and Adonis: Critical Essays*. New York and London: Garland, 1997.

Lanham R.A. *The Motives of Eloquence: Literary Rhetoric in the Renaissance*. New Haven: Yale University Press, 1976.

Leishman J.B. *Themes and Variations in Shakespeare's Sonnets*. New York: Harper and Row, 1963.

Lever J.W. *The Elizabethan Love Sonnet*. London: Methuen, 1956.

Lytle G.F. and Orgel S. (eds) *Patronage in the Renaissance*. Princeton, NJ: Princeton University Press, 1981.

Melchiori G. *Shakespeare's Dramatic Meditations*. Oxford: Clarendon Press, 1976.

Mortimer A. *Variable Passions: A Reading of Shakespeare's VENUS AND ADONIS*. New York: AMS, 2000.

Muir K. *Shakespeare's Sonnets*. London: Allen and Unwin, 1979.

Norbrook D. *Poetry and Politics in the English Renaissance*. London: Routledge, 1984.

Orgel S. and Keilen S. (eds) *Shakespeare's Poems*. New York: Garland Publishing, 1999.

Pequigney J. *Such Is My Love: A Study of Shakespeare's Sonnets*. Chicago and London: University of Chicago Press, 1985.

Ramsey P. *The Fickle Glass: A Study of Shakespeare's Sonnets*. New York: AMS Press, 1979.

Roche T.P. *Petrarch and the English Sonnet Sequence*. New York: AMS Press, 1989.

Schiffer J. (ed.) *Shakespeare's Sonnets: Critical Essays*. New York and London: Garland, 1999.

Schmidgall G. *Shakespeare and the Poet's Life*. Lexington: The University of Kentucky Press, 1990.

Schoenbaum S. *Shakespeare's Lives*. Oxford: Oxford University Press, 1970.

Schoenbaum S. *Shakespeare: A Compact Documentary Life*. Oxford: Oxford University Press, 1991.

Sheavyn P. *The Literary Profession in the Elizabethan Age*. Second edition revised by J.W. Saunders. Manchester: Manchester University Press, 1967.

Simone R.T. *Shakespeare and LUCRECE: A Study of the Poem and Its Relation to the Plays*. Salzburg: Universitat Salzburg, 1974.

Smith B.R. *Homosexual Desire in Shakespeare's England: A Cultural Poetics*. Chicago: University of Chicago Press, 1991.

Smith H. *The Tension in the Lyre: Poetry in Shakespeare's Sonnets*. San Marino: Huntingdon Library, 1981.

Spiller M.R.G. *The Development of the Sonnet: An Introduction*. London and New York: Routledge, 1992.

Stirling B. *The Shakespeare Sonnet Order: Poems and Groups*. Berkeley: University of California Press, 1968.

Taylor G. *Reinventing Shakespeare: A Cultural History from the Restoration to the Present*. London: The Hogarth Press, 1989.

Vendler H. *The Art of Shakespeare's Sonnets*. Cambridge and London: Harvard University Press, 1997.

Vickers B. *Classical Rhetoric in English Poetry*. Carbondale: Southern Illinois University Press, 1970.

Vickers B. (ed.) *Shakespeare: The Critical Heritage, 1623–1801*, 6 vols. London: Routledge and Kegan Paul, 1974–81.

Wells S. and Taylor G. (eds) *William Shakespeare: A Textual Companion*. London and New York: W.W. Norton, 1997.

Wilson K. *Shakespeare's Sugared Sonnets*. London: Allen and Unwin, 1974.

Winny J. *The Master-Mistress: A Study of Shakespeare's Sonnets*. London: Chatto and Windus, 1968.

Wright G.T. *Shakespeare's Metrical Art*. Berkeley: University of California Press, 1988.

Index